MARIO

MARIO

LAWRENCE MARTIN

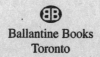

Ballantine Books
Toronto

To Kristina

Ballantine Books

Copyright © 1993 by Lawrence Martin. Originally published in hardcover in 1993 by Lester Publishing Limited

CANADIAN CATALOGUING IN PUBLICATION DATA

Martin, Lawrence, 1947-
Mario

ISBN 0-345-39802-5

1. Lemieux, Mario, 1965-   .   2. Hockey players – Canada – Biography.   I. Title.

GV848.5.L46M37   1994   796.962'092   C94-930949-4

Printed in Canada

CONTENTS

PROLOGUE

The definition of genius is that it acts unconsciously;
and those who have produced immortal works have done
so without knowing how or why.

—William Hazlitt

IN SEPTEMBER 1984 THE MEMBERS OF THE PITTSBURGH PENGUINS, the worst team in hockey, gathered in the weight room at training camp to begin pumping iron in preparation for the new season. The required exercise of the day was to bench press 180 pounds ten times. Even for this medley of hard-drinking journeymen, it was a relatively easy assignment. One after another, they passed the test, some doing more than ten lifts. Newcomer Marty McSorley, an Adonis defenseman, handled the bar like a toothpick. He looked as though he could have gone on forever.

Shortly after McSorley, another big kid, a rookie from French Canada, took his turn under the bar. This eighteen-year-old was being billed as the Penguins' savior. In his last year of junior hockey with the Laval Voisins of the Quebec league, he had orbited to an unheard of 133 goals, an average of almost two per game. The Penguins' management then selected him first overall in the junior draft. They were confident he would be "the franchise." The Penguins' veterans, always cynics in these situations, wanted some proof.

1

The rookie, the tallest player in camp, stood six-foot-four. He weighed over 200 pounds. No one expected he would have difficulty completing the bench-press exercise. No newcomer, certainly not one as exalted as he, would come to camp so unfit that he couldn't lift 180 pounds.

As he got under the bar, however, the rookie, Mario Lemieux, looked unsure of himself. He looked as if this was all very new to him. In fact, he had never seriously worked out with barbells before. He had never really trained at all. His Laval team doctor, fearful that Mario would have serious back problems, had once prescribed a series of strengthening exercises to help fortify him for a long NHL career. Lemieux couldn't be bothered doing them.

Now, as he exerted himself to lift the weights, he may have wished his attitude toward training had been different. His first vigorous push produced no result. The barbells remained stationary. He tried again, pushing harder and harder. Still, the bar didn't move.

As he struggled on, the wisecracks from the surrounding benches began. The veterans were enjoying the show. The hotshot rookie, the so-called savior, was turning into a jellyfish right before their eyes. One veteran began to chuckle, then another, and as Mario huffed and puffed to no avail, more joined in.

After one more failed attempt, Lemieux surrendered. He got up and, avoiding all eye contact, left the room. Though he must have been embarrassed, his teammates were surprised to see that he remained cool and pale. Anyone else in that situation, they thought, would have lit up like neon.

Shortly after the weight-lifting episode, Doug Shedden, one of Pittsburgh's better players, happened by Mario and asked him to come along for a jog. Sheddy wanted to do about three miles, but Mario barely made it to the halfway point before dropping out from exhaustion. Shedden, who had seen Lemieux smoking earlier at camp, bumped into him later. "Jesus, kid," he said. "You're only eighteen."

Paul Martha, the Penguins' vice-president, had once played football in Pittsburgh, including a stint with the Steelers. He went into the Penguins' dressing room that September to have a look at the prized rookie. He noticed that Lemieux's legs, from all the skating, were strong, muscular, well sculpted. But he was appalled at the French-Canadian's upper body. It was slender. There was no muscle. The contrast between the lower and the upper half, said Martha, "was freakish." Martha worried. The team was staking its future on this kid. He was supposed to be a model jock, yet he had a body that ran on smoke-coated lungs, collapsed under a 180-pound weight, and looked as if it belonged in a mime troupe.

First impressions were never an accurate way to gauge Mario Lemieux. What none of the Penguins could have been expected to realize in the early days of camp was that this player was different from the rest. For most athletes, a finely tuned, muscular body was imperative, but for Mario Lemieux a different set of rules—one that defied logical explanation— applied.

Long before Mario came to Pittsburgh, his bantam coach took note of his peculiar playing patterns. The coach, Ron Stevenson, observed that the more hurt, battered, and fatigued Lemieux became, the better he played. Stevenson found that in these depleted moments, Mario began to skate with greater fluidity. He lost his awkwardness. With exhaustion came grace.

Stevenson didn't want to overstate the phenomenon, just as, at a later date, others wouldn't want to overstate how Mario could possibly have played better in the wake of radiation treatments for cancer than he did before. But Stevenson would wonder on occasion, just as others would come to wonder, what kind of drummer the Lemieux boy marched to.

ONE
THE NATURAL

HOCKEY IN QUEBEC, IT WAS OFTEN SAID, WAS A RELIGION. THE great stars were gods and the organization supporting them, the hockey system, as devout as the church. Guy Lafleur put it all in perspective one day when he was asked about his top priorities in life. "I really love my family and kid," the Flower responded. "But first of all, it's hockey."

Lafleur was the third god. The first was Maurice (the Rocket) Richard, whose primitive, hell-bent rushes had a roar of destiny to them. The second was Jean Béliveau, the graceful and dignified counterpoint to the Rocket, the Joe DiMaggio of the game. The Flower was then the perfect complement to the first two, in that he combined the passion of the first and the polish of the second.

This was Quebec's hockey trinity. They all played for the Montreal Canadiens, a club that developed a success mystique as indomitable as that of any sports team on the continent. Only basketball's Boston Celtics rivaled the Canadiens in winning tradition. Like the Celtics, the Habs seemed predestined. Some days it was as if they won on aura alone.

Because of the Canadiens and the ambitions they aroused, minor hockey in Quebec became an integral part of the culture.

The hockey sacraments were administered as early as age three, with churches organizing hockey competitions on a parish-to-parish basis. Then the kids worked their way up through the ranks: atom, peewee, bantam, midget, junior, and hopefully, the pros. Only in the former Soviet Union, where they had hundreds of hockey schools, were the programs more sophisticated. Hockey was as much the Russian game as the Canadian one. While Canada liked to think it was the birthplace of the game, newspaper archives in St. Petersburg show that as early as 1865, perhaps earlier than in Canada, Russians were playing a sport with skates, sticks, and a small projectile to shoot into nets at either end.

Through the 1960s Quebec watched as Lafleur tore through the minor-league ranks and became the sure thing. But some years passed after that and no other minor-league phenomenon could be found. Instead, it was Brantford, Ontario, that produced the wunderkind, a youngster named Wayne Gretzky who by age ten was already being called the future star. Quebec waited until, finally, a dozen years after Guy Lafleur, four years after Gretzky, a boy appeared in west-end Montreal who looked as though he might be capable of ending the drought. He was a quiet boy with long arms, page-boy hair, and dark eyes, who lived and played in the district of Ville Emard. A low-income, low-key, very French quarter of the city, Ville Emard had a reputation for having the finest minor-league hockey teams. Many of the coaches and organizers were policemen, who instilled a sense of discipline in the teams. They walked the beat by day and came to the arenas by night, sometimes with their handguns still on their hips.

The boy, Mario Lemieux, was born on October 5, 1965. He took his first hockey steps when he was just past three. Pierrette, his mother, drove him to the Gadbois arena, which was located amid giant concrete stanchions supporting highways shooting out of Montreal to Quebec City. She put him under the watchful eye of Fernand Fichaud, a security guard who coached the children. Fichaud put little Mario, outfitted in a full red uniform, on the ice beside a chair, which served as the equivalent of training wheels on a child's bike. Mario held it tightly and tried to push it along while staying on his splaying feet. He fell to the ice several times, the chair tumbling down with him. Like the other boys, it took him a few sessions, four or five, before he could skate on his own. Fichaud then presented him with the instruments of the game: a stick and a puck. He wanted Mario to develop other hockey skills simultaneously with the skating. The stick, he believed, should be made to feel like an extension of the arms; the puck, an extension of the eyes.

Fichaud had taught the two Lemieux brothers who came before Mario. Alain and Richard both possessed talent, especially Alain. He had feathery moves and a beautiful skating motion. He would make it to the NHL. Richard, a lovable character, weighed too much and skated too awkwardly to advance that far, but from the blue line, he developed one of the hardest shots minor-league coaches had ever seen.

Knowing the brothers' talents and Mr. and Mrs. Lemieux's extraordinary dedication to hockey, Fichaud looked upon the arrival of Mario with special interest. Mario's father, Jean-Guy, was a house builder. He grew up on a farm, but suffered allergies and a lung ailment that kept him off playing fields and in hospitals for long stretches. Never a hockey player or athlete of distinction himself, friends wondered how he produced such a fine athletic brood. He did love the sport, however. He never missed a Canadiens' home game, and through his influence, his wife, Pierrette, not athletic either, came to have the same ardor for the sport.

Hockey was one of the few things they appeared to have in common. Jean-Guy and Pierrette were opposites. Jean-Guy was quiet, stern, stoic. Mario or Alain could score one or two goals, but that wasn't enough to warm their father. He'd sit in the arena like a frozen fish. Only a three- or four-goal night would bring joy to his face. Others in the stands would be moved to comment whenever his cheeks moved. "Did you see that?" someone would say. "Jean-Guy smiled."

Pierrette Lemieux, by contrast, was a loud and brassy dynamo, a bowling ball crashing through the pins. While her husband sat mute, Pierrette's voice thundered through the arena, urging her boy on while harpooning every opponent with vociferous, unholy vigor. Pierrette lovingly referred to Mario as "mon petit loup"—my little cub—but for the adversary, she'd turn the air foul with a ringing "colliste de tabernack!" or some other French-language zinger. Quebeckers often use religious symbols to curse and, literally interpreted, Madame Lemieux's invocation translated to a rather harmless "chalice of the tabernacle!" The real connotation, however, was something far more coarse. "No good son of a bitch!" was a reasonable approximation. Mothers at children's hockey games did not normally resort to such colorful phraseology. Muttered under the breath, maybe, but not with the decibel force that set the bells ringing at the neighborhood church.

But the Lemieuxs took their hockey seriously. The parents did everything so that their little boys could play the game every moment they were not at school. They attended every practice, every game, hoping, though not saying it, that maybe one day they could sit in the Montreal Forum and watch their sons play in the National Hockey League. The boys trampled so much snow into the house in the winter that they turned Pierrette's living-room rug into a slide. Not one to mind that, Pierrette was even prepared to take things a step further. According to local lore, when the snow got too deep to play hockey outside, Madame Lemieux transported shovels of snow into the house. She threw the snow on the carpet and pounded it down to a smooth surface that glistened like ice. With the heat in the house turned off and the doors opened to let the cold blow in, she had her boys, just past toddler age then, practice hockey on the rug. Outsiders could never believe the story. The Lemieuxs, they said, had wonderful imaginations. But after he turned pro, Mario would claim that he first learned to play in his living room. As for Pierrette, she too continued to talk about the old ice-carpet days. "They really did quite a job on my rug," she recalled. "But it was good for strengthening their ankles."

Pierrette and Jean-Guy surveyed Mario closely during his first lessons with Fernand Fichaud. That winter, early 1969, Fichaud led him through two one-hour sessions per week. His initial strides impressed the coach, but it was the autumn of 1969, when Mario turned four, that Fichaud knew he had something.

Mario was still learning to talk then. He stood not much higher than a fire hydrant. He took the puck, shuffled around two or three other squirts, and skated toward the goalie. He moved in quickly and confidently, shifting one way, then the other. At the goal mouth he pulled the puck abruptly to his wide right and yanked it back the other way. Then, with the netminder having moved precipitously on the first change of direction, Mario popped the puck into the vacant corner.

His motions on this play looked studied, rehearsed, groomed over a long stretch of time. Fichaud had never seen a four-year-old perform a deke, never mind one with such deft precision about it. He hadn't instructed the kids on how to deke goalies. That stage of the art wasn't to be contemplated until they had grown up a little more. He could only surmise that Mario had seen an NHLer perform such a maneuver on television, then had come to the rink and copied it to the letter, first try. But how was that possible for such a novice? Fichaud shook his head. There was only one possible explanation, he said. The young Lemieux was "a natural."

Fichaud remained astonished by what he had witnessed. "I think about that move all my life," he said, twenty-four years after it happened. "That was the greatest thing I ever saw." He didn't say a word to Mario about it at the time. He didn't want to swell the kid's head. But he did talk to Pierrette and Jean-Guy, who, of course, were there that day. He expressed his astonishment to Jean-Guy, who nodded solemnly. But Jean-Guy understood its significance, said Fichaud. "His parents knew how extraordinary it was. They could tell what it meant."

Following the day of the deke, Mario progressed swiftly. Everything came easy for him. He never even had to ask coach Fichaud a question. At age six he traveled to his first hockey tournament, a province-wide competition in St. Victor, near Montreal. Against other atoms, playing center, the position he would play forever, Mario scored four, five, six goals a game. Tournament organizers voted him MVP and the player most likely to succeed. This scenario was repeated at almost every minor-league tournament Mario attended. The word on the new prodigy soon spread. Roland Faubert, Mario's new coach, took him to an atom game in the Montreal suburb of Pierrefonds. At most, a few hundred people normally attended these games. That night three thousand came out to see Mario Lemieux. For the Montreal-area atom championships in Sorel, organizers were drawing eight hundred or nine hundred a game. For a Sunday match featuring Mario they drew five thousand. They remembered the night not only because of the crowd, but also because of Mario's shot. It was a shot that missed its target by ten feet. At his age, however, a shot's distance could impress the bystanders as much as its accuracy. Bobby Hull's slap shots, phenomenal power blasts, were all the rage then and kids like Mario Lemieux were trying to learn the big slapper themselves. Mario had one by age eight. In the game at Sorel he wound up at the center red line and fired off a missile that sent murmurs of astonishment through the crowd. The blast sailed clear over the plexiglass behind the enemy goal. What, the fans wondered, did the little guy have in him that could produce that kind of power? He was so small and thin. That kind of body wasn't supposed to produce that kind of result.

Given Mario's power, little goaltenders soon came to fear him. Carl Parker, a yellow-haired, blue-eyed boy who played net for the St. Joseph's team, had heard of Mario's reputation, his slap shot, his stunning scoring totals. When his team prepared to play Ville Emard, Parker grew uneasy. "I mean this kid was scoring six or seven goals a game."

On game day Parker looked up ice during the warm-ups to see Mario's teammates deferring to him. He noticed the star aura the kid had. Soon after the opening face-off, just as Carl Parker had feared, Mario broke in alone and cranked his stick back in a high arc, preparing for the slap shot. Parker winced as Mario's blast came at him very high, targeting the only vulnerable spot on his padded anatomy: the neck. The puck struck him there and Parker collapsed to the ice. The blow stung enough to make him cry. Players gathered around to console him, but Lemieux, the fallen Parker noticed, didn't number among the sympathizers. Having delivered the rifle blast, he had chuckled and slowly skated back to his zone.

Parker didn't wish to leave the game as a result of the injury. That would be a cowardly act and he'd probably get ribbed for it. So he stayed in the game, but shortly after the action recommenced, he began to doubt the wisdom of his valor. Mario had maneuvered the puck around two defenders and now descended on the goal once again. As he readied for the shot, Parker trembled. He didn't want to face this again. With his instincts screaming at him to make a move, the scared little goalkeeper did something only a fiction writer might contrive.

Mario Lemieux terrified him so much that Carl Parker jumped clear out of his net and sought refuge in the corner of the rink. Super Mario, immediately taking note, coolly drew his shooting action to a halt and continued skating forward. With a smile of scorn, he tapped the biscuit into the empty cage.

TWO

"BY THE SOUND OF HIS SKATES"

CARL PARKER WOULD NEVER GET OVER HIS PUSILLANIMOUS behavior that day. If he forgot about it for a time, somebody, come hockey season, was always there to remind him of his evacuation. He knew he could play better goal, though, and after that game, he set about proving it. He played well the rest of the season and the next year he made his way onto the status team in the area—Mario's Ville Emard Hurricanes.

Now, with the Natural on his own side, life changed considerably for Carl Parker. He watched in comfort as the other goalies froze. With Mario on his team, he set a league record for most assists by a goalie. It came easy. He stopped the puck behind his net, tipped it to Lemieux, and watched him weave up ice around all opponents and bury it in the enemy cage. In one season Parker got eight assists this way.

He lived in the same neighborhood as the Lemieuxs and, once on the same team, he and Mario became good friends. Not many got close to Mario. He was by nature an introvert. Normally, the local sports star also became the social star. Not so with Mario. When he was with his two or three best friends, "there were a lot of jokes and big talk," said Parker. "But when someone else came by who he didn't know so well, he was always quiet."

Parker spent a lot of time in Mario's house. In the Lemieux basement the two of them got on their knees and, using mini-sticks, played fiercely competitive floor hockey. After these games, they'd take their hockey elbow pads, put them over their hands, and use them as boxing gloves to pummel the heck out of one another. "I don't know why we did it," confessed Parker. "It was supposed to be for fun. But those gloves were thin. We were crazy. It was like having nothing on your hands and hitting your best friend in the face."

J. J. Daigneault, a future NHLer, and Mario's brother Richard joined in the games, the fights, and whatever other mischief they got into. One night a babysitter who didn't like hockey was looking after them. She had the gall to turn off "Hockey Night in Canada." Mario and the boys weren't going to let her get away with that. They locked her in the bathroom and turned the game back on.

Mario Lemieux, Parker and his other teammates noticed, viewed the game differently from the rest. Sure, he enjoyed playing hockey. Sure, he had fun. But he saw the sport, even before he turned ten, as business, serious business. It was evident in his demeanor around the rink. He would come to the games early, say hello, and barely utter another word until they were over. Once out on the street, he kibitzed with his close friends. But near the arena, seriousness and self-absorption marked him. He was solemn.

Something else stood out. He had an ironclad bond with his family, particularly his mother. Good-hearted Pierrette, some thought, exhibited a generosity to him and her other children that bordered on the extravagant. They thought she might be spoiling the kids, encouraging a self-centeredness that would later take its toll. Father Michel Fortin, a priest in Quebec City who came to know young Mario well, believed this to be true. He found him to be a great lad, but one "super-gâté par sa mère"—terribly spoiled by Pierrette.

Father Fortin housed Mario and other boys in the rectory when they came to Quebec City to play in tournaments. A grand event on the province's hockey calendar was the minor-league tournament in that city. The capital of the province gave itself over to pre-teen hockey for a fortnight. Crowds of fifteen thousand cheered on the kids and it was here, in the caldron of the Québec Colisée, that the French-Canadian stars of the future were anointed.

The boys attending the tournament loved to stay in Father Fortin's rectory because, even though they might have to attend church more often, the building had big hallways where they could play floor hockey and other games. On his first trip to the city Mario wanted to board there, but his parents, accompanying him, resisted. Finally, they struck a deal. If Mario played impressively in the tournament's first game against La Beauce, he would get his wish.

Mario scored seven goals. The performance stunned Fortin, who was also a minor-league hockey coach. He detected that day that the Lemieux boy possessed extraordinary gifts. He had a different hockey metabolism, the priest thought, a communications system from brain to eyes to hands to stick to puck far in advance of any other.

After the victory over La Beauce, Mario poked his head outside the dressing-room door. His parents stood there with the clergyman. "Father," Mario asked, "have I done enough to get to stay in the rectory?" He stayed there on every subsequent trip, building a special relationship with Father Fortin. "One time," recalled the priest, "he was tired of playing with the others. He came to me and said he wanted to sit with me, just the two of us, and leave the others to what they were doing. He was like that, Mario. He liked to stay quietly with me, not move."

Mario was always the most determined to find favor with the priest. Frequently, on car trips to and from the arena, a mini-controversy broke out over who got to sit up front with Father Fortin. Mario defiantly insisted that he be the one and always won the fight. In Pierrette's absence, Father Fortin found himself taking on a special role—that of the surrogate mother Mario had to have. Once, when Mario left Quebec City to return to Montreal, he broke into tears. The priest promised he would come to visit him in Montreal soon.

What the priest found striking were the contrasting approaches of mother and father to son. On a rare day when the Ville Emard team lost, parents of Mario's teammates grumbled that he had taken too many penalties. That, they said, cost the team the match. Mario was left crying in disappointment. His father told him that he had to learn to play with more discipline. He lectured his son sternly, as he did frequently on hockey matters, until Pierrette entered the room and stopped him in his tracks. "Leave it alone, Jean-Guy," she ordered him. "Drop it. I'll take care of this." She took Mario to her side, said soothing words to him, and gave him hot chocolate and chocolate candies.

Chocolate was a staple food for Mario, but in an effort to build up her pale and anemic boy, Pierrette often went beyond chocolate and hamburgers and fries. Father Fortin, along with several of Mario's teammates, noticed that she was forever plying him with vitamins, protein supplements, and other med-icines to keep him going. None of the other players needed this stuff and they wondered why Mario had to have it. It wasn't a major topic of discussion, but it was a signal to some that Mario's health might be different from that of the rest.

Visiting Montreal, Fortin noticed the Lemieuxs turned over the running of the house to Mario and his brothers. If Mario wanted to stay up and play cards with the adults, Mario stayed up and played cards with the adults. If Mario wanted to sleep in all day, Mario slept in all day. If Mario wanted medicine, Mario got medicine. Though he loved the Lemieuxs, Fortin thought it was too much.

Lemieux didn't talk to the priest or anyone else about dreams of one day becoming an NHL star, not then or later. But while there was no talk of it, everyone knew where Mario's future lay before he even reached age ten. His vocation was written in every stride he took. The coaches who followed Fichaud—first Roland Faubert, then Ron Stevenson—discovered, like the first coach, that there was nothing he had to be taught. His was a talent bestowed, "a gift of God," as his father once described it. Most exceptional players had at least a shortcoming or two to work on and grow out of. As a kid, Guy Lafleur couldn't shoot a backhand. It dribbled off the end of his stick. Finally, a coach separated him from his teammates and ordered him to practice his backhand with buckets of pucks and come back when he could do it. Wayne Gretzky worked determinedly to improve his wobbly skating and to build his frail physique. His father, Walter, trained him how to anticipate, how to read the play.

But all was right with Mario at the dawn. He had the wondrous hand-eye coordination, the sensitive hands, subtle and elusive moves, and a radar shot. He lacked breakaway speed, but had speed enough. Most importantly, he had an exceptional intuition about the game, instinctively knowing how and where to move. That intuition included something no coach could teach: a field of vision that took in what other players could not see.

His early coaches marveled at this. The eyes of an average hockey player might take in one-third, or 120 degrees, of the 360-degree circumference. Mario's eyes seemed to encompass much more, maybe 200 degrees. He had wraparound vision. He played, they said, as if his eyes were up in the press box viewing the whole ice surface.

One day in practice his coach watched in amazement as Mario skated in on two defensemen. Without turning his head, he laid a perfect pass back onto the stick of winger Stephan LePage. LePage had been trailing the play all along and Mario had not turned to look back at him. When Mario came off the ice, the coach couldn't help but ask, "How did you know LePage was there when you made that pass?"

"I could tell by the sound of his skate blades," Mario said.

The sixth sense impressed everyone, as did the delicate way he could maneuver his body and the puck. He had very light feet for a boy on his way to becoming so big, and he could glide and shift like a ballroom dancer. "I guess what impressed me the most," said Claude Côté, the manager of the Ville Emard bantam team, "was the way he faked and dribbled with the puck." He did little tricks, moving it forward and backward and between his legs, like a point guard handling a basketball.

Côté's son, Sylvain, was a linemate of Lemieux's. He remembered "the beauty" goals. "Mario and I didn't have to shoot from far out. We made our play in front of the net. Those beauty goals, you know what I mean? Those tic-tac-toe passes, then bang in the net, just like the Russians." With his treasure-trove of natural abilities, Mario needed only to grow and play a lot and have his game and his personality mature. One of the main obstacles he faced was the jealousy and bitterness his wealth of talents created among his competitors and even his elders. At a very early age opponents began acting like football linebackers to thwart him. They determined their team could only win by intimidating him or by forcing him to retaliate and thereby draw penalties. It got so vicious, recalled Claude Côté, that it became a scary thing to watch. "Mrs. Lemieux was a very excitable person, and when Mario was speared, it was certainly frightening for her. They didn't use normal tactics against him."

Mario sometimes compounded the problem because, coupled with his superior talent, he evinced an arrogant on-ice demeanor that fueled his adversary's contempt. Not suffering the slashers gladly in these early years, he sometimes toyed with them, faking his way around them three or four times on one shift, sometimes with an expression that said, "Come on, loser, I'll give you some more."

Albert Mandanici, who would later figure in Mario's career as a scout for the Pittsburgh Penguins, watched in despair as his son Joey tried, without much success, to check Mario. "It was his hands," Joey remembered. "It was the way he controlled the puck that made it so difficult. You'd go at him from one side, and suddenly he has the puck on the other." As Lemieux filled the net with pucks, the senior Mandanici grew angry. He could see himself in his son Joey, and see his own limitations. He went home frustrated.

Mandanici remained considerably cooler, however, than other parents whose sons were belittled by the Mario magic. Once, when he scored five goals in a game, a woman spat on him on his way to the dressing room. The woman had a special interest in the game. She was the losing coach's wife. Lemieux's coach, Roland Faubert, chased after his opposite number to tell him to calm her down.

There were other such spitting incidents. The abuse little Mario took off the ice meant that teammates sometimes had to act as bodyguards even when he went to a food counter for a hot dog or soft drink. Meanwhile, the abuse he took on the ice got so bad that Ron Stevenson, his bantam coach, once refused to let the *Ottawa Citizen* take his picture after a game. Mario, the coach felt, was too beaten and bruised. He would look awful.

The young Mario learned that he had to have ways of protecting himself. He became, in the opinion of teammates and opponents alike, one the dirtiest players in the league. Checkers like Joey Mandanici found he liked to use his stick when the referee was turned the other way. "He was easy to frustrate. When you just touched him, he gave you the cheap shot." He had a preferred spot for it, Mandanici recalled—"Just below your calf."

The quick temper and dirty play remained a source of controversy between Mario and his coaches. They hated to see him in the penalty box. Absorb the hits, they advised. Turn the other cheek. Mario could do it—but only sometimes.

In a peewee tournament, the provincial championships, his opponents from Verdun came at him as if their sticks were swords. Mario responded in kind and spent most of the first period in the penalty box. The coaches, tired of his revenge penalties, benched him. Mario was so disappointed, he cried. In the second intermission Ivan Gauvreau, the team's assistant coach, went to see him. "He was crying like a baby. I remember standing in the corner of the dressing room with him. He wanted to go on the ice so badly."

Gauvreau tried to calm him. He told him to control himself. "If you can play with discipline, we'll put you back in the game." Mario got back in and, with his team trailing 2–1, helped it toward a comeback victory. But he was still angry and so was his father. Sylvain Côté heard Jean-Guy dress him down. "We were good friends," said Côté, "and after the game I went to his house with his father. His father tried to tell him, 'You're the best, but you've got to stay on the ice. You can't retaliate.' Mario listened, but he was mad and when he played the rest of the tournament, then you saw the real Mario."

Though he shone in all the remaining games of that competition, he could not hope to match the performance he gave against Montreal North. As in the game against Verdun,

Lemieux fell into one of his dark, frustrated moods. He repeatedly fouled opponents and was booed by the fans. Mario was benched, Mario wept, and as was always the case in these situations, Mario's team fell behind. But this time it fell behind by an impossible margin. The score after two periods was Montreal North 6, Ville Emard 1.

The coaches sent Mario back out for the final twenty minutes. They had pretty well written this game off. With Lemieux on the team, they might have known better than to do that, but they couldn't have been expected to see inside him and know that the light had gone on. It didn't happen too often. Usually, Mario played a low-intensity game that was brilliant enough. Once in a while, however, the ego was wounded and he faced an exceptional challenge. Even as a boy, they said he sometimes needed a big challenge to make him go, something to snap his low-intensity cord, the cord that held him back.

In the Montreal North game it snapped. He came out for the final period and, using feints and hand-eye chemistry, he weaved around defenders to score two quick goals. It was 6–3. Then he scored another. He had put a hat trick together. Pierrette was screaming at her little cub and the stone face of Jean-Guy Lemieux was beginning to crack.

The kids on the opposing team had become too awed by now. They started playing cautiously, taking extra split seconds, thereby giving Mario time to work his magic.

After he had scored three in a row, the seas parted some more and Lemieux skated through. He scored again, to give him four straight and move his team within one goal. He scored a fifth to tie the game. Now, one shy of the double hat trick, he loosened himself from the grasp of his checkers and came face to face with a goalie who, like Carl Parker, must have felt like running for cover. He scored his sixth goal of the period.

Final score: Mario Lemieux 7, Montreal North 6.

THREE
THE BLACK MACHINE

MARIO LEMIEUX ALWAYS KNEW THAT NO ONE WAS BETTER. "I WAS always the best at the games we played," he would say. "Hockey or baseball, anything physical. As far back as I remember, I was always the best."

Always being the best meant gaining a degree of confidence that was extraordinary. It was simply a given that, if need be—but only if need be, only if he felt like it—Mario could rise above the rest. This total, unwavering self-assurance would sometimes leave teammates startled.

Through ages seven, eight, and nine, Mario's atom team under Coach Faubert, the Ville Emard Hurricanes, had won virtually everything there was to win, emerging victorious in six of the seven tournaments they entered. Mario was named MVP in all six. Before moving on to the peewee and bantam levels, however, he heard a lot of talk, just as Gretzky had at the same age, that he might not be able to cut it. Sure, he was good playing with the little kids, but just wait until he came up against some real competition. When Mario moved up to peewee, he quickly put such talk to rest. He scored four goals in his first game.

At the peewee and then the bantam level, which took him

through age fourteen, the Ville Emard Hurricanes he played on were a cocky group. They wore black uniforms and liked to think of themselves as tough. They had a nickname, "the Black Machine." They chanted it quietly as they came out of their dressing room and increased the volume until their skates touched the ice surface. There, in a dark, silent swirl, they began circling their zone.

They loved this moment. Just pulling on the black sweaters gave them a feeling of power. The crests on their jerseys featured a pelican flying wildly out of control. For good measure, it had a scar on its face. Coach Ron Stevenson liked to cultivate the rugged image. He didn't want a team fashioned after the elegant home-town Canadiens, but one more in the mold of the Philadelphia Flyers, the search-and-destroy gang of the mid-seventies, who laid waste to almost every team they played.

Stevenson's Hurricanes had a heated rivalry with the team from Granby. Through several close games during the regular season, a boys' brand of tension had developed between the two clubs. In one encounter a Granby forward rammed the butt end of his stick into a Hurricane player. Ron Stevenson forbade foul language from his charges, but witness to this infraction, a member of the Black Machine stood on the bench and cried, "Coach, the bastard is dead!" With that, he leaped over the boards, charging the Granby player.

Granby had a mean team, but Ville Emard had the toughest player, Sylvain Nantel. Nantel wasn't big, but he had shoulders of steel. For several years he served as the enforcer, protecting Mario from all the kid-goons on the other teams. Pierrette Lemieux appreciated this. Whenever an opponent fouled her son, Pierrette jumped to her feet, instructing Nantel, in her off-color French, to take care of him. Steel Shoulders was always up to his eyeballs in mayhem and Mrs. Nantel, whose vocal cords were every bit as coarse and loud as Pierrette's, was forever trying to restrain him. After games, Pierrette would have some explaining to do. She didn't mean for Sylvain to pummel Mario's assailants, she'd tell Mrs. Nantel, just ward the little buggers off.

After the tough season, the Black Machine met Granby in a tournament final. The game progressed in an air of crisp tension and the score stood tied at the end of regulation time. The teams played two five-minute periods of overtime and the score remained even. They played three more overtime periods. To most everyone's surprise, Mario Lemieux still had not put it away.

The rules now called for the outcome to be determined by a shoot-out: five shots for each club, most goals wins. After four, Ville Emard had one goal more. To tie, Granby had to score on its last attempt and hope the Hurricane shooter missed.

Before the finale, Mario Lemieux, who had his team's last shot, skated down to have a word with goalie Carl Parker. Parker, expecting a routine pep talk, welcomed the visit. He had become especially worried about this game, not just because Black Machine pride was on the line, but because of all the betting. The fathers of the Ville Emard players, so confident of victory with Mario on the team, bet big sums on the games. On this one Parker's dad had $200. During the break before the shoot-out, Parker had also been told that Sylvain Côté's father had put down $500 on it. "God," thought Parker, "it's all riding on me." As Mario approached him, the goalie lifted his mask and they had a brief chat. "Carl," said Mario. "We're up one goal. You stop this next guy and we win." Parker nodded. He wasn't so stupid that he hadn't figured that out already. But Mario hadn't finished. He looked at Carl Parker with an expression the goalie had come to know well, an expression of total confidence. In a cool, forthright manner, he said, "If you don't stop this guy, Carl, don't worry about it. I'm going to score anyway."

While Parker checked his ears, Mario skated over to the

bench to watch Granby's attempt. Their shooter came in and beat Parker cleanly. With the score tied, Mario readied for the final shot, gazing down at the Granby goaltender. The buzz of the jammed-in crowd gathered momentum as, with immaculate calm, Mario slowly made his way across the blue line and toward the target. He preferred, on most occasions, to close right in, fake the goaltender to one side of the net, and put the puck in the other. But this time, he slowed at about twelve feet in front of the goal, drew back his hands, and aimed a wrist shot at the net-minder's upper left side.

Carl Parker could barely watch. Even though he was confident of the outcome, even though he had just heard Lemieux's expression of ultimate faith, he was scared that once, maybe just this once, the Natural's genius would fail him. His fright seemed endless, but it lasted only the split second it took for the puck to quietly pulverize the white netting.

While there was no denying Mario Lemieux's abundant talents, other factors, as his years in peewee and bantam would illustrate, contributed handsomely to his development. By luck of circumstance, Mario had fallen into the most favorable of hockey milieux. In Ville Emard the minor hockey organization was superior, the quality of the coaching high. In Ville Emard the teams he played on were top-rate and the time devoted to hockey exceptional. In Ville Emard the support and protection Mario received from his family, his teammates, and his school proved extraordinary.

Though clearly the best player on the Black Machine, in the development of his abilities Mario was fortunate that his team had other superior performers. Two more future NHLers, J. J. Daigneault and Marc Bergevin, played with him. As line-mates, he had the speedy Sylvain Côté, who would also have made it to the NHL but for a virus that attacked his kidneys, and the small but deadly Stephan LePage, who had a way of getting to the front of the net and banging in Mario's precision passes. This trio skated together for more than three years. Even as atoms, they were taught an advanced collective brand of hockey with intricate passing patterns that Coach Faubert would have them walk through in a gym if ice wasn't available. The coaches wanted an offense of five equal parts, not one pivoting on a single player. Mario played unselfish hockey, demonstrating early on that he derived as much pleasure from the art of the pass as the art of the score. Coaches often had to urge him to shoot more. He passed off too much.

With playoffs and tournaments, Mario played close to a hundred games a season. Additionally, he had two practices a week and played in countless outdoor pick-up games near his home. The residence, a modest, semi-detached, brown-brick house on Rue Jorgue, lay within a five-minute walk of the small ice patch located out behind the church of St. Jean de Matha, a Byzantine structure fronted by a tower of bells. When not at the Gadbois arena, the Hurricanes played boot hockey there for as long as the daylight hours would allow. They took their hockey sticks to Madame Lemieux's and heated the blades over her stove to give them more curve, then returned to Pierrette's afterward for her delicious junk food—greasy fries and burgers dressed in everything and *crème caramel* for dessert.

Mario and his teammates also hung out at Dilallo's Burgers, which was across the street from the church. The Dilallo brothers, hockey enthusiasts who owned a small chain of restaurants, had sponsored Ville Emard teams since the early 1960s. As much as was possible, they modeled their teams on NHL clubs. Mario and the other Hurricanes wore jackets and ties on road trips and kept their hair trimmed. They faced penalties for breaking curfew, being late, getting low grades in school, and cursing.

Coach Stevenson, a friend of the Dilallos, was a father figure to the players, much admired by them. He made a special effort to ensure that the stars of his team did not receive preferential treatment. Stevenson meted out punishment like a cantankerous schoolteacher. Players had to write out fifty or a hundred "I must not" lines for infractions of the rules or miscues on the ice. Mario wrote as many lines as anyone. A young master of the "tabernack" vocabulary, he wrote "I must watch my language" hundreds of times, as well as "I must backcheck," which surprised none of his teammates, and "I must not get misconduct penalties."

Lemieux liked the coach, but because the boy was so quiet and withdrawn, few words were exchanged between them. Stevenson, a friend of the Lemieux family, picked up Mario and drove him to many games and practices. After greeting the coach, Mario would get in the car and not utter another word the rest of the way. Stevenson thought it was a bit unusual. Because little Mario was the coming superstar, many people wanted to meet and talk to him. Mario was so shy that he was often unreceptive, sometimes impolite. Finally, Stevenson had to take him aside and explain some basic courtesies. "He was the kind of guy who taught me a lot of things when I was young," Mario would later recall. "He wanted me to be polite with the older people, with the parents and people surrounding me. He said you should respect others and I think I learned that."

Although quiet and deadly serious about hockey, Mario was not without a mischievous side. He'd hide equipment or pull other stunts on his teammates in the hope that the coach would mete out a hundred lines to them. With Carl Parker, Sylvain Côté, Daigneault, or other teammates, Mario roamed the streets of Ville Emard looking for laughs. Besides Dilallo's burger store, a favorite hangout was the local roller-skating rink. One of the guys would sneak out some beers and Mario and the boys would put on their shades and have a few brews, on the way to the rink. Hijinks of one kind or another usually followed. One time they were walking the streets, sipping beers through straws, and giving the occasional slow-moving car a good kick, especially if it had a lady driver. The good time lasted until a horrified Mario peered through the window to discover that the car he and the boys were heavy-footing was his aunt's. This was one of the problems of fun-seeking in Ville Emard: he had a relative on every block. Seeing his close relative in the car, Mario dove to the pavement. He lay there for several minutes until the coast was clear.

He wasn't so lucky on a trip to Chicoutimi. He and some teammates found a local roller-skating arena with friendly girls and good music. They were stepping into their first teen years at this time and, while hockey remained their primary fixation, girls had become a relevant sideline. Curfew on road trips was nine o'clock, but at eleven o'clock, Mario and his teammates were still on roller skates. Mario's brother Alain, who was playing for a Chicoutimi team at the time, told the coaches the kids would probably be at the arena. When the coaches arrived at the door, some of the Hurricanes tried another exit. It was locked.

For their insubordination, they had their curfew put at seven o'clock the next night. They felt badly and knew that if they didn't win the tournament, their behavior would not be easily forgotten. Mario huddled with Sylvain Côté, Marc Bergevin, and others, and with the magnificent confidence he had displayed to Carl Parker after five periods of overtime, he told them he was ready to play. In the first game following the curfew violation, the Black Machine destroyed their opponent 12–1. Mario had six goals and five assists. His team went on to win the tournament.

They celebrated and, as they prepared to board the bus to return to Montreal, their transgression appeared to be forgotten. But just then, the girls from the roller-skating rink showed up to say goodbye. Mario was beginning to get tender with his "belle," getting a little "kissy, kissy," as one of the coaches recalled, when, bursting onto the scene like a hailstorm, came his seething mother. "Jesus Christ, my child! What on earth do you think you're doing?"

Didn't he realize he was still just a boy! He was too young! These girls would be his ruination! As the tongue-lashing continued, Mario could see the grinning faces of his teammates in the bus windows. The boys on the bus were cracking up, Mario's girl was ashen, and Pierrette wouldn't shut up. Didn't he know, she stammered, that he could fall in love, that his love for a girl could supplant his love of hockey? Didn't he know this?

Pierrette's singular ambition for her son would brook no female interference for several years to come. Nor, for that matter, interference of other sorts. If girls got in the way, girls had to go. If school got in the way, school had to go.

Mario liked to go to bed late and sleep late the next morning, which meant missing a lot of school. But with his mother's blessing, he was allowed as much snoozing time as he wished. He became almost as good at hooky as at hockey. The other members of the team would drag themselves to class after a long night at the arena. "We'd look around," recalled Sylvain Côté, "and, oops, no Mario. He'd show up for a couple of days, then we'd look around and, oops, no Mario." After the record-long Granby game, Carl Parker, trying to stay awake, surveyed his classroom the next morning and discovered, without surprise, that Mario wasn't there. "If only," Parker thought, "I had a mom like Pierrette."

Everyone sensed that Mario was a bright boy, easily as smart as the other players. He had a studious, thoughtful way about him and could size things up intelligently. With an effort, he might have been a top-rank student. But the mind was always on the rink. "You want to know if there is anything else besides hockey that interests me," Mario would one day tell an interviewer. "The answer is no. At the age of six I separated myself from the others thanks to the way I could handle a stick and puck, and never did the idea of doing anything else other than play hockey ever cross my mind. My life is one long skating rink."

Mario not only got help from Pierrette, who, some of the players maintained, even helped write out the lines assessed by Coach Stevenson, but also from a junior-high principal who was a hockey fan. In order to play on the Hurricanes, coaches required that the boys maintain their grades. Despite all his absences, Mario kept getting sufficient marks. His teammates couldn't understand it, until they got the word. "It was the principal," said Parker. "She loved hockey, went to a lot of the games. She wanted to help Mario."

A lot of effort went into the protection of Mario Lemieux. It was a constant theme song of his early years. Sylvain Nantel recalled a confrontation in a restaurant prior to a peewee game, when Mario and the Hurricanes accidentally met up with their opponents from Notre Dame de Grace. NDG star Sergio Momesso, who would play for several NHL teams, tried to provoke a fight with Mario. Instead of taking him out during the game, Momesso thought he'd give things a new twist and try to do so beforehand. Before he could lay into him, however, J. J. Daigneault leaped across the table at Momesso, getting Lemieux out of harm's way.

The players liked Mario. He may have appeared arrogant to others, but not to them. To them, he was low key, humble, and the best in the game. So Daigneault, while small, was prepared to fight to save the star. For his effort, he was rewarded with deep scratches around the eyes. But he accomplished his mission. His Hurricanes, led by their god, went on to crush NDG that evening.

By age twelve, Mario had caught the attention of the Montreal Canadiens. Yvan Cournoyer, the Habs' cannon-propelled winger, attended a Hurricanes' game and returned to the Forum to tell Coach Scotty Bowman that he had seen the future and it was Mario Lemieux. Bowman went to Granby one night to see the wunderkind for himself and Mario put on a clinic for him. Bowman agreed with Cournoyer. He told *Le Journal de Montréal* that the Habs had scouts running around all over the place, but the best prospect in the world was sitting right in their own backyard. The Montreal Canadiens hosted a big night for minor-league players. The player of the month was given the honor of appearing for a photo session with the Habs' player of the month. Mario's appearances included one with his idol in the 1970s, Guy Lafleur. He was at the Forum sitting right behind the Canadiens' bench when, for the third consecutive season, the Flower scored his 50th goal. Pierrette Lemieux treasured a picture showing Lafleur in celebration and her son in the background reacting to the goal. In her home, which would become a shrine to her boy's story, it took a proud place.

As impressive as he was in those days, as brazen as his confidence level appeared, Mario couldn't come close to matching Wayne Gretzky's staggering minor-league output. When Gretzky was ten years old, he scored 378 goals in eighty-five games. He averaged four and a half goals a game. He edged his nearest rival in the scoring race by 238 goals. Those who witnessed his exploits remarked on Gretzky's unremitting intensity. If he had six goals in the game and his team was ahead by a dozen, Gretzky would be pressing for goal number seven. It was always Maximum Wayne.

Mario's numbers were closer to those of ordinary superstars like Guy Lafleur. One of his most productive seasons came in his second year as a peewee, when he had 150 goals and 90 assists. A much different type of player than Gretzky, Mario played a moodier game. On some nights, like when he played his final game for Coach Stevenson, the mood was right and the result was preordained. He badly wanted to win that last game for Stevenson. After two periods against St. Leonard, however, his team was behind by two goals. During the intermission Mario, who usually never said anything between periods, went over to the coach. "Don't worry, Mr. Stevenson," he said. "I'll make sure we win this game for you." And of course, having willed it, Mario Lemieux went out and made it come true. He scored three goals in the final twenty minutes, just enough for the Ville Emard Hurricanes to win again.

On other nights, when the stakes were not as high, Mario leisurely roamed the neutral zone for long stretches, as a sea gull does the shore line. Maximum Mario was never as easy to get as Maximum Wayne. He inherited, as did his brother Alain, his father's low-key, passive approach to life. It was rare to see the eye of the tiger in Mario or Alain. Alain possessed marvelous natural abilities, but was standoffish. He didn't like to go into the corners. Coaches talked about him in the same vein that Toronto Maple Leaf boss Harold Ballard once talked about Inge Hammarstrom, a Swedish winger. "He could go into a corner with a half-dozen eggs in his pocket," said Ballard, "and not break any of them."

Mario didn't shy away from the corners, but he was, for the most part, a low-intensity player. His lack of passion could be found in his bloodline, in the fact that he was coddled by so many around him, in the fact that he was bequeathed too much talent to begin with. He had a problem, a nice problem to have, but a problem just the same. Without hard work, he could still conquer. He could play at 60 percent capacity and still be better than the rest.

FOUR
NUMBER 66

BOB PERNO, AN IMPORTANT FIGURE IN MARIO LEMIEUX'S LIFE,
part brother, part father, and agent for him, owed his status as a
hockey agent to Wayne Gretzky. He deeply admired Gretzky.
He would try to mold Mario in his image because, for him, there
could be no better model. He would try hard, but perhaps he
should have realized that Wayne and Mario were different in
every way, except in their genius for the game.

Perno, a short, stocky man with dark, sad eyes, had once
entertained thoughts of becoming a pro hockey player himself.
But while playing midget, he broke his arm at the elbow after
falling backward over an opponent. The doctors then reset it the
wrong way. They had to break it and cast it again. When Perno
finally did get back to hockey, he went out and fractured the arm
one more time. He decided he had had enough.

After a couple of years at Concordia University in Montreal, he got a job in the advertising department of the *Montreal
Star* newspaper. The paper folded in 1976. Perno sold ads for a
publication called *Camping Canada* until, through a contact, he
was hired by a hockey stick manufacturing company, Titan, as
sales director. Lean times followed. Lightweight sticks, white in
color, were in vogue and Titan produced dark-colored sticks.

Players, Perno analyzed, associated dark colors with weight. To effect a badly needed image reversal, he was convinced the company needed the endorsement of a budding star. He had heard about Wayne Gretzky, the whirling kid phenomenon then playing his first year of junior in Sault St. Marie. Following one visit to the Sault—Gretzky scored four times—Perno came back and told his boss: "We gotta gamble on this kid." He talked to Gretzky, who said he would only use a stick under 650 grams. Perno had a dozen sticks made to this featherweight specification. Gretzky liked them and kept ordering more. After the season he signed an endorsement contract worth the small sum of $2,000 to promote Titan's product. As Gretzky's career took off, so did the sales of Titan sticks. Perno had his break. He had shown initiative, it had paid off, and more good news was on the way.

Gretzky's agent was the Toronto-based Gus Badali. Badali was looking for a presence in Quebec, someone who could spot and sign the rising young stars in that province. Gretzky had just the guy: Bob Perno. Through the recommendation of Gretzky, who had come to be friends with the hockey stick salesman, Perno was hired as Badali's main man in *la belle province*.

Some time later, as he was reading through old newspaper files in his suburban Montreal home in St. Lucie, Perno came across the evaluation Scotty Bowman had made of young Mario Lemieux. Perno knew of the Lemieux boy, but now his eyes lit up. "Christ," he murmured, "if Bowman thinks this. . . ."

That spring, 1981, he went out to see Mario, now fifteen, at a hockey school at the University of Montreal. Mario wasn't having an oustanding camp; he was by no means dominant. But Perno got very enthused watching him. He sensed Mario had Gretzky qualities. In the way Mario thought on the ice, in the way he saw, in the way he handled the puck, in the way he passed it, Perno sensed extraordinary hockey intuition.

Jean-Guy and Pierrette were attending the camp, following

their son's every move. Perno arranged a meeting with them in the living room of their house on Rue Jorgue. He knew a couple of other agents had been trying to sign Lemieux, but he felt he had the ace card. When he casually mentioned to the Lemieuxs that Wayne Gretzky (164 points in his previous season with the Edmonton Oilers) was a client with his agency, the Badali agency, he noticed a change of mood in the room. Now the Lemieuxs were sitting up in their chairs. Gretzky was not only a client, Perno continued, but a personal friend. Mario would get to know him, he would learn from him, they would become friends.

Mario hadn't said much, but when he spoke, Perno was struck by his cocksure nature. Mario hadn't played a single game of junior yet, but he declared that day that he could break the Quebec junior scoring records and become the number one junior player in the world. If he did those things, he asked Perno, "How big a contract do you think you can get me?"

Most fifteen-year-olds didn't talk this way—especially with their parents in the room. They might say they could be as good as any other junior, but not the very best. They might, on the question of money, feel around a bit to get an idea, but not ask a pointed "how much?" Not at fifteen years old. Perno stalled for time. "Well, it's hard to say," he responded. "But if you break the records and are the first pick in the NHL draft, I think you will become a millionaire with your first contract."

Mario's eyes jumped. It was the number he wanted to hear. "A million dollars!" he said. "I'll get a million dollars? You're sure?" He looked at his mom and dad. More discussion followed. "Yes," Perno vowed. "I'll get you a million." Mario shook Perno's hand and declared, "You are my agent." The handshake was the extent of their agreement. Perno would regret the simplicity of it some years down the line, but for now, he was delighted. He had, he was sure, the hottest prospect in the province.

Mario had just completed a year of provincial Midget Triple A hockey for the Montreal Concordia team. He was the top scorer in the loop with sixty-two goals in forty games. In the playoffs he suffered a slash across the hand, which left a gash with considerable swelling around it. The blow came in the final minute of a game that was going into overtime. The doctor, Réal Lemieux (no relation), came into the dressing room, examined the wound, and pronounced Mario unfit to play. Mario said he didn't care, he was going to play anyway. In the overtime period he went out and, playing with half a hand, set up the winning goal. It was a vignette of valor every great athlete is supposed to have in his or her scrapbook.

In the draft for the Quebec Major Junior Hockey League, the owner of the Laval Voisins, Claude Fournel, debated between taking Lemieux or Sylvain Turgeon of Hull first overall. The manager of the Ville Emard Hurricanes, Claude Côté, told Fournel: "You got no one showing up at your rink. If you want to pack the barn, there is only one thing to do. Pick Mario."

Fournel's display of confidence in Mario prompted another manifestation of the young player's bravado. He promised the owner that he would bring Laval the ultimate prize in junior hockey: the Memorial Cup. He didn't know Fournel's reputation, but others, like Perno and Marc Lachapelle, the junior hockey writer for *Le Journal de Montréal*, were not enthusiastic about him. They thought he was pompous and tight with money. Perno expected problems with Fournel, and alerted Badali in Toronto.

That summer, Perno quickly took Lemieux under his wing. They saw or spoke to each other virtually every day. Mario was taking his first steps out from under the gaze of his mother and father. He would watch TV at the Pernos', he'd play ball hockey on the street with Perno's kids, he'd sometimes stay overnight. Perno introduced him to a new sport, one which would come to rival hockey in Mario's esteem. He took Mario and his brother Alain to the St. Hyacinthe golf links. Mario fired a 116, a noteworthy first-time score. He soon came to love the game, demonstrating a talent for it almost as natural as that for hockey. He swung in a smooth, graceful, classic rhythm. He had feel, extrasensory feel, and he had power. After a few times out, he was breaking a hundred. Within a year, he was breaking eighty. Within a few years, he was breaking par.

Golf, in the form of Gus Badali's annual Toronto tournament, provided the occasion for an introduction to Wayne Gretzky. Gretzky was in training for the 1981 Canada Cup tournament at the time and was slated to do a TV commercial the day before the golf get-together. More than happy to greet the young Quebec star, Gretzky invited Mario to follow him during the commercial shoot to get a look at what might be in store for himself some day. He had first seen Mario Lemieux some weeks earlier when, at the bidding of Badali and Perno, he dropped by a summer-league hockey game in Montreal. He watched the big kid for a while and said some obligatory nice things, noting in particular his size advantage.

During the filming of the commercial, Perno and Badali instructed Mario to closely observe the professional manner with which Gretzky comported himself: the modesty, the politeness, the good nature, the sensitivity to the feelings of others. Gretzky then surprised Mario by inviting him to dinner. Totally unknown outside of Quebec, a kid who spoke only broken English, Mario wasn't exactly prize company at the time. But Gretzky followed dinner with an invitation to join him for a few beers at Ports, the trendy singles bar of the day on Yonge Street. Mario was fifteen, several years below the legal drinking age, but this was Wayne Gretzky. No one was going to ask a friend of Wayne Gretzky's for proof of age.

As a young bachelor, Gretzky was highly active on the social front. After he had given Mario some advice on stardom, public relations, endorsements, and whatnot in the bar's Kon Tiki room, he fell into conversation with a couple of adoring girls, both of whom knew of him, of course, but not of his friend Mario. Continuing his performance as the perfect host, Gretzky introduced one of the girls to Mario. The four of them then adjourned to the Westbury Hotel, where they spent the night and, if what Mario later told a friend was true, a big moment in his young life took place. It had only been a year previous that young Mario had been lectured by his mom for venturing a kiss with a girl outside the bus in Chicoutimi. As a chaperone, Mario discovered that night in Toronto, the Great Gretzky was leagues ahead of Pierrette.

On Mario's favorite-player chart, Gretzky had been gaining ground on Guy Lafleur, who was beginning a slow and painful decline with the Canadiens. That night, the transfer of allegiance was complete. With little in it for himself, Gretzky had given an entire day over to entertaining Mario, a kid who hadn't even played a game of junior. Mario was dazzled.

The highlights from the Toronto visit, however, were not yet complete. On the train trip home with Perno, Mario wanted to discuss his jersey number. Throughout his minor-league career, he had worn number 27. His brother Alain wore 27 and Mario had continued the family tradition. But now both he and Perno agreed it was time for a change.

"Well," said Perno, "what number do you want to wear?"

Mario thought for a few seconds. "How about 99?" he asked.

Perno frowned. He was once again taken aback by the kid's presumptuousness. Here was an untested midget, whose visions of grandeur already extended to sharing in the glory of Gretzky's own distinctive trademark. He shook his head. "There already is a 99, Mario," he told him. "He's setting records, he's in a class by himself. Why put that kind of pressure on your shoulders?"

Mario asked Perno to suggest a number. Perno hadn't given it much thought, but Mario's mention of number 99 got his imagination working. He did like the Gretzky connection, but didn't want to be so brazen as to copy it. So he flipped it over. "How about 66?"

A smile came over Mario's face. If not 99, number 66 would be the ideal compromise. He agreed to it on the spot, and 66 would be his number for life.

The summer of '81 saw the dispersal of Mario's old Ville Emard gang. As testimony to the talent of the Black Machine, two out of every three players on the team moved up to the Quebec major-junior level. Without his old friends nearby, Mario became more reliant on Bob Perno. Because Laval was on the outskirts of Montreal, at the opposite end of Ville Emard, he could no longer be cared for and live full time at home. He sometimes stayed at a boarding house in Laval, sometimes at home, sometimes at Perno's.

Linemate Sylvain Côté was off to Granby; Marc Bergevin to Chicoutimi; Carl Parker and Sylvain Nantel, Mario's body-guard, suited up for Trois-Rivières. Parker had been Mario's opponent, teammate, and now had to face him in the nets again. He had grown up considerably since the terrible day Mario had come hurtling in on him and he had evacuated the cage. Having played with him, having studied his moves, Parker felt he could now stop him. As he dressed for his first junior-league confrontation against Lemieux, he thought how delightful it would be if he could shut him right down. His Trois-Rivières coach played up the rivalry, telling the media he was counting on Lemieux's old friends to win the game for their team.

Mario quickly crushed the hopes. He beat Parker six times. His Laval team ran over Trois-Rivières. After the game, Parker went over to the other dressing room to see him. He found

Mario with a grin on his face. "You're an animal, you know that?" Parker said. "You really piss me off." He went on, calling Mario "shithead" and a variety of other honorifics, but he couldn't keep a serious face. The two old friends finally broke out laughing.

Mario had lost his long-time protector, but Sylvain Nantel had good memories and it was indicative of the loyalty Mario inspired that even now, playing on an opposing team, Nantel was prepared to help out his old friend. The Trois-Rivières bunch Nantel had joined were gangsters, a mean group of raw-meat hunters, the dirtiest team in the loop. In a game following the one in which Mario beat Parker six times, the true nature of this team was made manifest when it chose an early moment—the pregame warm-up—to start the game's first pitched battle.

The Laval netminder had left his helmet at center ice, near his team's bench. A Trois-Rivières player skated by, took it on his stick, and began passing it around among his teammates as if it were a puck. When Laval players came to retrieve it, the brawl erupted. Lemieux, of course, was a prime target. Trois-Rivières had several players who wouldn't have minded putting him in the hospital for the evening. Acutely aware of the possibility, Nantel skated quickly over to Lemieux, jostled him off to the side, and commenced a phony war, a pretend fight. The diversion worked. The other head-hunters on the Trois-Rivières team left Mario to Nantel. Some of Mario's teammates sustained match penalties or bad wounds from the fracas, but not Lemieux.

Nantel thought he was entitled to a vote of thanks from his old friend. But while checking Mario during the game, in which four hundred penalty minutes were assessed, Mario responded with a wicked slash across the legs. Nantel exploded. "What are you doing? You know I've got a job to do out here. Are you forgetting what happened earlier?" Lemieux acknowledged his old friend had indeed helped him out, and at game's end apologized for the slash. Nantel, however, still had to face his own teammates, some of whom were angry he hadn't finished off Lemieux for the evening during the pre-game hostilities. Accused of being a traitor, Nantel replied that he respected Mario Lemieux too much to maim him. Quebeckers had to have pride in their best, he argued. "He's our superstar. He's our bread and butter. He draws the fans. He makes us known. Let's be proud we have one like him."

He went on. "I'll beat the piss out of anyone, but not guys like Mario Lemieux. I'm not going to dirty my name doing that."

Playing on a weak Laval team, Lemieux recorded a respectable first year in junior hockey, but was unable to provide the output and the spectacle some expected of him. He looked alert on some nights, tired and inactive on others. He showed himself to be a splendid playmaker, counting sixty-six assists in sixty games, but his goal scoring was a disappointment. He had only thirty. Still, his ninety-six points led all new-comers in the league, and when he and his parents and Bob Perno went to the year-end awards banquet, they were sure Mario would walk off with the rookie-of-the-year title. This would constitute an important honor for Lemieux. It would be evidence to support his claim that he could be the best junior. It would vindicate Fournel's selecting him number one over Sylvain Turgeon in the draft. So when they announced Turgeon as the winner, a feeling of shock swept the Lemieux table. Jean-Guy remained impassive. His eyes didn't move. But Pierrette was devastated. She wept openly. Perno tried to calm her, but it was no use. At home, her tears continued to flow. Her son, she said, had been cheated.

Mario was bitter. "I know I'm a better player," he said. "I'll show them. I know I'm better." Perno tried to explain to the family that the award was not so significant, that, yes, Mario deserved it, but that disappointments were part of life. "You have to learn from it," he told Mario. "You have to prove them wrong." But it took a long time for the Lemieuxs to get over it. Most everyone, not just the Lemieux circle, agreed that Mario merited the award. Speculation suggested that management on other teams cast votes for Turgeon out of spite for Fournel, whom they disliked.

The disappointment of the first season contributed to Mario's decision to leave school with a grade ten education. He complained that having to combine classes with hockey had made him tired, depriving him of playing to his potential. "I want to be the best in the world," he told Perno. The only way he could do that, he said, was to be free to concentrate all his efforts on hockey.

The decision, as Mario himself recognized, constituted a big gamble. If hockey didn't work out, he was stuck. Perno and Badali tried to dissuade him. They talked to Gretzky, who had also quit in high school. Gretzky felt Mario could attend classes and still stay sharp for games. The agents passed on Wayne's message to Mario. But Mario wasn't convinced and after much discussion, his own view held. His parents supported him. His father had been confident since Mario was six years old that he would one day be an NHL star. As a compromise, Badali and Perno got him to take English courses. With the type of career he had ahead of him, learning English, they stressed, was imperative. Mario agreed and devoted considerable energies to the study of the language.

His effort in this regard was an exception to the norm. As much as Perno liked his client, he was becoming uneasy about Mario's work habits. While he badly wanted to be number one, Perno felt he simply was not prepared to work hard at developing his talent. Mario had said, for example, that quitting school would allow him more time to skate every day. The team owner, Claude Fournel, made sure ice time was available every afternoon at the

Laval arena so Lemieux could get that skating done. But Mario frequently missed his afternoon skate for the unlikeliest of reasons—he slept in! "He'd stay up all night watching TV," said Perno. "He'd go to bed at two in the morning and sleep till two or three in the afternoon. It was just a habit he had."

Athletes were becoming more diet-conscious in these years. Grains and fruits and vegetables supplanted beef and butter and saturated fats. But Mario, a cholesterol king, paid no heed. He also began, despite Perno's protests, smoking cigarettes at age sixteen. Soon, the habit extended to cigars, big, fat stogies that the teenager would suck on, leaving Perno shaking his head. "Smoking is like a little sex," warned Perno, who hated to see such young, pink lungs blackened. "You're never, never happy. You'll always want a little more." Mario would defend himself, saying, "I don't smoke too much. It won't hurt me." He'd claim he had quit at times, but Perno always found out otherwise.

Carl Parker, who would later reunite with Mario on the Laval team, spent a lot of time with him. He never once saw him jog or work out. Parker could understand why. "He didn't need that stuff. Everyone who saw him play realized he didn't need it. He was just too good. He was a natural."

Even so, Perno didn't find the composite picture a pretty one: no exercise, junk food, tobacco, poor sleep habits. Perno was always, of course, comparing the new prodigy to Gretzky. Gretzky worked with intensity. Gretzky stayed in condition. Gretzky didn't smoke. Couldn't Mario be more like Wayne? It was a sentiment Mario would hear ad nauseam. The comparison would forever stalk him.

In his second year, when he began playing forty minutes a game, Mario felt a sharp pain in his lower back for the first time. At Mario's insistence, the Laval team doctor, Réal Lemieux, administered pain killers so he could still play. "I remember one time when we had to do an infiltration to relieve the muscle spasms," recalled the doctor. "It was very rare to do [what we did]. That's why I remember it very well."

Dr. Lemieux sensed at the time that the back problems would likely return and possibly plague Mario throughout his career. He talked it over with the young star and recommended physiotherapy to condition and strengthen the back and build it up for the rigors of the NHL. He gave Mario a program of stretching and reinforcing exercises and advised him to do a lot of swimming. But despite the potential seriousness of the condition, Mario neglected the program.

"He was not doing the exercises we asked him to do. He did not work." Dr. Lemieux would also have liked Mario to do weight training to tone his muscles, as well as running and jumping exercises. But he found, like Perno, that Mario had no interest in this and was developing "a soft body." Mario's smoking also distressed the doctor. "There are some specialists," he said, "who feel there is a bad influence on the circulation from smoking and that it affects the back. We have a surgeon in our group who forbids smoking by his back patients." Mario would continue to smoke throughout his career.

Perno could understand his own advice being ignored, but when he heard that his prize client disregarded the doctor's as well, he grew more concerned. On game days Perno would often suggest Mario rest up and prepare mentally and physically so he would be primed for a big night. "Don't worry," Mario would respond, "I'll get a couple of goals tonight." Once, Perno had his comeback well prepared. "Well, maybe you will score two goals tonight. But maybe if you really bore down and started taking care of yourself, you'd score four."

Perno, who was investing a great amount of time in his client, would not receive any payment for his services until Lemieux signed his first pro contract. In the meantime, there were some things he had to bear in mind. He had to bear in mind that there had been many sixteen-year-olds in the past who enjoyed a spectacular minor-league career and didn't make it to the NHL, much less dominate it. He had to bear in mind that Mario's first year in junior was not exceptional. He had to bear in mind that he was essentially a big, lazy kid.

Still, he had a faith in Lemieux paralleled perhaps only by that of the player's parents. He was convinced that, in Mario, he had the Gretzky equivalent and more—a Gretzky with size and strength and twice the reach. That's what was beginning to unnerve opponents. Size. Having blossomed to six-foot-four, Mario had added an asset that no superstar in hockey had enjoyed. He had been able to master all opponents in the peewee leagues when he was the same small size as they were. Now, while keeping his superior gifts, he towered over them.

Given these natural gifts, given what he could do without working hard, Perno tried to convince Mario of the need to maximize his abilities. Making such points to the player, whose stubbornness was a family trait, seldom had an impact. Like any spoiled boy, Mario would do things on his terms, the way he thought they should be done, not the way anyone else suggested they be done.

When Perno, for example, chose to criticize Mario's sometimes flagging intensity, Mario didn't respond. If Perno pressed the matter, Mario, he said, would just walk away. On other shortcomings, such as his alleged lack of defense, Mario had a ready response. "I've got the puck about seventy-five percent of the time that I'm out there. That's not such bad defense." Perno could hardly disagree.

FIVE

THE CLAN

MARIO'S DAD DROVE A RATTLING, WHEEZING OLD BUICK WITH A rusted-out floor. Cold air whipped up through the gaps in the winter and Mario froze. Sun rays glowed off the horrid yellow body in the summer and Mario cringed. He called it the "air-conditioned canary," and it embarrassed him deeply to pull up in front of a girl's house in the beast and usher her into it.

He received his driver's license shortly after turning sixteen in 1981, but since his junior hockey salary was only fifty dollars a week, he couldn't afford a car of his own. Certain hockey club owners found under-the-table ways to remunerate their junior stars with more than the paltry stipend league rules permitted. But Claude Fournel wasn't that sort.

Mario was beginning to sow some wild oats at this time. He'd confide in Perno about his sex life and share dirty jokes with him. With his dark, tall, classic look, his reserved comportment, and his hockey fame, he easily drew females to him. On more than one occasion, young ladies came on to him so aggressively in bars that he pulled away and left. But usually he enjoyed them, as any young hockey star might. "He'd spend all night with some broad," said Perno, "get two hours' sleep, and go out and score two or three goals."

Mario got hooked early. At one of the many Lemieux family get-togethers, cousins introduced Mario, seventeen, to their friend, the tall and trim Nathalie Asselin, a fifteen-year-old schoolgirl. After one minute with him, Nathalie, as she would one day testify, knew he was "the one." She would make every effort to ensure, despite the sometimes protesting Pierrette, that he didn't get away.

When taking Nathalie out, Mario became more and more irked about the yellow car. A Mercedes on the ice, he hated being an eyesore on the road. Finally, Bob Perno tossed him the keys to his own automobile, a Buick Regal. Mario was relieved. "He was a proud person," said Perno. "So to use this car made him feel much better. He was all happy when he went to pick her up." Mario took Nathalie to family gatherings, junk food outlets, or arcades where he could play pinball and other electronic games. Fittingly, given the magnificent hand-eye synchronization he had shown in hockey, Mario soon became a pinball wizard, and later, master of the Nintendo game. Nathalie, meanwhile, became an ardent hockey fan, going to all the games and defending Mario as vehemently as his mother did. Once, she got into a scrap with a woman who was heckling Lemieux during a game against Trois-Rivières. Nathalie told the woman to shut up, which led to various other exchanges.

Bob Perno liked Nathalie at first, but he worried about her crowding his boy. An upbringing in modest Ville Emard with clannish parents had yielded a youth who, like so many others his age, was sheltered, naive, and poorly educated. Perno wanted to expand Mario's horizons. One night he had Mario and Nathalie over for dinner at his St. Lucie home, and quickly discovered how unvarying some of the player's habits had become. Perno's wife had prepared a rich dish of seafood, baked to perfection. Mario looked at it with apprehension. He confessed he'd never laid eyes on this kind of thing before. The dish lay there for the longest time while the Pernos tried to convince him to eat. Finally, helped along by a fine white wine, he did so. Soon, he was quite taken by this fish stuff, and by night's end, had taken another step beyond Ville Emard.

Perno was surprised to see that Nathalie was still around after a few months. "She seemed like a nice girl," he said, "but like most young girls in a hockey player's life, I figured she'd come and she'd go . . . Mario used to see other girls. He used to really like other girls. That was another reason why I thought it would never last."

When it did, Perno began to worry. "I said to myself, 'What is she here for? Does she smell the money? Is she like a lot of these young girls who just hang around the hockey rink hoping to make it with the star?' I could see that big pro contract coming and I thought she might have ulterior motives. I guess it is natural for agents to think that way because sometimes we have to protect our clients and, in a lot of cases, we may even end up overprotecting them." Mario, he was convinced, had to focus on hockey and public responsibility. Girls could wait.

Perno was coming off a searing, grieving experience at this time, an experience that would put the game in a broader perspective and shape his thinking on the lives of young players. Besides Mario Lemieux, one of his big-name clients was Normand Leveillé. Leveillé had played a fine rookie season with the Boston Bruins in 1981–1982. His next season, the first nine games of it anyway, had begun splendidly and Leveillé looked to have a gilded future. When he phoned Perno after game nine, he brought more good news: he was planning to marry a lovely girl he had met. He was excited and wanted some advice. "What do you think, Bob? You don't think it's too early, do you?"

The only cautionary note about the call was Normand's mention of a headache, a strong, persistent pain. He had been cross-checked in the head a few nights earlier in a game against Edmonton and was carried off the ice on a stretcher. "Do you think it's the hit?" Perno asked him. "I don't know," Leveillé said, adding that he would ask the trainer for some pills. "But don't worry about it, Bob. I'll be okay."

The next morning Perno turned on his radio and heard that Leveillé had suffered a brain hemorrhage, was in a coma, and wasn't expected to live. The player regained consciousness some time later, but the stroke had crippled him and left him in a wheelchair, barely able to speak. The tragedy touched a lot of hearts and in Boston the fans came out for a Normand Leveillé night. Leveillé, who had been so audacious on the ice, such a hard skater, was wheeled out in his helpless condition and stationed behind the boards in a corner of the arena. In the tense quiet of the moment, as thirteen thousand spectators sat in silence and stillness, a Bruins' player skated alone toward Leveillé. When he reached the rink's corner, where he could see the expressionless, stricken visage of his former teammate through the plexiglass, the player banged his stick furiously, again and again, against the glass. Then another Bruin skated in and did the same, and then another and another, and as the banging of each grew louder and shattered the air, tumultuous roars cascaded in sheets from the Bruins faithful, leaving Bob Perno shivering from the raw currents of emotion that tore through him and the fans in the Boston Garden wrenched and lachrymose and heartened.

Perno came to love the indomitable spirit of Leveillé. His tragedy further sensitized Perno to the need for altruism on the part of those blessed with extraordinary gifts. That again brought him back to Gretzky, and how he cared about charity work and helping others. If he saw a boy in a wheelchair trying to make his way over to him, he would go to the boy and pose for a picture and spend time with him. Perno wanted to get

Mario on the same track, to inculcate some of that public-spiritedness in him.

Meanwhile, in discussing his relationship with Nathalie, Mario assured Perno that everything was under control. Nathalie, he said, didn't lead him to trouble, but kept him out of it and was a good adviser. "Nathalie doesn't let anything pass," he said. "When I play badly, she is the first in line to tell me. But she is very positive and helps me a great deal." He gave no indications of being a young man given over to rash impulse. "I read, I watch television, I eat, and I sleep," he said of his lifestyle at Laval. "I spend a lot of time thinking about things, wondering whether my attitude in life and on the ice is the right one."

In his second year playing for the Laval Voisins, the arrival of Nathalie in his life was one of two significant developments. The other was the arrival in Quebec of a player, an American, about half his size. Pat LaFontaine, whose family lived near Detroit, had a game predicated on bursts of acceleration, lightning lateral shifts, and a prescient hockey sense. "Hockey," said LaFontaine, "is a game of anticipation." Along with his talent, he came with a champagne smile and a natural exuberance for life, which so contrasted with the pall of reluctance enshrouding Mario Lemieux. The Quebec hockey journalists took quickly to the little Yankee's breezy brilliance. Playing for Verdun, he scored in torrents to open the season, matching Mario point for point. To sell papers, the press needed a rivalry. Now they had one: the tiny, perfect American vs. the big, brooding home boy.

Marc Lachapelle, the most important junior hockey writer in Quebec, stoked the story. In a decade at *Le Journal de Montréal*, Lachapelle had developed the junior hockey beat into a prime piece of newspaper real estate. A meat-and-potatoes reporter who talked in staccato bursts, Lachapelle worked hard and shot straight. His style did not allow him to get too close to the players. Some hockey writers became bar-time companions with the stars, thinking this was the best ticket to the inside story. Lachapelle didn't see it that way. "It's dangerous to get too close. Maybe you hang around with them and get some insights. But those insights, can you write them? Can you say he played bad because he got drunk the night before?"

LaFontaine's surge at the start of the '82 season prompted Lachapelle to focus more on the American than Mario. The boy's accessibility, his energy, his cheeriness, made the journalist's decision all the easier. Lachapelle liked him more than Mario. Though certainly admiring Lemieux's hockey brilliance, the journalist detected a selfish streak in Mario, an attitude that suggested he was prepared to do his job and nothing more. "He played the game," said Lachapelle, "and he came to the rink to practice. That was his task. And that was it."

Lachapelle saw Mario as dominated by his family coterie, inextricably bound to the Lemieux clan at the expense of everything else. The clan encompassed the immediate Lemieux family and nearly a hundred relatives and close friends who prayed together, partied together, and cheered Mario on together. Tightly woven, indefatigably loyal, they held Mario in tight embrace. Rather than socialize with teammates or others after games, Mario would melt into the clan and be gone.

His steadfast allegiance to the clan contributed to the image of Mario as a player encased, a step removed. His teammates didn't mind. As was the case in atom, peewee, and bantam, Mario was well liked by the Laval players, in good part because he never strutted his superiority. When Steven Finn, a defenseman who would go on to a career with the Quebec Nordiques, joined Laval in 1982, he was nervous about meeting Mario because of his wondrous reputation. But Mario greeted him in such a low-key, warm, and friendly manner that Finn felt at home with him the first day. "Mario had his two feet on the ground," remembered Finn. "He was liked by everybody. The thing that impressed me most about him was his confidence."

The Lemieux–LaFontaine scoring duel continued vigorously through the autumn of '82. But on a night in Drummondville in mid-November, Pat LaFontaine, who skated faster than Lemieux, faster than probably any player in the league, played an inspired game. He screamed past everyone, as if on destiny's wing. Taking the game entirely in his own hands, he posted eight points and, shooting ahead of Mario in the scoring race, soon buried him. "We didn't see Lemieux the rest of the year," Lachapelle recalled. "I can never forget that night."

Mario, in fact, continued to score at an impressive pace, impressive even for the Quebec junior league, which traditionally yielded a high-scoring brand of hockey. He was scoring almost two and a half points a game. But by Christmas, LaFontaine was at more than a three-a-game pace. He had 131 points in forty-one games. He scored in forty-three straight games to break a league record. He had a 30-point lead on Mario. The surge brought the American even more publicity, which the Lemieux clan found hard to tolerate. Some in their number came at Lachapelle. "How can you do this? You give so much ink to the American? What about Mario?" Although a strong Quebecker, sensitive to the intolerance of English-Canadians and others, Lachapelle was not about to play the role of patriot at the expense of a good story. Ignoring their wishes, he faced cold words and cold shoulders for the rest of the season.

Lemieux had stayed within reach of LaFontaine until shortly before Christmas, when he had to take a two-week break to play for Canada in the world junior tournament in Leningrad. The tournament marked his first step into international hockey, an arena that would be riddled with controversy for him. In Leningrad, Dave King, a sophisticated coach of the game, demanded disciplined play and a strong defensive effort. He didn't feel he was getting this from several players, including Lemieux. He put him on the fourth line.

Mario was furious. This criticism, that he was lackadaisical, was one he was beginning to face frequently. It would dog him forever. Yves Courteau, an excellent player who was a Laval teammate of Mario's, was among those who felt the criticism was justified. Courteau noticed that while LaFontaine flew the ice looking for opportunities, looking to implicate himself, Mario the Condor slowed and glided, waiting for the play to come to him. "When he didn't have the puck, he was an average player," said Courteau. "Mario was there, but you didn't see him." He was the same way in the dressing room in his junior days. "He'd stay in the corner," Courteau remembered, "and not say very much. He didn't really want to mix with the guys. He liked to be with his family. But he was a nice guy with everybody."

Steven Finn thought the problem had more to do with Mario's size. If he seemed as if he wasn't working or was slow, said Finn, it was because you can't make a big body look fast. "But he was a strong skater. If he got a step on you, that was it."

Jean Béliveau also faced occasional criticism that he wasn't pushing himself hard enough. So did Frank Mahovlich. But bigness didn't necessarily mean that a player had to appear lax. Phil Esposito was a big, lumbering skater, but he played eager, vigorous hockey. He was a more emotional player than Lemieux and the other big men. What created the impression of slowness was not so much the player's effort, but his temperament. Neither Lemieux nor Béliveau could sustain a proactive, hyper pace that would make them look industrious and hardworking. Their personalities were too relaxed. Their size exaggerated that relaxed state.

While acknowledging occasional lapses in intensity, Mario

believed his game was misunderstood. In a rare bit of self-analysis while he was in junior, he defended his style. "It's not easy when you are bigger than the others. The strides are longer, each gesture appears slower, and mistakes are easier to pick out. But I have the same mind as a small player. The same heart. They say I'm overloaded with talent. But they forget sometimes that I work as much if not more than the others to polish my game, to be at the top of it, to get the results that everyone expects of me."

At the world championships he hurt his knee and sat out most of three games. When he did get to play, he was scoring, which made his rare fourth-line appearances all the more frustrating.

The setting compounded his misery. Leningrad is the embodiment of melancholy at that time of the year. The city darkens at three in the afternoon, and a dank, unremitting cold breathes in from the Baltic Sea. The hotel beds are a foot short for a player of Mario's size. The bath water is rust-colored and cold. The food, when compared to Pierrette Lemieux's oily delights, is rubbery.

The juniors lost 7–3 to the gold-winning Soviets, and went home with only a bronze medal. On his return, Mario found that LaFontaine had benefited enormously from the extra games and was now practically out of reach. Mario was tired. He was hurt. The first experience in international play had left a sour impression. He told his family and his agent he would never play in the world junior championships again, nor would he ever play for Dave King.

For the rest of the season, though scoring at a high rate, he played moodily, prompting the media to sometimes question his attitude and effort. Lachapelle wrote an open letter to Mario in his newspaper, making these points. Mario was incensed, the family was incensed, and team owner Fournel, who never liked Lachapelle, was incensed. Perno had seen some merit in

Lachapelle's earlier criticisms and he hoped Mario was learning from them. But Lemieux, after all, was scoring almost three points a game and now Perno, too, thought Lachapelle had gone too far. Still, Perno didn't want to go to the lengths of Fournel. The owner's anger drove him to confront Lachapelle's employers to try to get him fired. His visit yielded the predictable result. *Le Journal*'s editors let him present his case, then told him where he could find the door.

The controversy prompted more discussion between Perno and Mario about the business of public image. The agent found that though Lemieux craved public esteem, he showed no interest in working to cultivate it. He complained frequently about being hounded by the media, about life in a fishbowl. For this very reason, he talked disparagingly about the possibility of having a career with the Montreal Canadiens. While it was every Quebec boy's dream to play for the Habs, Mario said there would be too much pressure, too much spotlight, too much attention. "To play in Montreal would be an incredible challenge. But I would certainly have less pressure in the United States and [fewer] taxes to pay."

Playing in the States would also mean living in a new culture, speaking a foreign language, leaving the clan behind. Quebec players who had previously tried to make the culture transfer—Gil Perreault, Marcel Dionne, Mike Bossy—had found it difficult. They never achieved the fame they might have in Montreal, where the Rocket, Béliveau, and Lafleur, more comfortable in their own cultural milieu, were immortalized.

When Mario minimized any aspirations toward a career with Montreal, friends thought he was only playing games. Though it was true he didn't appear to relish the media spotlight, this was a player who welcomed pressure, who, through his early career, had demonstrated he could raise his game in the climactic moments. In those situations, he wanted the puck. This was sport's great litmus test. The players who had supreme talent and supreme confidence in that talent wanted the football, the basketball, the puck, in the pivotal situations. And when they got it, when they had the final shot to win or lose the game, they showed why they had coveted the opportunity.

If he played a particularly inspired game, Mario wanted it to be noted. He'd see Perno after such games and, half-kiddingly, he'd say, "Did you see that show I put on?" Or he'd make a remark like, "How about that deke?" Or, "Did that move turn on the crowd or what?" Though he said these things laughingly, the message registered. As introverted and aloof as he was, Mario Lemieux enjoyed the roar of the crowd.

Though he lost the scoring race to LaFontaine in the 1982–1983 season, he led the Laval club to a first-place regular-season finish. This constituted a considerable accomplishment. Mario had joined a last-place team. Now, in only his second year, it topped the standings. His work was complemented by that of Courteau, a strong two-way player and the team's moral leader. He had been Laval's star when Mario arrived, and had been naturally reluctant to give up that status to the new sensation. He felt the rivalry with Lemieux. Though Mario was noted for being unselfish with the puck, when he played with Courteau the trait was less evident. Courteau couldn't figure out what Mario was going to do with it, and complained that he frequently got lonely out there. He found out, he said, what many others would—that Mario wasn't about to settle for anything less than number one.

The team celebrated its first-place finish by drinking the city of Montreal half-dry. Many players were in a stupor for days. One had to be taken to the hospital. Courteau didn't think this was the best note upon which to begin the playoff drive. As it happened, Laval never recovered. The team played Longueil, a club of inferior talent, but one that was expertly coached by

Jacques Lemaire, who would soon take over behind the Canadiens' bench. None of Lemieux's skills could make up for the discipline and hard work manifested by the underdog team. Laval fell. The classic final match-up between Laval and Verdun, between Lemieux and LaFontaine, never materialized. Mario's second campaign in junior ended, as had the first, in disappointment. He'd scored a raft of points, a club record 184 in 66 games, but finished second to LaFontaine, who had 224. He'd suffered a miserable experience in his first sampling of international hockey. His team made a quick exit from the playoffs.

Mario's two main rivals, LaFontaine and Sylvain Turgeon, both moved on to the NHL. Had Mario been born three weeks earlier, he would have, by virtue of the age rules, been moving on with them. He would have been entering the pros on the heels of an unspectacular junior career. He likely would not have been the number-one draft pick. His pro contract would have been worth substantially less money. His confidence level would not have been so high. But because he was not turning eighteen until October, he was eligible for another year of junior. Thus, he had another chance to accomplish what he had set out to do when he began his junior career. He had promised Perno he would break the scoring records and be the number-one pick. He had promised Fournel he'd make Laval a Memorial Cup champion.

In the summer of 1983, the summer before his final season, Perno impressed upon Mario the need to prepare better, to devote some time to conditioning. Smarting from the results of year two, Mario decided to put in an effort. While most of his summer was casually spent on the golf course, there were days when an occurrence as rare as a UFO sighting took place. Mario Lemieux could be seen in the parks of Ville Emard, running.

Before his third campaign at Laval began, a point of contention had to be resolved. Everyone conceded that he was responsible for the increasing crowds Laval was drawing. But Fournel maintained that Mario could not be paid any differently than any other junior. That, he argued, would violate league rules. But Mario's teammates, including even Courteau, were of the opinion that, given his value, Lemieux should be getting something extra. They wouldn't mind seeing the rules broken for their friend Mario.

Jean-Guy Lemieux also wanted to see his son rewarded. He took the matter up with Fournel, but got nowhere. Mario responded by missing a practice in protest. Gus Badali, Perno's boss, came in from Toronto. A loud and inflammatory meeting followed. Mario would sit out the season, his agents threatened, if Fournel didn't bend. He'd play the year with the Canadian Olympic team, they said, even though there was no intention of having him do so.

Fournel gave in, but just a little. He wouldn't flagrantly violate the rules and give Mario straight cash payments, he said, but if Mario played well, material benefits would come his way both during and at the end of the season.

Fournel didn't know, nor did anyone, just how well Mario could or would play.

SIX

HEIR APPARENT

BEGINNING HIS THIRD AND FINAL YEAR AT LAVAL, A CAMPAIGN that would have enough drama in it for any eighteen-year-old, a new attitude seized Mario Lemieux. Even during the pre-season games, coaches and the media detected an enthusiasm in his manner. His play was purposeful. There was a driving imperative to his every move.

In his first three regular-season games, Mario amassed sixteen points. He followed a lone assist in his next encounter with another three-game gallop, averaging an astonishing six points in each. He had thirty-five points after seven games. Fed by wingers Alain Bisson and Jacques Goyette, he had three four-goal nights.

The exceptional beginning continued, stirring talk of his possibly breaking the junior scoring record of Guy Lafleur. The Flower registered 130 goals in the 1971–1972 season with the Québec Remparts. In chasing St. Guy, Mario had the advantage. Lafleur's accomplishment was made over a sixty-two-game season. The schedule in 1983–1984 had eight more games. After the first twenty-two games, Mario had the exact same number of goals Lafleur had at that stage—forty. Mario also targeted the regular-season points mark of 251 set by Pierre

Larouche. In his twenty-two games he had ninety-four points, an average of more than four a game.

Mario was perhaps the least surprised of anyone by the spurt. In a remark reflective of his unshakeable inner confidence, he told reporters that he always knew that he was as good as he had been since the start of this season. Others weren't so sure. Michel Morin, coach of the Hull Olympiques, had served as an assistant coach at the world championships in Leningrad. "There is no comparison with the Mario Lemieux of this year," he noted. "This is a rejuvenated player who has brought a total new determination to the fore to complement his natural abilities." Mario no longer waited for the puck to come to him, Morin analyzed. Now he was reading the play more intensely, looking for the open ice when he didn't have the puck and jumping into the gaps. He began wearing contact lenses this year and they helped his game. "Now I see the faces of the players," he said, "and I can guess what they are going to do."

His play naturally increased the calls for him to represent Canada at that year's junior world competition in Sweden. Brian Kilrea of the Ottawa 67s had replaced Dave King as the national team's head coach. But Kilrea had narrowed any hope of luring Mario when, before the new junior season began, he made an observation that struck number 66 as dismissive. Kilrea said that if Lemieux didn't want to play, it was up to him. In a conversation with Perno, Mario gave his response: "Well, fuck him." He had vowed the previous year never again to play in the tournament. Now he was retaking that vow.

Kilrea tried to repair any damage, visiting Lemieux to explain how important he would be to the team's chances of success. Mario gave the question some thought, but came back with a categorical no. Besides his dismal experience the previous year, other factors influenced the decision. He would miss four games of the Quebec schedule, diminishing his prospects of breaking Lafleur's record. Moreover, he would miss, he said, being able to spend Christmas at home with his family. Though he had stated at the start of the season that it was time for him to become more independent, that his parents should no longer be the ones to tell him what to do in life, Mario was still a homebody.

Because he was judged the hottest junior in the country, his decision to boycott the team sparked a highly publicized controversy. He was labeled selfish and unpatriotic. The Quebec junior hockey league's executive decided if he wouldn't play voluntarily, it would try and force him. League president Paul Dumont argued feebly that a clause in the standard players' contract stipulated that Mario had to undertake acitivities that were in the interests of the image of the league. Representing Quebec and Canada in international hockey was one such activity. In not going, Lemieux would be violating his contract. Not stopping at that, the league's board passed a resolution stating that any player refusing to play for Team Canada would not be allowed to play in regular-season games while the international tournament progressed. The board then followed up, suspending Lemieux for four regular-season games as well as the all-star game.

The league fathers hadn't anticipated having to go this far. They thought Mario would have buckled to the pressure, joined the team, and flown off to Sweden. They didn't know Lemieux. The streak of stubbornness that ran through him was a steel cord. "If somebody yells at me to hurry up," Mario said once in a comment that applied always, "I slow down."

Lemieux promptly sought an injunction to have the league's decree overturned. The eighteen-year-old's chutzpah rocked the hockey hierarchy, further heightening the controversy's already heady profile. The league governors were not accustomed to being dragged off to Superior Court by a teenager. They didn't suffer badly in the court of public opinion, however. Mario's gambit failed to generate much sympathy. On the contrary, he was viewed as putting his own interests first, ahead of those of his province and his country. No one could remember another case of a Canadian athlete going to court to protect himself from having to play for his country in world championships. No one could remember a gesture so unpatriotic. It was supposed to be a privilege to compete for one's nation in such prestigious international events. Personal concerns were supposed to be secondary.

Most athletes regarded such competition as not a sacrifice, but an honor. There was the glory of being selected for the national team, and of wearing the country's colors. There was the educational experience of time spent abroad, the taste of foreign competition, the advantage of enhanced media exposure.

Mario rejected all such reasoning. His action was consistent with his character. He was essentially an outsider, a young man who never ran with the crowd or pandered to the pack mentality. While reviled by many, his court action was admirable from the perspective of the exercise of individual rights. And as was apparent in the verdict of the judge, it was also admirable in legal terms. Quebec Superior Court Justice Frazer Martin ruled that Lemieux's contractual obligation was only to the Laval Voisins and not Team Canada. Nor was the player compelled by any league ordinance to miss playing four games. The moral obligation to carry the colors of one's country cannot be confused with legal obligations, ruled the judge. Judge Martin made clear, however, that he too viewed Lemieux's act, while lawful, as a selfish one. "Being a professional, Mario Lemieux has to make sacrifices and being far from his loved ones at Christmas is one of them."

Mario was now free to play for his team. In the four holiday-season games he scored only two goals, but added nine assists. The crisis passed, but despite his court victory, Mario's image suffered enduring damage. Some might have been able to get away with what he did—rebels can sometimes win—but Mario did not have the charm to play the maverick role. His demeanor was too distant to connect with the people. His talent could win their admiration, but winning their hearts was another matter.

Early in the new year, Bob Perno took a step in image rehabilitation by getting Mario to sponsor a charity golf tournament, with proceeds going to Normand Leveillé. Wayne Gretzky agreed to be honorary president of the event. All the big hockey names were invited, as well as, with one major exception, the heavyweights of the Quebec hockey media. The exception was Mark Lachapelle. When Mario saw his name on Perno's proposed list, he said, "Take him off. He's not coming to my golf tournament."

Mario's spectacular play in his third season helped smother the memory of the Christmas controversy. As the Lemieux clan watched their prince scale unseen scoring heights, unpestered this time by comparisons with the tiny perfect American, there was ample reason to celebrate. The parties were frequent and Mario, with Nathalie, who was smooth on a dance floor, would spin to old Elvis Presley hits. Integrating Nathalie into the Lemieux clan was not easy, however. Concerned that the relationship could affect Mario's hockey, Pierrette Lemieux was unhappy with the influence Nathalie was coming to wield over her son. Bob Perno, who shared some of Pierrette's concerns, appeared at the Lemieux home one day to find Pierrette and Nathalie in heated argument. The Lemieuxs were planning a trip to Chicoutimi. Nathalie wanted to accompany Mario, but Pierrette wished to have her son to herself this time. Perno greeted the two of them and proceeded to Mario's bedroom, where he found his player as upset as he had ever seen him. He was distraught over all the bickering between his mother and Nathalie. When they began to talk, Mario broke into tears. Perno took him and held him, "just like I held my own son." The pressures of the season, the court case, the media, and now the family feud were spilling over. "It hit me," said Perno, "to see Mario, who usually gave the impression on the outside to everybody that nothing bothered him, to see him cry just like any other kid." Mario pressed for Nathalie to come on the Chicoutimi trip, but his mother had her way.

Through the winter and the early spring his torrid scoring pace continued, and he kept the records well within sight. One of the few concerns was the condition of his lower back. Pain was infrequent, but it was a serious enough problem that Mario tried switching skates. His doctor suspected that perhaps the lie of the old blades tilted his body in such a way as to aggravate the back. But different skates with a different blade angle didn't seem to help. Still, whatever the blades, whatever the back condition, his hockey didn't suffer. His game had matured so much since he came to Laval. He had settled comfortably into his big body size and had come to terms with what it took to make that body size work. His growth spurt had not deprived him of the subtlety of movement he had always possessed. While most players, even the exceptional ones, had a repertoire with limits, one that opposition defensemen could often guess, those who played against Mario confessed to bafflement. He rarely used the same move twice. To have such an extended reach, and to be able to regulate its movement with the ease and fluidity that Mario did, left him with an almost unlimited potential.

The only goalie who could stop him in his third Laval season was Carl Parker. The two friends were reunited when Parker was traded from Trois-Rivières to Laval. The Quebec television network, TVA, was preparing a news feature on Mario. They wanted to film him scoring spectacularly on some guinea-pig goalie. Parker volunteered, but wanting the scene to be realistic, thought he might try to make Mario sweat a bead or two to get his goal.

The day of the shoot came. They readied the lights, the cameras, and signaled for action. Mario took a breakaway, but Parker stopped him. He took another. Parker stopped him. He took a couple more. Parker stoned him again. As Parker chuckled behind his mask, enjoying every minute, Mario fumed. The producers were getting impatient. "Come on, for Christ's sake," they told Lemieux. "Put one in."

"It was so funny," recalled Parker. "I think it took fifteen shots for him to beat me. The TV guys were shouting and Mario was all pissed off at me. He eventually scored a couple of goals and that's all you saw on the news—the two I let in."

They'd have done better to film Lemieux in live action, where he had no such scoring difficulties. He surpassed Pat LaFontaine's record of collecting a point or more in forty-three straight games in a single season. Extended over two seasons, Guy Lafleur had the overall record—sixty games in a row. Lemieux cracked that mark as well. He was just nine games short of completing the entire seventy-game season without being shut out when his roll finally halted in game number sixty-two against Verdun. He hit the post with one shot and set up teammates who were unsuccessful on several opportunities. His regular coach, Jean Begin, was absent for the match. Although the Laval players didn't like the high-strung Begin, he had been smart enough to give Mario all the ice time he wanted. The most under-reported component in a scorer's arsenal, ice time was critical to Mario. His fantastic jump in point totals in year three was partly attributable to a corresponding jump in ice time.

In the Verdun game Begin's replacement, Denis Dubic, kept Mario on the bench for most of the first half of the third period. Afterwards, Mario commented, though diplomatically, that this obviously didn't help his chances of scoring.

His next milestone was Larouche's 251 points in a single season. Lemieux passed Larouche with five games still remaining on his schedule. Unlike most players, who, upon setting a mark, trot out the standard cliché that "records are made to be broken," Mario evinced a stronger pride. Vowing to work hard in the remaining games to boost his totals, he was frank: "I don't want my records broken. I know that by the time I'm finished this season, the statistics could be pretty astronomical. It's going to take quite a hockey player to beat these marks."

As he came to the last week of the schedule, however, the big one, the Lafleur scoring record, looked almost out of reach. With four games left, Mario was still twelve goals behind the record of 130. He had been averaging slightly less than two goals a game to this point. Now he needed more than three a game in the remaining ones to beat the Flower.

Against Chicoutimi he erupted for four goals, but followed that with only one against Shawinigan. Now two games remained and he needed seven goals just to tie the mark. In the first of the two, against Lafleur's old Québec Remparts club, he kept the hopes alive with a spectacular four-goal, seven-point night. It set up, in Mario's words, "the biggest match I will play since I have put on skates." The sportingly correct remark would have been, "Sure, the record would be nice. But my own stats are not important. All that matters to me is if we win as a team." But again, with Mario, such false humility had no place. Instead, he was saying what most players would have said were they as honest as he.

He was ready, feeling primed the day before the game. Playing hockey had been so much easier this year, he noted, than when he always had to read about the comparisons with LaFontaine. It had been such a poor comparison. "We have two completely different styles. His game is speed. Mine is finesse." On the day before Mario's try at his record, Guy Lafleur told the papers he had never seen him play. But he did say, somewhat prophetically, that "the Canadiens need someone like Lemieux to replace me." Implicit was a rebuke of the Habs' management team of Ronald Corey and Serge Savard, who appeared to be moving Montreal away from the high-scoring, star system of old to a close-checking, defensive style. The superstar system of *les Glorieux*, Lafleur believed, had succeeded. The torch had been passed from Richard to Béliveau to Lafleur and now it was paramount that a successor be found. But the Habs weren't listening to their history. They wouldn't get a crack at Mario in the draft and, under the new regime, could never land the one sublime player to continue the line of succession. They would win two Stanley Cups in the decade that followed, but not with great teams. By luck of circumstance, they didn't have to face any of the league's best teams in the playoffs in either of the Cup-winning years.

Unlike Lafleur, Wayne Gretzky had seen Mario play. During the regular season he had gone to Laval at Perno's invitation. Assessing Lemieux's game, he told journalist Tom Lapointe of *La Presse* that "this is the guy who is going to take my place." At this stage the two players were getting along very well. "I consider him as a friend," Mario said of Gretzky. "He's just as impressive off the ice as he is on it. He has given me a lot of advice and encouraged me to never quit working with intensity. He has opened my eyes to all kinds of things."

By coincidence, Gretzky's Edmonton Oilers were in town to play Montreal at the same time as Mario's last game of the season. For the most important game of his life, Mario would have the brightest star in hockey in attendance. Perno picked up Gretzky and also Paul Coffey at their hotel and took them out to Laval. Gretzky had a curfew that night because of the game against the Canadiens the following day. He told Mario to "make it quick," because he had to get out of there.

This, obviously, was a night of fantastic pressure and importance for Mario, but that didn't stop Carl Parker from coming over before the game to issue a vote of non-confidence. "I didn't think he could do it, break that record," said Parker, "and I told him so. I said, 'You won't break the record,' and I made a bet. I said, 'I'll give you ten dollars for every goal you score more than the record, if you give me ten for every one under.' And you know what? He took the bet. The guy was that confident."

Playing against Longueil, number 66 scored his first goal at the forty-three-second mark. His second came at 2:03, sending the four thousand spectators into a frenzy. Mario was making it quick. Opening the second period like the first, he scored at 1:18. He had 130 goals. The Lafleur record was tied. At the seven-minute mark, not yet halfway into the game, he took a face-off to the right of Daniel Brazeau, the Longueil goalie. Face-offs were a weak point in Mario's game—he lost more than he won. This time he won it, however, and sped the puck over in front of the goaltender toward teammate Jacques Goyette. But miraculously, the puck hit a skate and slid back to him. "Then I just fired at the net and it hit the post and went in." He lifted his arms in triumph and was quickly covered in teammates and the roars from the stands. The greatest season in the history of Quebec junior hockey was sealed.

Wayne Gretzky wouldn't have to miss his curfew and Carl Parker had lost his bet. But Mario wasn't finished. He scored two more goals and, on yet two other occasions, when he had an empty net staring at him, Mario, not wanting to be the glutton, passed off to teammates who scored themselves. His display of talent that night was staggering. He completed the game with eleven points—six goals and five assists. Everything was working: the touch, the deft feints, the vision, the shooting eye, the intensity, the passing artistry, the intelligence. The best word his players and teammates could find to describe the performance was "scary." "It was scary the way he played," they said. "He was so good it was scary."

But Mario himself made the most telling remark. "When I have a prestigious record within reach," he said, "I give three times more effort." One of sport's most numbing clichés, fashioned over decades of inane repetition, was the one suggesting athletes always tried to exceed the limit, as in, "He always gives 110 percent." But after his postgame statement that night, no one could ever accuse Mario Lemieux of numbering in that pack.

Following the game, a surging crowd filled the lobby. Mario opened the dressing-room door, saw Bob Perno, and waved him over. With his face a fabulous glow, Lemieux said, "Bob, remember three years ago when you met me in my house? Remember you told me how much I'd get if I broke the records?" Perno nodded. "Well," said Mario. "I've done my job."

Gretzky had come to congratulate him after the second period and left, so as not to break his curfew. In his comments to the press, observing how Mario's style was comparable to his own, Gretzky made a noteworthy observation. He singled out Lemieux's vision. Mario, Gretzky noted, could see the entire ice surface and use every player on it.

He was paying tribute to the very thing Scotty Bowman and a few other observers of the game had: Mario's eyes. The great majority of coaches assessed players on their skating, puck handling, intensity, size, and so on. Far down on the list came the question of how the player saw the ice. For Mario Lemieux and Wayne Gretzky, this quality separated them from all the rest. They could read and anticipate the play better than the others. Many players had the ability, but none to their degree. Joe Sakic of the Quebec Nordiques was a player with an exceptional sense of vision. He had a better read on the action than anyone else on his team. He was a joy to watch until one day in early 1993, when he suffered an eye injury. The injury, it seemed, took away that special quality that marked Sakic out from the rest. For the remainder of the season Joe Sakic was an ordinary hockey player.

Though Gretzky spent only a brief moment with Lemieux on the night of the triumph, he had another meeting with the junior sensation before he left Montreal. After the Edmonton–Montreal game the next night, Gretzky took Mario, along with Perno and Paul Coffey, to the Chez Paree. He brought along a bottle of champagne to toast the king of junior hockey. The Chez Paree was an upscale strip bar. Here, the men sat and drank while women undressed on a hotly lit, slowly turning dais in the center of the room. For an added fee, one of the beauties would make her way over and provide the patrons with an exclusive, up-close performance. The Chez Paree was a favorite spot of many NHL players and coaches. Gretzky, a bachelor at the time, thought it was terrific. "It was Gretzky's office when he came to Montreal," said Tom Lapointe, the *La Presse* journalist who came to know him well. "He went there all the time."

Gretzky was no different than a great number of NHL players who liked going there, explained Bob Perno. "Wayne loves it there. . . . It's one of the only places where he doesn't get bothered. He'll go into a restaurant and everybody is going to bother him. He goes into the Chez Paree and nobody bothers him."

Though many hockey players frequented the club, it would have been a public-relations disaster for someone like Gretzky, whose image was unsullied, to be photographed there or be publicized as a regular patron. But he was prepared to take the chance, as Lemieux would be after he turned pro. To guard against the possibility of an aggressive young journalist crashing a Chez Paree party, the doormen were given the word when Gretzky or any other stars arrived and were told to take care that no photographers or writers got in. Of the Great One's visits to the bar, his agent, Mike Barnett, said, "That's Wayne. You know, he's a fun guy and a typical hockey player."

On the night following Mario's heroics, they stayed at the club for two hours. Gretzky and the others toasted the eighteen-year-old heir apparent while all around them clothes fell. The 133-goal scorer soaked up the praise from the premier star in the game, and asked him questions about money and endorsements. Coming from a modest background, Mario had a keen interest in these matters at the time. The discussion was light for the most part, but Gretzky did not let the evening pass before sizing up the significance of the moment. Toward the end of the evening, he talked about what was ahead for both of them. He said, as Perno recalled the conversation, that he considered Mario a friend. "But come October, when the new season starts, I know you're going to be after my records. You're my friend now, but from that time on, it will be different." He was talking in a friendly, almost jocular way, but the message rang clear. The competition would be tough between them. The strain on the friendship would be immense.

There had been many outstanding juniors in recent years, but Gretzky was insightful enough to realize then, before Lemieux was even drafted, that Mario was the one.

The regular season had established Lemieux as the record scorer in junior hockey, the best player in junior hockey, and the NHL's number-one draft pick—everything he had cockily promised Bob Perno three years earlier. Mario finished with 282 points, easily surpassing Larouche and eclipsing LaFontaine's brilliance of the season before by 58 points. In his second year at Laval, Mario had set a club record with 184 points. In his third he smashed his own record by 98 points.

Two promises remained to be fulfilled. One was to win the

Memorial Cup; the other was to get the million-dollar contract that Perno had promised him.

As the season approached its final stages, the Pittsburgh Penguins, the team most likely to have first pick in the NHL draft, focused on Lemieux. Albert Mandanici, who had watched his son play against Mario in the kid leagues, was now Pittsburgh's Quebec scout. As a long-time enthusiast of Mario's play and a friend of the family's, he heartily recommended Mario as the Penguin choice. General Manager Eddie Johnston agreed fully, but others in the Pittsburgh organization weren't convinced. They said Mario wasn't backchecking, that he tended to float along the center red line. They thought Kirk Muller of Kingston might be the preferable pick. Though Mario was playing with more intensity this year, his style still had too casual a look about it for the tastes of many eminent hockey people, including Serge Savard. Having watched Mario in several games, Savard was uncertain. For long stretches, Mario would do nothing, Savard told the press, then he would explode. Perno's response was simply, "Look at his numbers." As for Mandanici, he told the dissenters in Pittsburgh what Claude Fournel had been told when he was wondering who to pick in the junior draft. "You're averaging six thousand fans a game," Mandanici said. "If you want to fill the barn, you've got to pick Mario."

Laval, meanwhile, progressed through the Quebec league playoffs to win the provincial title and move on to the elimination tournament in Kitchener, which would decide the Memorial Cup. In fourteen Quebec playoff games, Mario scored twenty-nine goals and had twenty-three assists, establishing another league record.

The Laval Voisins appeared ready for Kitchener. They were a pre-tournament favorite, they were injury-free, and if the day of the disappearing smoke was any indication, they were in apparent good humor. The team prohibited smoking, but

Mario was enjoying a cigarette in their Kitchener hotel during a card game with teammates when a rap on the door warned them that the coaches were coming by for a check-up. Sensing Mario's predicament, the players quickly came to his aid. In a madcap scramble, they waved their jackets, they waved bed sheets, they thrust open the windows. They then quickly regrouped around the card table before opening the door. The coaches came in, smiled, looked around, nodded approvingly, and moved on.

The tournament was supposed to showcase the player many people outside of Quebec had heard about, but few had seen. In the first game against Kitchener, however, in front of everybody who meant anything in the NHL, in junior hockey, and in the North American hockey media, Mario went into his phantom act. He cruised the mid-zone, far away from the drama. He didn't come in contact with the puck often and when he did, there was no magic in his wand. He had played eighty-three games (including playoffs) in 1983–1984 and had scored at least one point in eighty-two of them. Now, for the second time in eight months, he laid the goose egg. His team fell behind Kitchener by two goals in the first three minutes and couldn't rally from the shock. Kitchener won 8–2 and Jean Begin, the Laval coach, couldn't contain his anger. In the dressing room he started berating his veterans, pointing the finger in particular at Mario Lemieux, the same Mario Lemieux who had set all the records and hadn't played a bad game in months. In front of everyone, the coach accused him of lazy play, of play that would get him nowhere in the NHL. Mario angrily rebutted Begin and soon all his teammates, with Yves Courteau in the lead role, were coming to his defense. They shouted down the coach and he left the room.

Outside, Begin told the media, "My veterans let me down." He advised them to wait a while before they saw Lemieux and the rest of the players because they needed time to cool off. But Marc Lachapelle went straight to the big guy. "Mario, the coach says you and the veterans let the team down," he reported. Mario looked at Lachapelle. "You tell Begin he better shut his fucking mouth."

Without the expletive, the headline appeared in *Le Journal de Montréal* the next day: "Begin Would Be Better Off To Keep His Mouth Shut—Mario Lemieux." In the article Mario said that it was he and the veteran players who had carried the club all season. "It can happen that on one night nothing works."

The confrontation with the coach drained the spirit from Laval. They lost the next game 6–5 to the Ottawa 67s. With a goal and an assist, Lemieux played considerably better, but not with the brilliance people had come to expect. The team had to win its next game to stay alive in the tournament, but lost 4–3 to Kamloops. Mario had one assist, bringing his total to three points for three games. It was his lowest three-game output of the entire season.

Perno rarely saw Mario as down as he was during the series. Part of the problem was the scale of competition. The Ontario and western Canadian teams featured bigger wingers and defensemen who played a more robust, tight-checking game than in the offensive-oriented Quebec league. Lemieux had less room to maneuver. He also had developed a chest cold in the series, and had had the feud with the coach. But he was devastated that he hadn't performed to expectations. Now all his doubters, including some NHL scouts who said he was a floater, had their day. Yet another year in junior, this one so spectacular, had concluded on a sour note.

The split between players and coach was so severe that Begin did not return home from Kitchener with the team. He got a ride with Marc Lachapelle. Mario stayed on for some solace, receiving the award as the best junior player in Canada. "Our loss in the Kitchener game killed our confidence," he said in his acceptance speech, adding how his team wasn't used to the more physical style of play it confronted. "[But] we can leave with our heads high. . . . We have worked hard the whole year." As for his own showing, he said, "I am satisfied with my effort. I gave everything I had."

Claude Fournel, acting on his promise to provide Mario with some material rewards if he played well, came through, however modestly, with a new set of golf clubs. Earlier in the season, the owner had purchased some fine clothing for Mario to spiff up his wardrobe.

The big prize, however, was still very much a question mark. Bob Perno had promised Mario Lemieux a million dollars. No rookie entering the National Hockey League had received close to that amount. Despite his setback at the Memorial Cup, Mario was convinced he deserved that much. NHL team owners weren't so sure. But Mario was prepared to meet this challenge with the same stubbornness he had shown in refusing to represent his country abroad.

SEVEN

MY WAY OR THE DOORWAY

MARIO HAD BEEN THINKING ABOUT THE BIG MILLION-DOLLAR CON-
tract for the three years since he entered into the quiet pact with
Bob Perno. He had complied with his half of the bargain and now
he fully expected that the other half would be upheld. It was this
expectation that brought on another public crisis in the life of a
young man who simply wanted to play the game and be left alone.

The desperate Pittsburgh Penguins won the first pick in the
draft of junior players. They had to finish in last place to have
Mario Lemieux available to them. Helping to ensure this
outcome, to ensure defeats right up until the end of the season,
were two changes by Eddie Johnston, the GM. First he traded
away his best defenseman, Randy Carlyle, for players he
wouldn't see until future seasons. Then he sent Roberto
Romano, his best goaltender, down to the minors and brought
up the untested Vincent Tremblay. Tremblay promptly rang up a
goals-allowed average of six per game. The Penguins lost their
last six games to finish 16–58–6, the most dismal record in their
seventeen-year history.

Having won the rights to Lemieux, Johnston received
many handsome trade offers for him. The manager, however,
was aware of the Penguins' bleak history of trading away

first-round choices. The previous season they had dealt their first-round pick—who could have been Pat LaFontaine—for Ron Meighan and Anders Hakansson, two stiffs from Minnesota. In fact, rather than build through the draft, the Penguins had bled through the draft. Between 1967 and 1984, the club traded away its first-round draft choice a remarkable eight times. While the value of building a team through draft selections was often overstated (a case can be made that perspicacious trading can be just as effective), the mediocrities the Penguins received in return for their first-round picks were evidence of the folly involved. In 1972 they got Bob Woytowich, in 1979 it was Hartland Monahan, in 1981 Rod Schutt, and in 1983 Meighan and Hakansson. Johnston vowed there would be no more deals. "I've had guys say, 'We'll give you six players for Mario.' I tell them, 'Stick it in your ear.'"

The Penguins averaged only 6,700 fans per game. They were so anxious to start waving the Mario banner to attract new customers that they asked to begin contract negotiations before they had even officially drafted him. Unwisely, agents Badali and Perno agreed.

Edward DeBartolo, the owner of the Penguins, had real estate, shopping malls, and other interests worth close to a billion dollars. But he had been losing several million a year on the hockey team. He was prepared to offer Lemieux $700,000 split over three seasons. He was not prepared to offer him a million. Badali and Perno rejected his offer, but thought they could make it work as a basis for negotiation. If DeBartolo threw in an attendance clause, stipulating a cut of the gate should Mario's presence substantially increase the number of spectators, they could put the case to Mario that the contract was worth a million dollars. But the Penguins rejected this counterproposal, leaving the two sides at a stalemate as draft day approached. In the meantime, leaks to the media had a pro-Penguin look about them.

They made Mario look greedy. Junior hockey players weren't in the habit of asking for attendance clauses, the journalists wrote. Who does Lemieux think he is?

Kept abreast of the failing negotiations, Mario declined to lower his demands. To him, it was a matter of straightforward logic. He had the best three-season junior record in the history of Quebec. He was worth what he was asking. If the Penguins couldn't pay the amount, then they should trade their rights to him for someone they could afford. Informed that Eddie Johnston would not consider a trade, the stubborn and proud Lemieux dug in. He told Perno his next step. "I will not go to the draft unless we have an agreement. I will not be a hypocrite like a lot of other players and go to the draft and put on a happy face."

The night before selection day, Mario's agents met Eddie Johnston. Johnston said he simply couldn't go over $700,000. Badali and Perno said they'd be open to new offers until ten the next morning. "If we don't have the offer we want, he's not coming to the building."

Mario spent a quiet evening at his parents' home. He ate dinner, then went out on the street in front of his house. It was June, and it was hot, but the most celebrated junior star in the world played road hockey with some young cousins. Johnston, meanwhile, phoned Mario's agents to inform them of a final offer—$760,000. Badali leaned toward accepting it, but Perno knew it wouldn't work. "Gus, I promised him a million. He's not going to accept $760,000." He phoned Mario to make sure. Mario repeated that it was either a million or nothing. "If I don't get it, I'm not going. I've booked a golf date. I'm going to play golf instead."

The NHL draft showcased the sport's new talent. National television would be covering the draft for the first time. Recent tradition required the first player selected to enhance the spectacle by coming to the draft table and, while brandishing his biggest smile, putting on his new team's jersey and posing for a thousand pictures. But now the same Mario Lemieux who had antagonized the hockey establishment with his crusade against playing for Team Canada was prepared to deprive the NHL of its day in the sun and embitter its ruling class. Mario would leave the whirring cameras with a phantom for a first pick. He'd be on the fairways honing his silky smooth swing.

No junior player had displayed such arrogance before. Perno tried to talk him out of it. "Mario, to refuse the contract is one thing; to not show up is another." At the same time, he repeated the message to the Penguins: no more dough, Mario won't show.

Badali and Perno got on the phone to Gretzky. Gretzky, they knew, might well be able to change Mario's mind and have him avoid the pending calamity. Gretzky gave them his thoughts. He said he understood Lemieux's position, but he thought Mario owed it to the game, the public, his parents, and the Pittsburgh fans watching on closed-circuit TV to show up. Whether he goes to the table to put on a Penguins sweater is another matter, Gretzky said, but he should at least be there. The agents relayed Gretzky's words to Mario, who rethought the matter. He canceled his golf game. He'd show up, but he wouldn't go to the Penguin table.

At the Montreal Forum on draft day the tension of this climaxing story was evident. The newspapers were still pounding Mario hard. The journalists didn't know the background to the story. They didn't know about Perno's vow three years earlier to get Mario a million. They didn't know it had become a point of principle with him. Most of what they were getting had the Penguins' spin. Mario was losing another public-relations battle. He had already lost one such battle during his refusal to play in the world junior tournament. Now this. What he needed at this time, and in the years to come, was a good image weaver to do his public-relations work. He would never find one.

At the Forum he sat between his tight-lipped father and Badali. They all looked for a signal of flexibility from the Pittsburgh table, but could see none. Mario talked about leaving right then, but he could see Albert Mandanici in the Penguin group. Mandanici had spent many evenings at Mario's home with his parents. He had golfed with Mario. They had become friends.

As planned, Pittsburgh went ahead with their selection. Eddie Johnston announced the name Mario Lemieux. Mario stayed in his seat. As if someone hadn't got the point, Johnston pronounced it again. Mario remained seated. Some in the Forum began to boo. Mario's mother started to cry. "For Christ's sake, Mario," Perno pleaded. "Don't spoil the day. Look at your mother." Mario stood up and waved to the crowd, but sat right back down. He wasn't going to the table.

Now Albert Mandanici, in his brown suit, headed upstairs toward the Lemieux box. He stopped a couple of rows below the clan and, in an authoritative manner, told Mario that he had to come down to the table and put a sweater on. "He doesn't have to do anything," Perno shot back. Mandanici's attitude had angered Perno and the entire Lemieux box. Now Mandanici snapped at Perno, "It's none of your business." Mario jumped in, telling the Penguin scout it was very much Perno's business. Unless he was paid properly, he did not belong to Pittsburgh and he wasn't going anywhere.

The bitter exchange continued. Gus Badali gave Mandanici a vulgar hand signal, suggesting he should hurriedly move on. An enraged Mandanici was tempted to jump at Badali but, restraining himself, turned away.

The draft had now moved on to new selections. The moment when Mario could have gone to the front to put on the Pittsburgh sweater had passed. He and his entourage left the Forum, with Mario stopping to talk to reporters on the way out.

"I didn't go to the table because the negotiations are not going well," he explained. "I'm not going to put on the sweater if they don't want me badly enough."

He felt correct in defending the point of principle. To do otherwise would constitute an act of hypocrisy. Why should or would anyone make a grand gesture of allegiance to a team not even coming close to putting forward what he or she considered a good faith offer? While his family agreed, the media didn't. They savaged Mario. The *Globe and Mail* labeled one report "Lemieux Behaving Like A Petulant Prima Donna." A French-language headline described Lemieux as a snob. In a column entitled "Mario Snub A Tasteless Act," Red Fisher, Montreal's dean of hockey writers, a reporter who could normally be counted upon to follow the management line, lashed out. "Mark this down. His refusal to join the people around the table who rated him number one . . . is the biggest mistake he has ever made." Lemieux's agents no doubt steered him astray, Fisher reasoned, "but Lemieux isn't blameless. An 18-year-old with grown-up talent can make up his own mind. It was a tasteless demonstration of bad manners, unmatched by anything I've ever seen."

Fisher turned Mandanici and the Penguins into martyrs. "Night after night he [Mandanici] sits in drafty arenas, often after driving hundreds of miles through swirling snow, and dreams of the day when his employers can call out the name of Mario Lemieux. . . . This was to have been the day for Mandanici." On reading the Fisher column, Mario was furious. Perno felt like throwing up.

The day following the draft, a viciously hot Sunday, Perno sat by the swimming pool Mario had helped him build the previous summer. Perno was trying to forget about what had happened when Mario phoned and said he wanted to talk. He came out to St. Lucie with his mother, father, and brother Richard. They sat by the water, agreed on the need for a compromise solution, and kicked around some alternatives. They came up with a new proposal Mario could live with: he'd accept the base amount the Penguins wanted to pay him, provided it came with healthy bonus clauses for goals and assists. Under such terms, if Mario did exceedingly well he would get his million.

Perno phoned Eddie Johnston and put the poolside compromise to him. Johnston took the offer to DeBartolo. By the end of the week, terms were agreed upon, and the ill feelings between the two parties were soon forgotten. Before too long, Mandanici called Mario and they went out to dinner. Mario paid.

Mario was satisfied. He hadn't been forced into a contract he didn't want. He had stood his ground. But as was the case with the world junior tournament, his fight against the hockey establishment cost him support from the press and the public. While on principle he could perhaps feel victorious, on the important matter of image cultivation another story was being written.

Before making his first visit to Pittsburgh, Mario cast himself in a more positive light by hosting a golf tournament. As most such tourneys do, Mario's went off smoothly. They played it at Piedmont in the Laurentians, an hour from Montreal. In his role as host, Mario arrived a day early to pump hands and make small talk. With Gretzky as tournament president, the entry fee was a neat $66.99. The event, which drew some media attention, raised six thousand dollars for Normand Leveillé, who had become a beloved figure in Quebec.

Mario's golf game had sharpened to the point where he was now shooting in the seventies. Every chance he got he played golf, sometimes showing more intensity on the links than on the ice. Gus Badali had never played with such a concentrated golfer. He hadn't realized the depth of Mario's competitive spirit until he saw him trying to match par. Gretzky demonstrated less talent for the sport and took it less seriously.

He'd shoot eighty one day and a hundred the next, relaxing while doing so.

The Piedmont golf club sat close to one of the most popular bars in the Montreal area for hockey players. The Bourbon Street bar, not a strip club like the Chez Paree, attracted many NHL stars because it offered the right stuff: beautiful women, atmosphere, overnight rooms, star treatment for star people, and a most popular owner in Sean O'Donnell. Perno introduced Mario to O'Donnell and they soon became friends. Mario liked him and he liked the bar. Chez Paree and Bourbon Street became two of his favorite spots, something that Bob Perno, in his role as guidance counselor, was not enthused about. Mario never struck anyone as a rollicking partyer, as one who would fall prey to the seedier dimensions of the sport. Usually, he sat unobtrusively in a corner with a friend or two, had a couple of drinks, ate peanuts, and left. But Perno still felt compelled to warn him of the obvious hazards of such places. Perno wanted not just a superstar, but a saintly superstar.

The golf tournament out of the way, Mario made his first visit to his future home. Accompanied by his father and Bob Perno, he was met at the Pittsburgh airport by Paul Steigerwald, the Penguins' marketing director. Steigerwald's interest in Mario was obviously keen. His livelihood could well depend on him. With the Penguins' attendance at less than seven thousand a game, Steigerwald knew that neither the team nor his job would be around for long if things didn't improve quickly. He knew that the future of the franchise was dependent upon the young man he was meeting.

At the airport he saw a reticent teenager who had a certain sensitivity and royalty about him. Far from the stereotypical muscle-bodied, muscle-minded athlete, Mario had a sophisti-cated, almost elegant way of carrying himself. Steigerwald took particular note of the size of his hands. Though he was very tall, his hands looked huge, as though he had yet to grow into them—like the feet of a puppy, Steigerwald thought.

The marketing director listened anxiously to how Mario performed in English. Like most apprentices of a language, Mario had his quirks. Though no such prefix was warranted, Mario would begin many of his English sentences with the same three words: "Well, of course. . . ." It was his way of getting his English motor started. He understood most English words and, albeit with several errors in grammar and word choice, he could get his point across. But the concern, however, did not involve Mario's being understood or misunderstood. It involved his confidence level. How much did having to perform in the second language affect the social personality? Mario Lemieux was withdrawn to begin with. Away from his home turf, and trying to communicate in a foreign language, it seemed likely that he would become more introverted.

Starting his NHL career, the portents were hardly propitious. Mario was coming off the world junior controversy and the draft fiasco and he was heading into a new culture. He had three strikes against him. Probably no other number-one draft pick had started with as many image handicaps.

He showed no lack of confidence his first days in town. Introduced to the media the day after his arrival, Mario wore the white Penguins sweater over a shirt and tie. He looked regal and confident and immaculately handsome. The dark hair curled forward and formed a perfect line a half-inch above the top of his eyebrows. The dark eyes locked easily into a bold and noble pose. The nose was not so bashed out of shape as to be indelicate. The lips were comfortably pursed and the skin as clear and fresh as a five-year-old's. He wore the number 66, which raised a few eyebrows because everyone made the connection—the upside-down Gretzky. Of the draft controversy in Montreal, he told the press, "It had to be done. It's all history now and we're all happy. Eddie's happy and I'm happy." Of the pressure of stepping into the NHL under such towering expectations, he said, "I think I can handle it."

Much had to be done: marketing for the team, finding a Pittsburgh home, getting a car, getting settled into a foreign country, learning more English. Mario visited some local malls with Steigerwald and shook hands and signed autographs and tried to be appealing. He worked out an arrangement with a local Chev-Olds dealer. Mario would do some radio spots and appearances at the car lot. In return, he received a four-wheel-drive Blazer.

Because Mario was only eighteen, Johnston, the Penguin GM, preferred to have him live with a family, rather than on his own. With a family he'd learn more English, he'd be taken care of, he'd be able to concentrate on hockey. Johnston interviewed several possibilities before settling on the well-to-do Tom and Nancy Mathews. They were a model American family. Tom was a highly successful executive with a construction firm and Nancy was the perfect homemaker. They lived in the posh Virginia Manor section of Mount Lebanon and had three sons, two of them hockey players. Johnston felt certain they would provide a healthy environment for Mario, and Bob Perno expressed satisfaction with the arrangement as well. The experience, Perno felt, would be a much-needed offset to the narrow world of Ville Emard's Rue Jorgue. Mario would learn how a successful family lived, how it managed finances, how it did things. Perno was pleased. What he didn't know, however, was that Tom Mathews was closely connected to Tom Reich, the fast-rising sports star agent. Had he known that, he would have had a different view of the living arrangement.

Perno planned on coming to Pittsburgh frequently to help his client through his first year. Steigerwald and others in the

Pittsburgh organization felt Perno was good for Mario. They could see that he was clearly not out to exploit his client for his own purposes. They could see a bond, a rapport between the two that was much tighter than the usual agent–athlete relationship.

With the opening of the Penguins' training camp, Perno received unsettling news. Nathalie Asselin wanted to remain in Pittsburgh with Mario. She wasn't doing much in Montreal—she had left school and rarely worked—so she planned to rent a small apartment to be close to Mario and his new Mount Lebanon home. Perno informed his boss, Gus Badali, of her plan. Badali was adamantly opposed. "There's no way, Bob. Mario has an obligation to his team and they're paying him a big dollar. Mario can't be worried about getting home after practice. He can't be worried about anything else but the team. You tell her she has to go home."

Perno did not want to be the messenger. His relationship with Nathalie had already seen some dicey moments. "Gus, I can't tell her that," he said. "You tell her."

"Well, I can't speak French, Bob. I think it would be better if you told her. You speak the language."

"I can't tell her."

"Well," Badali suggested, "tell Mario's parents to tell her."

Perno spoke to Jean-Guy and Pierrette, but they didn't want to let her know either. At long last, Badali agreed to do the deed, even though he spoke no French and Nathalie spoke little English. Though he tried to word it gently, it didn't help. As he informed her, he could see the tears filling Nathalie's eyes. She objected, pressing her case strongly, saying she would be more of a help to Mario than a hindrance. The agents didn't cave, nor did Mario become overly obstreperous about the issue. Nathalie returned to simmer in Montreal, bitter toward the agents. She knew it was they who had changed her young man's mind.

Now Mario was left alone with a family of Pittsburgh strangers for a home and a family of strangers for a team in the form of the sad-sack Penguins.

The Pittsburgh Penguins were one of modern sport's most gruesome franchises. They were a club plagued by a history of last-place finishes, pitiful attendance, human tragedy, drunks on skates, bankruptcy. Their exercise in folly had begun with the expansion of the six-team NHL in 1967. The first Penguin name players—Andy Bathgate, Ken Schinkel, Earl Ingarfield, and the skater with the name more akin to a flying trapeze artist than a hockey player, Val Fonteyne—toiled through a string of losing seasons. The team appeared to be on the right track by the mid-seventies, however, posting a 37–28–15 record in 1974–1975. They had assembled a respectable cast by then in Syl Apps Jr., Jean Pronovost, Vic Hadfield, and Rick Kehoe. To complement the veterans they had a rookie sensation, a French-Canadian savior in the form of "Lucky" Pierre Larouche.

Larouche, in fact, was the second French-Canadian savior. The first had been Michel Brière, a centerman from Shawinigan Falls. In his rookie season, 1969–1970, Brière showed fine promise, leading the club in assists. Team management saw him as a player to build the team around. But no sooner were the possibilities registered than the tragic news came. A month after his first season, Michel Brière was involved in a serious car accident which took his life.

Lucky Pierre Larouche arrived with more fanfare and more talent than Brière. He was an extraordinarily light-footed ice dancer, a scooter who left enemy defensemen in Elvis-like contortions. In the pre-Lemieux era he set the points record in the Quebec Major Junior Hockey League. In the NHL he led all rookie scorers, with sixty-eight points in his first season. In his second campaign no sophomore slump plagued him. Lucky

Pierre topped the fifty-goal plateau with fifty-three and added fifty-eight assists.

Larouche and the Penguins appeared well placed when they began the playoffs in 1975. They won their first series handily and quickly jumped to a three-games-to-none lead over the New York Islanders in the second. Only one other team in league history had ever squandered a three-game advantage and lost a seven-game set. These Penguins emulated the feat. After game three they had a three-day break. Rather than returning the short distance to Pittsburgh, General Manager Jack Button elected to have them stay in New York. Their chief place of residence, as it turned out, was a well-known Long Island drinking hole, the Salty Dog Saloon. Reports of a premature victory celebration emanated from the Salty Dog. The Penguins never recovered, blew the series, and the Islanders, not they, became the team of the future.

Pittsburgh management had been desperate for playoff money to stay alive. With the debt at $6.5 million, the team declared bankruptcy on June 13, 1975, becoming the first NHL club in the postwar era to do so.

New buyers came in wanting to build the team around Larouche. They sponsored a "Date with Pierre" contest to promote the team. But success had come too fast for Larouche, who had achieved fame at age nineteen. Lifestyle problems set in. Pierre missed practices, Pierre played no defense, Pierre liked to party. There were too many dates with Pierre. His play precipitously declined in his third year, and in the next, Lucky Pierre was gone, traded to the Montreal Canadiens for two Peters—Peter Mahovlich, who was winding down his career, and Peter Lee, a scorer with half the Larouche potential.

In the late 1970s the spirit of the Penguins had plunged to such depths that Mahovlich, who was schooled on Montreal's winning tradition, felt compelled to walk into the general manager's office one day and insist that he banish the team's drunkards. Mahovlich, not realizing that a player outside the office was eavesdropping, singled out the free-spirit goaltender, Dunc Wilson. The eavesdropper informed Wilson, who promptly found Mahovlich and attempted to knock him out.

When Mario Lemieux arrived, the Pens had posted losing records in thirteen of their seventeen years. They were coming off the worst record in their history. They had gone through eight coaches and almost as many owners and general managers. Baz Bastien, the last GM before Eddie Johnston, had died, like Michel Brière, in a car crash. Bob Berry, the new coach, had been fired from Montreal, picked up by the L.A. Kings, fired in the same season by them, and now snapped up, right after his second canning, by the Penguins.

Edward DeBartolo, the owner, had said that "as an investment, a hockey team stinks," and had seen his words come true. Between 1978 and Mario's arrival in 1984, he watched as his team lost an estimated $18 million. Usually, he watched from afar. "I don't understand these owners who get so involved," DeBartolo said. "You know, we have a few other projects going from time to time that are a little bigger than a hockey team."

Lemieux didn't know all the details of the Penguins' dismal history. He tended to look upon the situation with an air of equanimity. "No, I wasn't disappointed with being drafted by Pittsburgh," he reported. "It's hard, you know, to start with a team that is last. But we have to build this team. I like to play with a team that is very low and get the team up in a few years.

"I think first of pride, not pressure. A lot of guys, they can't take the pressure. I think I can . . . I'm the kind of guy who isn't very nervous, who takes life as it comes."

EIGHT
FIRST SEASON

THE TEAM'S FIRST WORKOUTS TOOK PLACE IN SUBURBAN MOUNT Lebanon. The Penguins brought two other first-round draft choices besides Mario Lemieux to camp: Doug Bodger, a promising defenseman, and Roger Belanger, a center. Lemieux's press build-up was enormous. The team's veterans tended to view the premature anointing of superstars cynically. Doug Shedden, one of Pittsburgh's leading scorers, had seen Mario perform at the Memorial Cup a few months earlier and had come away, like most everyone else at that event, decidedly unimpressed. He didn't have many good things to report to teammates about him. Mike Bullard, the Penguins' hard-shooting, hard-drinking, fifty-two-goal scorer of the previous season, stood to lose his ranking as his team's top player if forecasts of Mario's brilliance proved accurate. Like Shedden, Bullard was not overly enthusiastic about the Quebecker's arrival.

Before the actual camp opened, the Penguin veterans gathered at the rink for some informal warm-up drills. Mario Lemieux, eager for an early start, joined them. As he made his way from the dressing room to the ice surface to spend his first moments skating with NHL players, all eyes were on him.

After all the build-up, the moment had finally arrived. Lemieux strode confidently to the ice's edge, but as he stepped onto the practice rink, he felt his skates fly out from under him. As if in a slapstick comedy routine, he crashed to the ice, rear first. All that was missing was the drumroll and the boom. The doubting veterans could not have hoped for more. "Oh yeah!" said one of them. "He's going to be a great one all right."

In those early days there soon followed the episode in which Mario proved to be the only one on the team who could not lift 180 pounds. He came away from that particular incident both surprised and depressed. "He just couldn't understand," recalled Perno. "I remember he said, 'Bob, you should have seen this Marty McSorley. He just discouraged me. He lifted that bar like a toothpick. I couldn't even budge it, not even budge it.'"

Perno was surprised himself to hear what had happened. "Mario was strong. I'm sure he could have lifted that bar. I think it was the situation he was in, the pressure of the moment—that and never really having done it before."

After the barbell session, there was the further embarrassment of Mario's long-distance run with Doug Shedden, when he proved capable of only short distances. But what mattered most, of course, was how he looked on the ice, not in gyms or on tracks, and in the early workouts his performance excited Penguins' management. They expressed immediate confidence that they had made the right choice. Fans packed the arena just to watch practices. Paul Steigerwald returned home from seeing Mario on skates for the first time and excitedly called a friend. "He's another Gretzky!" Steigerwald shouted. "He's just like Gretzky! He makes those long passes! He has eyes in the back of his head! He sees everybody on the ice!" Like Scotty Bowman, everyone marveled at how he saw the ice. "There's not another player who's close," Bowman had said of the 1984 draft picks. "Mario seems to have that extra sense of knowing where all his teammates are and opponents are at the same time."

For GM Eddie Johnston, Mario's practice perfomance stirred memories of 1966, when Bobby Orr broke in with the Boston Bruins. Johnston played goal for the Bruins, a dismal club at the time. "We'd heard about this eighteen-year-old kid, Orr," he recalled. "He was going to save the franchise." The build-up made skeptics of the veteran players, who wondered aloud what the kid could do among the pros. The attitude lasted two practices. After that, Johnston remembered, it was "Wowww! Look what we've found."

"That," said Johnston after watching Mario in a couple of practices, "is a pretty good analogy to what I saw out there today."

Despite Mario's talent, breaking in presented difficulties. Mario's language discomfort, his age, and his private personality separated him from the clique who led the Penguins. Unlike Lucky Pierre, Mario was not the type who could ingratiate himself with the boys by heading off to the bar for a half-dozen Bud. Mario did go to Walt's, the Mount Lebanon hangout for many of the players during camp, but instead of drinking, he played pinball.

He injured a knee in preseason, an insignificant development, but somewhat symbolic of what was to come. This was a player who couldn't get past preseason without a mishap. In the four exhibition games he did play, Mario scored three goals and counted five assists, for a two-points-a-game average.

On Thursday, October 11, 1984, he suited up for his first regular-season NHL game. The opponent was Boston, a tight-checking club, and the site was the Boston Garden, a small rink favoring close-checking players. It wasn't, as Mario noted over a pancake breakfast the day of the game, the best place to start. With his passive look, he showed no outward sign of nerves. But he would say later that he really felt uneasy that day.

At 1:41 of the opening period, he made his first appearance. Ray Bourque, the Bruins' anchorman, their best defenseman since Orr, attempted a pass in the center zone. More by luck of position than anything else, Mario got his skate in the way of the puck, knocking it in the other direction. Suddenly, he found himself alone, the puck ahead of him, nothing between him and the goal except it and the Garden air. Now it was easy. He had done it at age four, he could surely do the same now, especially with his size advantage and the porous Pete Peeters in the Boston goal. A player's reach, if he has enough coordination to control it, gives him the edge on the breakaway. One quick shift of the arms and the puck has transferred from one side of the net to the other, faster than a goalie can possibly move.

With his great expanse, Mario the Condor swooped in on Peeters. With a sharp shift, he drew Peeters to his knees. Now he had the puck on the other side of the goal, the backhand side, and he snapped it up into all that empty space that poor Peeters could not cover.

First game, first shift, first shot, first goal. He played unremarkably the remainder of the game, but added an assist to make it a two-point inaugural. The Penguins lost 4–3, but nobody cared as much about the result as the debut of the big guy. "You've got to like that sixth sense he's got," said Bruce Crowder, once a Bruin, now just a Penguin. "There are guys who can skate and shoot and do everything, but they don't have that hockey sense." Peeters noticed the wingspan. "I stood in there, forced him to make a move, and he made a move. The thing I forgot was that he's got that great reach." Mario saw Tom Lapointe of *La Presse* after the game. A Pittsburgh–Boston encounter normally offered limited interest to Quebeckers, but *La Presse* had wanted a man in Boston for Mario's first game. Mario perked up when he saw Lapointe, somebody with whom he could relax and speak his own language. "You came all the way here to see me in my first game, Tom?" he said. "I really appreciate that."

Two nights later he played badly, by his own admission, in his first appearance as a pro in the Montreal Forum. He had been concerned about the reception he would be accorded, given the uproar and bad press at the junior draft. When about one-quarter of the spectators in the Forum stood and applauded his introduction, he was relieved. But already, after only a few exhibitions and a couple of regular-season games, Mario was beginning to feel limited in what he could do by what his surrounding cast could do. There was no one to feather the passes to him, no one to read the play smartly and move the way he hoped they would move, no other stars. "It was tough because the team didn't play well, so it was hard for me to play well," he said of the Montreal game. At the same time, he retained his composure and perspective. "I would have enjoyed playing well, but it's all part of the game and I can't do anything about that. There will be other chances."

He wore his baseball cap on the flight back to Pittsburgh following the game, the team's second straight loss. While he slept, a teammate poured mounds of shaving cream onto the peak and stuck a cigarette in the top of it like a candle. When Mario awoke, he wondered what everyone was laughing at. He wore the cap a lot, especially following rookie initiation day. One of the standard ways the old guard officially welcomed newcomers to the team was with scissors and electric razors. In the dressing room one day Mario noticed that Shedden, Bullard, Dave Hannan, and Randy Boyd were readying the tools. Before they could pin him down, Mario jumped onto the trainer's table and volunteered his scalp. Given his status and the potential management reaction, the veterans hesitated. But they eventually gave Mario a nice, gnarled trim.

For his home debut, he faced the Vancouver Canucks.

Nothing quite caused the eyes to glaze over as much as the prospect of a Canucks–Penguins clash. In Pittsburgh, a Canucks appearance normally drew only 5,000 fans. This being opening night, however, and Mario's opener, 14,741 passed through the doors of the Civic Arena, or the Igloo, as it was commonly called.

Coach Bob Berry put Mario out for the opening face-off. Eighteen seconds into his home inaugural, he moved down the left side of the rink and slipped around Canuck defenseman Doug Halward at the blue line. Doug Shedden had moved over from his wing position and was powering down the middle toward the goal. Mario saw him. His crisp radar pass struck Shedden's stick blade, Sheddy buried it, and the Igloo went nuts.

During Mario's next shift, Vancouver's little Gary Lupul began pestering him like a bee: a stick to the legs, a stick to the gut, a stick to the forearm. Mario had had enough. He turned on Lupul and used him as a punching-bag. Lupul folded himself up like a turtle. Now Mario had a point and a TKO in just three minutes on Igloo ice, and the patrons roared some more. As the fight continued, the Penguins' Rod Buskas tag-teamed with Mario, skating in and suckering Canuck Michel Petit with a haymaker that sprayed his teeth five rows up in the stands.

After his jellyfish performance in the weight room, Mario had wanted to send a message to his teammates, and his adversaries, that he wasn't a puffbag. Though he had chosen a small guy, he'd done a good job. "I would say I got in about ten uppercuts," he said of his square-off with Lupul. He was happier with the results of the fight than the game itself. He got only the one point, marking the third outing in succession in which he hadn't quite met his own high standards. More modest performances followed. On the night of Ronald Reagan's election to a second term, Wayne Gretzky and the Edmonton Oilers came to Pittsburgh. The first 99–66 confrontation produced a

3–3 draw, with Mario getting one assist and Gretzky a point on a late goal to tie the game.

"In an eighty-game schedule he's going to find out there are a lot of peaks, but there are also a few valleys too," said Gretzky. "He's going to find out you're not going to win every game and score four goals a night like in junior. If he keeps a level head, he'll be all right." Glen Sather, the Edmonton coach, didn't like the idea of Mario wearing number 66. "I think that it's a mistake to have him try and compare himself to Wayne, one way or the other. He's not Wayne. He has to be his own man. Don't try to live in Wayne's shadow. Wayne is a unique hockey player and there's not going to be one like him." But Sather wasn't denigrating Mario's talents. "He handles the puck great. He's big and strong. He may end up being better than Wayne."

"It isn't very fair to compare me to Wayne Gretzky," Mario said. "He's the greatest. I'll try to be the best, but it will take me more than a year to do that."

Coach Berry had trouble finding the right linemates for Lemieux. But a few games into the campaign, Mario took note of the play of Warren Young, a twenty-eight-year-old rookie free agent who had traveled the roads of the minor leagues for years without catching on in the NHL. Mario noticed that Young was scoring points and, at the same time, playing a physical game, a game that could give a linemate room to maneuver. He asked to play with Young and Berry assented. Young could not have been more pleased.

The two played well together from the first day. They had a quiet rapport. There were no long discussions about who should do this and who should do that. Mario just had one piece of advice, which he repeated to Warren Young time after time. It became known as Mario's number-one commandment: "Just get me the puck," Mario said in his French accent, "and go to the net."

Young obliged him. The unheralded minor leaguer became a *cause célèbre*, the surprise of the Penguins' early season. He scored more goals than Mario, partly because Mario set the table for him and partly because Mario wasn't scoring himself. Number 66 was setting up goals. He had twelve assists in his first eleven games, but only one goal. After nineteen games he had five goals, but not one of them on home ice. In November he was smashed by Washington defenseman Darren Veitch, hurt a knee, and had to sit out for seven games. When he was back from the injury, the goals came a little easier. At long last, more than two months into the season, he ended the Igloo drought by scoring against the New York Islanders on December 14.

He was averaging more than a point a game, commendable enough for a rookie. But besides playing short of his own expectations, Mario was not leading his team out of the hellhole it had been in for so long. The Penguins started the season well enough, but then won only one in their next fourteen games. They had an encouraging December, winning five in a row in one stretch, but early in the New Year they went winless in twelve.

Mario analyzed his play. "The first ten games were really tough because I felt a lot of pressure on me to do well and maybe I was trying too hard. I guess I ran into all the things that players do when they come in from junior hockey. The pace is faster, the players are bigger, stronger, and smarter, and if you make a mistake, they take advantage of it.

"At first I felt that the things I had done in junior hockey just wouldn't work in the NHL and that limited me a lot. Then I started to realize that they would work, but that I just had to do them that much faster and not hold onto the puck so long." He had been passing too much early in the season, he said. He had to get comfortable enough to shoot more.

Bob Berry worked with him on defense and face-offs, the two weakest parts of his game. In his first NHL season he faced the same criticism he did during his Laval years: without the puck, he tended to look lazy and uninterested. Teammates sometimes spoke among themselves about his lack of defense. "He has a somewhat laconic attitude," noted a veteran. "He's a bit too easygoing at times and that reduces his effectiveness. Gretzky never relaxes on the ice. He's always on the prowl, looking for any little opening. Mario lacks consistent hunger." Critics said Mario treated his own zone like a minefield. Mario and perspiration were total strangers, they complained. Lemieux countered with arguments he had used before: his big frame gave him the appearance of being slower and less intense than he actually was; he played so much with his brain that he didn't need his legs as much as the other players; and "Pittsburgh is paying me to score goals, not to play defensively." By and large, the local media supported him. "Asking Mario to play defense," cracked Dave Molinari of the *Pittsburgh Press*, "is akin to asking Sinatra to sell popcorn at intermission."

Mario got along well with the Pittsburgh media, and always would. They were—unlike some reporters in other cities—easy to get along with. But Pittsburgh was a small hockey market. It would be the media elsewhere who set the overall image.

His first year was mostly business. Mario didn't go out a lot in Pittsburgh. Living with the Mathews, he didn't want to be late getting home. Besides, there was his age. As he discovered one evening with Perno and Young, he was too young to enjoy the hot spots. Perno and Young took him to Confetti's, one of the trendy bars of the day. As they entered, the proprietor looked at Mario and said, "Sorry, but I can't let you in." He had read in the papers that Mario was only nineteen, and explained to him that he could lose his license if he served him. Warren Young stepped forward. "Hey, look, you're talking to Mario Lemieux."

The man said, "Yeah, I know it's Mario Lemieux, and I know he could buy this bar tomorrow, but I can't let him in."

Embarrassed for Mario, they all trooped back to the Mathews' house and drank beer, watched TV, and got slaughtered by Mario in Nintendo. Despite the regular flow of girls who drove down the Mathews' street honking their horns for the bachelor, this evening was representative of Lemieux's social life that first year in the steel city: beer, TV, video games. He spent so much time at the Mathews' that they became real family to him. "We didn't plan to get attached," said Nancy Mathews, "and we didn't want to get attached, but somehow it happened." She found Mario quiet, classy, cooperative, and mature for his age. Pierrette and Jean-Guy were welcomed to the Mathews' home whenever they came to town, and got along splendidly with them as well. Still, as Mario told many friends back in Montreal after his first year, he often felt lonely. On the team he hung around a bit with Warren Young, especially on road trips. They were friends, quiet friends, but Young never got too close.

By the all-star break Mario had twenty-one goals and thirty-five assists in forty-two games, enough to get him named to the all-star squad by Islanders' coach Al Arbour. In the days leading up to the game, Don Cherry, the devotee of "rock-em, sock-em hockey," picked up on the criticism of Lemieux's laid-back style. Normally Cherry, the king of "Hockey Night in Canada," saved his best shots for Europeans. But this time, he leaned into the households of the nation and pronounced Mario "the biggest floater in the NHL."

Mario heard about it. His ire was up, and at the all-star game he responded the way he normally did when the stakes had been raised. The so-called biggest floater floated like a butterfly and stung like a bee. He scored two goals and had one assist and was named, at age nineteen, playing against every superstar in the league, the game's most valuable player. After

the game he told reporters, "That was for him." He was referring to Don Cherry.

Gretzky was typically gracious. He and Mario were still
good friends at this time. "Mario played a great game," Gretzky
said. "He was really deserving of the award." Coach Arbour
called him "the future of the game."

When Mario returned to Pittsburgh from that game,
Warren Young noticed a transformation in him. "Up to that
point, he was still a little unsure of what he could do. The all-
star game gave him the confidence that he could do anything."
But even with him scoring more, the team's losses continued.
The players and the management realized that they simply
didn't have the talent. Mario grew frustrated with his opponents'
clutching, grabbing, and highsticking. Finally, he tried dropping
a hint to management that a bodyguard would be a welcome
addition to the team. "Right now, I have to take care of myself,"
Lemieux explained, thinking of Edmonton and how Dave
Semenko protected Gretzky. "Maybe that's what we have
missed, a tough guy on the team. We have some tough guys in
Baltimore [Pens' farm team]. I don't know why they don't bring
those guys up." GM Johnston was quick with the rebuttal.
"We'll run the hockey club. Let Mario play hockey."

Young had enough size to deter some who tried to crowd
the superstar. Mario, however, valued Young too much as an
offensive contributor to see him serving a lot of penalty time.
On several occasions, when the opposing team sent out an
enforcer with the apparent intent of getting something started,
Mario would skate over to Young and say, "Stay on the ice." He
didn't want Young to fall for the fight bait, but rather to concentrate on going to the net. Mario was nine years younger than
Warren Young, but assumed the role of adviser on other occasions as well. In Toronto Young was awarded a penalty shot
against the Maple Leafs. Toronto was his home city. Young had

every friend and every relative looking on from the stands. He had never been so nervous. As he lined up for the shot, Mario skated by and said, "Go in with speed." Young listened. Going in with speed loosened up his nerves and he scored. He felt better after that goal than any he could remember.

The Penguins didn't make the playoffs. Their record, 22–48–10, was almost as pitiful as the year before. Mario had not been expected to bring about a renaissance in only one season, but the Penguins had expected to win more than twenty-two. As it was, playing without strong winners, with pluggers who had half the talent of Gretzky's early season linemates, Mario finished the season with 43 goals and 57 assists—an even 100 points in 73 games. Even with the seven missed games, his total was the third highest for any rookie in league history. To no one's surprise, he was named rookie of the year. And to no one's surprise—and his own dismay—he was named to the team to represent Canada in the world hockey championships in Prague.

NINE
SIXTH SENSE

BY THE MID-1980S THE ANNUAL WORLD HOCKEY CHAMPIONSHIPS had become a sideshow of diminishing significance. They were staged every April, the same month the NHL playoffs began. Canada could only send players from teams that didn't make the playoffs or were eliminated in the first round. Consequently, the Soviet Union or other nations defeated Canada at the tournament every year. Canada hadn't won the gold medal—even though everyone knew there was no better hockey nation—since 1961.

Despite the semi-farcical nature of the Canadian presence in this tournament, a measure of national honor was still deemed to be at stake. If called upon, Canadian players were expected to volunteer their services and, in the name of their country, go over to Europe to get trounced. Not all players answered the summons, but most stars, including Phil Esposito and Wayne Gretzky, made the effort. If for no other reason than public-relations damage control, the trip was worthwhile.

Mario Lemieux's patriotism had already been questioned. He could ill afford another controversy involving his participation in international hockey. Nonetheless, he greeted his invitation to the 1985 tournament in Prague unenthusiastically. He had just completed a long, first NHL season. He complained of fatigue, homesickness, a need for relaxation and golf. His agents countered that attendance at the world tournament was a price the big stars had to pay, that he was in no position to snub another such competition, that Gretzky wasn't the type to stay at home. Alan Eagleson, Canada's czar of international hockey, lobbied Mario, as did his Pittsburgh landlord, Tom Mathews. Mario finally relented and headed for the Czech capital.

Once there, he was quickly bored. Not keen on culture, having developed few interests outside of hockey, Mario was hardly one—nor were most other players, for that matter—who could enjoy the sights, sounds, and smells of Communist Prague. He was the only French-Canadian on the team. He didn't relish playing third-rate competition like the Germans. He suffered a groin injury and sat out two games. His outfit played poorly and was crushed by the Soviets in the qualifying round.

Mario brooded and finally told Eagleson he wanted to go home. He asked to be booked out on the first flight back to Canada. Eagleson agreed, only to report back that no flights were available. Mario phoned Bob Perno—at three in the morning Montreal time. "Get me out of here," he ordered his agent. Perno sighed. "Jesus," he thought, "here we go again." Didn't Mario know that deserting the national team during the world championships would bring on a deluge of media condemnation? Didn't he care? Did he want to be viewed forever as an ingrate, as unpatriotic?

Perno plunged into a morality lecture. "You owe it to the team, you owe it to your country to stick it out. If you can't play because you are injured, then your job is to give support to those who can." Mario said that he didn't care, that he was tired, bored, hurting.

Perno knew well the stubborn nature of Mario Lemieux. Its genesis was in the common urge to be free of the control of others. "There are some men," wrote Jean de La Bruyère in *Les*

Caractères, "who turn a deaf ear to reason and good advice, and willfully go wrong for fear of being controlled." He may well have been writing a message for Lemieux. In all the time that Perno was with him, Mario had never changed his mind on a major issue.

While sitting in the stands watching his teammates getting beaten by the United States, however, Mario got frustrated and angry. He turned to Eagleson and told him he was going to stay.

The next game was against Finland. Though he was still hurt, Mario played a substantial role in a win that set up a medal match against the Soviets. The Soviets had won the first game over Canada by a 9–1 margin and were rightfully disdainful of their opposition. They had enjoyed a monotonous monopoly of this competition. The team they had this year, gold-medal winners from the Olympics the year before in Sarajevo, was among the best they had ever iced. In world championship competition, Canada had not beaten the Red Machine since 1961.

No reason to think anything would change now, but for the fact that Mario Lemieux was in one of those moods in which, extricated from his dispassion, his game vaulted to new levels. Despite his complaints, the conditions in Prague were right for him. His clean, artistic, purist style comfortably fit the European type of play; his size fit the larger dimensions of the European ice surfaces.

The game against Russia would teach him that there could indeed be life on foreign ponds. The nineteen-year-old got in the flow of the game. He demonstrated to Coach Viktor Tikhonov and the other Russian masters the level of harmony and control his game could reach. It was one of those games in which Mario looked as though he was monitoring his moves from the press box above the ice. He scored two of the three Canadian goals. On the first, he lasered a Larry Murphy pass, without first stopping it, into the Soviet net. On the second, he was put in open ice with a relay from Kirk Muller and descended alone on the Russian goaltender. Final tally: Canada 3, Soviets 1.

"It's not every day you get a chance to beat the Russians," Mario beamed afterwards. "Maybe I wasn't so happy when we first got here. We were playing against the German teams and there wasn't any pressure, and I was hurt and wanted to go home." His team lost the gold medal when it fell to Czechoslovakia, but the Canadians still brought home an unexpected silver and Lemieux had turned what had all the markings of a disaster into a triumph. He had demonstrated some national pride and had shown he could expertly compete—even at such a young age—with some of the most brilliant hockey players in the world. "Doing this is a greater thrill than I ever dreamed of," he told the press. Would he do it again? Without hesitation, Lemieux responded, "Of course I would come here again."

Perno and Mario's family members greeted him at the Montreal airport. He appeared wearing a proud face and the silver medal around his neck. He hugged Bob Perno and thanked him, telling him that the pressure Perno had put on him to stay in Prague was the best advice he had ever given him. They all went back to Rue Jorgue for a party. Perno and his wife then flew to Daytona Beach, Florida, for a week's vacation with Nathalie and Mario. They played golf and dined on fine food and enjoyed the beaches. On the surface, all seemed well between the agent and Nathalie, who had cooled her heels in Montreal during Mario's first year in Pittsburgh.

Mario spent some of the summer of 1985 back in Montreal. First, he had to cart up many of his belongings from Pennsylvania. With Perno, he jammed everything he could into his Blazer and set off on the eleven-hour drive. At the border crossing in Buffalo Perno told Mario he had unfortunately chosen a lane that would take them to a female customs officer. Perno had always had bad luck with women in these situations. "There could be a long delay getting through here," he warned Mario.

"Don't worry, Bob," the star replied. "Just watch me. I'll charm her to death."

At the gate Mario put on his best superstar smile and was exceedingly friendly as the officer asked what he did for a living in the United States. "I'm a professional hockey player, Mario Lemieux."

"Do you have some proof on you?" she inquired. "Where is your pro contract?"

Mario replied that it wasn't something he normally carried around with him.

"Well, I need to have it," said the woman. "You'll have to pull over." Mario's pleas got nowhere. He and Perno had to empty the Blazer of almost every scrap. Then Perno had to phone Pittsburgh and have a copy of the hockey contract faxed up.

Three hours later they were back on the road. "Some charmer you are!" Perno told Mario. Lemieux fumed all the way back to Montreal.

They had another big party at the Lemieux residence to celebrate Mario's first season in the NHL. As master of ceremonies, they brought in a reporter Lemieux trusted—Tom Lapointe of *La Presse*. Mario and his clan were confident that they could give Lapointe a close-up view of the hockey star's personal life without fear that they would one day read about it in the newspapers. Mario's brothers had gotten to know Lapointe and they had confirmed that Tom was okay. Lapointe was only too pleased to come and do the MC honors. Lapointe's style, the opposite of Marc Lachapelle's, was to get tight with the stars. He had carved out a close relationship with Wayne Gretzky. He figured that somewhere down the line this would pay off in a big story, a scoop. Now he was getting close to the heir apparent, a player very few knew well. Most other Quebec journalists had ruined their chances with Mario with criticisms of him during one of the controversies that had sullied his young career.

At the party a small band played and Mario was loose, as he always was with the Lemieux clan. When the beers flowed smoothly and he relaxed, Mario would break through the shyness barrier and do something hardly in character for introverts: impersonations. He was good at them, and especially liked doing Elvis Presley. That night the clan presented him with a diamond ring in recognition of his fine first season in the NHL. He wore it proudly. Despite all the complications, Mario felt he had proved that his advance billing was no mistake. More importantly, he had convinced himself that he could be a star at the NHL level. It had taken some time. For almost the first half of the season he had played somewhat tentatively, but then he had found his game and discovered that his skills in junior could indeed carry over to the NHL and dominate there as well.

"I want," said Mario, speaking of hockey's tempo, "to be able to go out and control the game. After maybe thirty games I really started to play well, started to control the game a little bit more. That's what I did in junior."

For year two there would be changes: a new home, a new car, Nathalie's presence, an effort to be outgoing, an increased consistency in his hockey performance.

Language shyness and the usual problems associated with being a rookie in an entirely new environment had held Mario in the background to a degree which, even for him, was unusual. Now, with some seasoning, he could be more assertive. Though he had a working knowledge of English, he had suffered through many embarrassing moments the first season. One came on Myron Cope's local Pittsburgh radio show. Mario didn't know that he should never have agreed to appear on this program. With his speeding Pittsburgh twang, Cope was sometimes difficult even for the natives to comprehend. For Mario, it might just as well have been Swahili. To Cope's blurred assaults, he chose one of three responses: a "yes," a "no," or, for variety's sake, an "I think so." Confessed Mario after the appearance: "I didn't understand a word."

He moved out of the Mathews' house and into a condominium, one nearby because he liked the idea of having the Mathews in the neighborhood. He'd be close to the fine meals made by Nancy Mathews. In the new home, the plan was to have Nathalie Asselin join him for much of the year. Nathalie couldn't get a work permit in the United States, so she couldn't be a formal, full-time resident. But she could still spend much of the time in Pittsburgh with Mario. She would no longer have to idle in Montreal. They could set up house, and she could help him organize his life.

This at least was the plan. She didn't realize, however, that Perno was working behind the scenes to scuttle it. The agent was bending Mario's ears about the dangers of any close living arrangement with Nathalie. Did Mario know anything about laws in the United States as they concerned common-law relationships? Did he know that in the event of a split, Nathalie could perhaps have a major claim on Mario's income? The questions got the big guy thinking. Maybe it wasn't such a good idea. Perno then came forward with a compromise proposal: "Get Nathalie to sign papers waiving any and all claims she might have on you under a common-law living arrangement." The suggestion was cold-blooded, mercenary. Perno may have been trying to protect his client's interests, but how could he expect the two of them, still teenagers, still kids, to enter into such a pitiless compact?

Since that day when the fifteen-year-old Mario asked Perno how big a contract he could get if he broke the junior scoring records, he had always demonstrated a special concern for money matters. Nothing had changed. He agreed to have the idea put to Nathalie. Perno did the deed, and Nathalie went ballistic. She wasn't prepared to sign anything. How could they even suggest it? Did they have nothing but dollar signs in their eyes? Did they really think she was in this relationship just for the money? Her anger was chiefly directed at Perno. Who was this goddamn agent to pry his way into their personal lives like this?

Eventually, the idea of having Nathalie sign the waiver papers was dropped. She would come to Pittsburgh and stay at the condominium when she pleased. She no longer wanted to have anything to do with Bob Perno. The agent, it appeared, had stuck his nose in once too often. In a test of Mario's loyalties, he could hardly expect to come out the winner. He had babysat, nurtured, and schooled Mario through three years of junior hockey without a penny in return. Now, just as Mario's career was about to blossom, he stood to lose him.

Though many had noticed that the Mario–Perno bond was much tighter than the usual player–agent relationship, questions had surfaced about whether Lemieux was being well served by his friend. Around the Penguins office, some eyebrows were raised when Mario signed his first contract. A $100,000 signing bonus came with it, but for many weeks no one picked up the check. It lay there while the interest it could have earned was frittered away. In his role as Mario's landlord and friend, Tom Mathews was keeping a close eye on the quality of service Mario was receiving. It was no secret that, after Mario's first year, Mathews talked about this matter with his good friend Tom Reich, the Pittsburgh super-agent.

Meanwhile, with Nathalie's help, Mario set up the condominium. It wasn't ostentatious. Mario was developing a taste for fine wines, wines finer than the Blue Nuns of Ville Emard, but most everything else reflected his age and his working-class heritage. Outside of hockey, his interests remained few, as shown by his answers to a series of questions put to him by the *Pittsburgh Post-Gazette*.

Your first job?—"I didn't have a job. I played junior hockey."

Your dream vacation?—"Play golf for a week at Myrtle Beach."

What people may be surprised to know about you?—"I'm really shy."

The book you want to read when you get time?—"I never read."

He watched "Three's Company" and "Miami Vice" and soap operas. He played with Oscar and Casey, his Himalayan cats, until he found he was allergic to cats and had to send them away. He kept friends older than himself and not on the hockey team. Bill Kelly, a Pittsburgh car dealer, was one. He and Mario worked out an arrangement whereby Mario got the use of a high-quality car in exchange for doing ads for the dealership. Kelly, who was more than two decades older than Mario, became a good friend. He did have to lower his flamboyant personality a few notches to make Lemieux feel comfortable. Though Mario was terribly shy, Kelly found him remarkably cooperative. He'd have Mario out at his showroom on a promotion night and hundreds of people would show up wanting autographs and pictures. "It was tough," remembered Kelly. "You know the routine. 'Here, hold the baby, Mario. Now stand with Grandma and smile. Now here, sign this.'" Other celebrities Kelly had used for promotion left at the earliest opportunity. "You get some flunky football player or baseball player and there'd be a hundred people standing there, but if it was nine o'clock, bang, they're gone."

He never had a problem with Mario. He was patient and polite—and a disappointment to every girl who came through the showroom door. "I've been there when girls came up and flaunted themselves at him," said Kelly. "They came over and actually propositioned the guy. Like 'Here, I'm available.'"

I mean, we're talking about perfect tens here, not nines. Mario would stand there and respond, 'No, thank you. No, thank you.' I think he'd rather play nine holes of golf than have some woman hanging around him."

Unlike other athletes, Mario always returned Kelly's cars in pristine condition. For his second year on the Penguins, he replaced the Blazer with a Cadillac convertible, sports model. But he couldn't get excited about it and wanted a sports car instead. He had always talked, despite his size, about owning an old English sports car. One of his relatives knew how to make replicas of them, and Mario asked him to custom-build one for him. With all his earnings, he also wanted to see his family members driving in style. He gave the car he won at the all-star game to his brother Richard, who traded it in a few weeks later. He bought his father, who had developed a bad back, a Pontiac Parisienne to replace, at long last, the old canary. He wished to buy his parents a new home, but Pierrette and Jean-Guy preferred to stay in Ville Emard in their modest duplex with their friends and their memories. Mario had a big TV dish installed on the roof so that they could have the clan over to watch all the Penguin games.

In the first year Mario's presence drove up Penguin attendance by roughly three thousand a game, from seven thousand to ten thousand. Now the Penguins no longer had to worry about being overtaken in popularity by the Pittsburgh Spirit, an indoor soccer team. The jump in gate receipts, in combination with his quality of play in the first season, prompted the Penguins to begin renegotiating Mario's contract. He would soon sign a deal worth $500,000 a year. Ironically, however, despite the team's more promising outlook, the owner was threatening to move the franchise to Hamilton, Ontario. To remain in Pittsburgh, DeBartolo wanted a better lease arrangement with the city on the Igloo and a major increase in season ticket sales. To save the franchise, the team's managers called upon Mario to help promote a ticket drive. Their campaign theme was "The Best Is Yet to Come," the added twist being that Mario's last name translated in English to "the best."

He responded enthusiastically to the call for help. He became convinced, like Terry Bradshaw of Pittsburgh football in the previous decade, that he was the one to save the franchise. "When he became aware of that," said Tom Rooney of the team's marketing department, "he would have opened a phone booth at a shopping mall if we [had] asked him." Mario worked the malls and the radio stations. He continued to hold a particularly strong attraction for young females. At a suburban shopping center one day fans swarmed after him as if he were a rock star. "He was bigger than the Beatles!" said Eddie Johnston.

Mario only had to crack the smile and be nice on such occasions. In spite of his private nature, he realized—or at least appeared to realize—that, as he himself put it, "being nice to people is part of everybody's life, including an athlete's. It's good for publicity too because if people like you, they'll help you."

The deeds and the words signaled an apparent maturation in Mario's attitude. But not much could be read into his public-relations effort. What he did in the isolation of Pittsburgh, where he was becoming more comfortable and where he was adored by the media, could not be confused with the larger picture. No sooner had signs of his new attitude begun to appear, than a reversion to the old ways took place. In the summer of 1985 he decided to cancel his charity golf tournament. He couldn't be bothered making the effort to continue it. He had hosted the second annual tourney, again at Piedmont, and it too had been successful. But he didn't enjoy himself. While everyone else was having a good time, Mario complained to Perno that he was too busy glad-handing and was weighed down with official duties, things he didn't enjoy. He didn't want to do it any more.

The tournament put Mario front and center, and the only time Mario Lemieux was comfortable in that role was on the ice rink. Beyond that, he sought no limelight. Beyond that, he would just as soon shut the doors and darken the room.

As a typical kid, Mario didn't understand, nor could he really have been expected to understand, the importance of charity, from the point of view both of altruism and his own public image. He wouldn't understand this until later in life, when things happened to him that would make him understand.

Nothing could have been more simple, more ideal for Mario from the point of view of philanthropy than the hosting of a charity golf event. He needed only to be nice to people for a couple of days and, in return, he got to spend a day on the golf course, he raised money for charity, and he enhanced his public image. But Mario loved golf because the game offered him privacy, solitude—the very things that hosting a tournament for a cast of hundreds took away.

He once made some observations on golf that illuminated his pensive, private nature. "I would like to play golf professionally when this [hockey] is over," revealed Mario. "That is my dream anyway. There is something clean and bright about golf. It is a game where you are alone and within yourself. That's something I like sometimes, to be alone and to see what is inside myself.

"Sometimes with hockey—although I try not to let it be so—there is no time for reflection. Thinking is important. Thinking what you are." His private, introspective nature was central to his make-up. But this, his natural way, was something others couldn't understand or wouldn't accept.

As the crisis over the team staying in Pittsburgh passed, Mario was less needed by the Penguins for public-relations purposes. Management now wanted him to devote his full energies to hockey. Promotional obligations could be set aside. The Penguins had to win games and make the playoffs. They wanted to shield the star. This approach suited Mario well and he welcomed it. To be left alone to hockey, to Nathalie, and to Nintendo was what he desired. And what, he wondered, was the fault with that? What was wrong with being a private young man who came to the rink, did his job marvelously, and then left the rink behind?

In theory, it was fine. But in real life, sports superstars could not get away with it—especially if they were not well fronted. If there was a public-relations department to soothe media egos and nicely explain the star's no-shows, or a coach who could take the heat for the star, or a star who could smile and transmit occasional warmth and convincingly explain his need for solitude, then perhaps it could work. But Mario couldn't do this and he couldn't get help. The Penguins' coach, Bob Berry, had no time for the visiting press. They needed a public-relations director like Bill Tuele of the Edmonton Oilers, who shielded Gretzky when he needed shielding. Tuele could say no without making Gretzky look like the offending party. Mario had no buffer, no front person, no one to sell his side of the story, no one to present him as an honorable solitary man.

His second season began more optimistically than the first. New skaters had come to the team, including the promising first-round draft pick Craig Simpson, who took Mario's boarding spot at the Mathews' residence, and the young Finnish defenseman Ville Siren. The team also added veteran goaltender Gilles Meloche, a French-Canadian who became friends with Mario, and Terry Ruskowski, a small but rugged winger. Forwards Lemieux, Bullard, Shedden, and Simpson gave the Penguins, weak defensively and in goal, respectable offensive potential. But for all his excitement over Mario, Eddie Johnston was still unable to find two wingers to complement his game. Moreover, the GM still hadn't fulfilled Mario's wish for an incredible hulk to act as his bodyguard.

In his first season Lemieux had been on the ice for thirty-five more goals scored against his team than for it. He wanted to improve on this unflattering number by playing with more of an eye toward defense. He appeared to bring a greater energy level to his work. Even Serge Savard was impressed. Following an exhibition game, the Montreal GM said he detected a new number 66. "Eddie," he remarked to Johnston, "you always heard the guy was lazy, but he's not lazy anymore. He's become a complete player."

Despite his efforts, however, the season started poorly. The Penguins won only three of their first ten contests, and on a late October night, when Lemieux played an untypically horrid game, he bolted from the Igloo, speaking to no one. The Hartford Whalers beat the Penguins 4–3. They scored all four of their goals when Lemieux was on the ice. The Whaler line of Ron Francis, Sylvain Turgeon, and Ray Neufeld blew by Mario's new line, which featured Troy Loney and Jim McGeough.

In the postmortems, Francis, the crafty centerman who would later play for Pittsburgh, said, "Lemieux is unbelievable in our end, but in his own end he is more the type to hang high. You tend to get an extra second to work with it." He capped the analysis with a direct slam. "It's kind of like five on four." Another Whaler who was to become a Penguin teammate, Ulf Samuelsson, criticized Mario for taking dives. Samuelsson received a penalty when Lemieux, skating through the crease without the puck, brushed Samuelsson's glove and dropped to the ice like a sack of potatoes. "I couldn't have knocked over a two-year-old with that one," Samuelsson complained.

Fake falls to draw penalties became one of Mario's defensive mechanisms to deter players from cheap fouls. Because of

Lemieux's skyscraper size, opposing coaches didn't hesitate to hunt him down with their enforcers. With Wayne Gretzky, who was small, wore a halo, and was surrounded by Semenko, there was considerable hesitation.

Late in the first season, Winnipeg's Jim Kyte skated in from behind Lemieux and, with the glove still on his hand, sucker-punched him with a left hook. Mario collapsed to the ice and lay motionless for several minutes. Kyte later claimed he was paying Mario back for cross-checking one of the Jets' smaller players. Barry Long, the Jets' coach, said Mario behaved like a baby. "That shot that put him down was a whiff shot. It was a left-handed shot, for crying out loud. Anybody and their dog could take it. It wasn't even a punch. . . . That thing was a powder puff."

Following the depressing experience of the Hartford game, the Penguins journeyed to Detroit, where Mario was promptly leveled by the right fist of Reed Larson, the Wings' defenseman. He wasn't hurt as badly as in the Kyte episode, but these and other assaults again got him thinking how nice it would be to be number 99.

Mario played an exemplary game in his first trip to Montreal since the poor showing in his debut there. He scored a goal and set one up, displaying all the while the genius of his hand-eye work in threading imaginative passes to targets no one else could see. It was these types of passes that Warren Young now missed so badly. Because of the success he enjoyed playing with Mario, Young, the minor-league journeyman of all those seasons previous, had hit the jackpot, moving from the Penguins to a million-dollar contract with the Detroit Red Wings. Young liked to think that maybe his own talents had something to do with his forty-goal season in Pittsburgh, but in his first sixteen games with the Red Wings, he went goalless. Reports of the big goose-egg stared at him from the pages of every paper in every city the team visited. Desperate for a goal, he kept thinking back to the previous year and yearning for a little help from his friend. His Red Wings played in Vancouver on November 13 and he was blanked again. He knew that Pittsburgh was flying into Vancouver the next day and, before leaving the visitors' dressing room, he took a piece of chalk and wrote a message on the blackboard: "Mario, help!—Warren."

The inheritor of Young's position in Pittsburgh was a player of about the same age, twenty-nine-year-old Terry Ruskowski. Orval Tessier, the Chicago coach, had dispatched him from the Hawks saying Rusko was pretty well washed up. The rugged winger worried Tessier might be right until he found himself on Mario's line, scoring at the rate of very nearly a point a game. Rejuvenation had set in. As he had with Warren Young, Mario handed down one instruction to Ruskowski. It was Lemieux's one and only instruction: "Rusko, just get me the puck and go to the net."

Mario constantly surprised Ruskowski. The former Hawk would be skating along, far afield of the play, and suddenly feel a thud against his stick. Couldn't be the puck, his instant reaction suggested. Four players had been between him and Mario, who had been skating with it. But of course it was the puck— Mario had feathered it through the maze. Mario's passes often arrived when Ruskowski was near the enemy goal. The split second Rusko lost between the surprise of finding it on his blade and reacting to shoot cost him dearly. "I probably would have scored another ten or eleven goals had I reacted in time."

One night in Pittsburgh, Ruskowski was forewarned. He lined up in the right face-off circle, opposing his checker in the enemy zone. Mario was taking the face-off, but before he did, he skated over to Ruskowski. "Rusko, when they drop the puck, you spin off the guy and go to the net. And remember, keep your stick on the ice."

"What?"

"Just do it," Mario said. "Keep your stick on the ice."

Rusko followed the instruction. He got by his checker and crashed toward the front of the goal, stick grounded. He didn't look back, but as he was about to, the puck hit his stick blade and deflected into the goal. Rusko was so surprised he didn't even raise his hands to celebrate. "I just kind of looked in awe back at him. Mario looked at me with a smirk and kind of shrugged his shoulders and skated back to center ice."

The excitement of playing with Mario on the ice was contrasted by the boredom of being with him off it. Ruskowski roomed with Lemieux. All Mario did was sleep. "He lives for sleep," said Ruskowski, who had to tiptoe around to keep things quiet. "He hits the bed and that's it." For most of the road games, Mario's routine was automatic. He'd get into town the night before, have dinner and a drink, watch TV, and sleep. After breakfast he had the morning skate, watched TV, lunched, slept, played the game, slept. The big guy was so naturally low key that teammates put his resting pulse at one. Ruskowski sometimes got so excited and hyper the night before a game that he couldn't sleep. Looking at the softly snoring Lemieux, he realized that this was a player whose nerves would never fry, who would remain cool forever, who would have an NHL career until he was forty. Mario, he concluded, ran on a different motor.

On the road Lemieux had to survive without his best friend, Nintendo. At home, in the months when the links were frozen over, Nintendo dominated the agenda. Bob Perno would go to Pittsburgh, where he and Mario would play Nintendo for six or seven hours at a time. "We'd play all day until an hour before he had to leave for the arena, when Nathalie would make him some spaghetti. Then we'd come home from the game, he'd have something to eat, and he'd say, 'Let's play Nintendo.' We'd play from midnight till four in the morning. He'd just whomp me every game, but he still wanted to keep playing. He never got bored of beating me. That's what I found amazing. He kept giving me the jabs and he'd laugh and we'd have another beer and he'd whomp me again."

While struck by Mario's endurance, Perno was more astonished by his skill. Mario's sense of anticipation, so evident in hockey, was manifest in remarkable fashion in the Nintendo room. "It was as if," Perno recalled, "he knew what was going to happen before it actually happened." Perno didn't know anyone who could beat Mario at Nintendo or pinball or anything keyed on hand-eye synchronization or extrasensory perception.

Terry Ruskowski saw Mario's sixth sense at work in the games. It was said of all great players that the puck followed them. There were moments, particularly when players were in a gaggle battling for the puck, when Ruskowski would see Mario standing calmly off to the side of the pack, fully confident the puck would come to him. He was all eyes, following it like a pinball or a Nintendo gnome, and it was as if he had his hands on the controls. Sure enough, most of the time the puck would emerge from the disarray onto Mario's stick and he would move on with it. If Ruskowski or any other of the game's muckers tried playing that waiting game, it would never work. "The puck," said Ruskowski, "would be sure to go the other way."

At times, rare times, Mario demanded the puck. It usually happened after he had been fouled and wanted to make the perpetrators pay. On these occasions Mario turned up the intensity level. Opponents, for example, would dump the puck into the Pittsburgh zone and a Penguin defenseman would move to collect it behind the net. Mario would be out at the blue line and would shout, "Leave the puck! Leave the puck!" He would then determinedly skate back, pick it up, and irritably work his way up ice to score or set up a goal. His teammates marveled at the inevitability of these moments.

In the second season Lemieux was scoring at a pace half a point a game better than in his first. This was enough to invite more and more comparisons with Gretzky, even though Gretzky was still thrashing him in points output. The comparisons angered Mario, Ruskowski found. He didn't say it in so many words, but he would shake his head or get annoyed when he saw the talk in the newspapers. "Why are they doing this?" Mario would wonder.

On January 22, 1986, the Penguins visited Edmonton. Mario scored a goal and had three assists in a 7–4 Penguin win. He was named the number-one star. Gretzky, who had two points, was number three. When he skated out, many of the fair-weather Edmonton fans, spoiled through the years by the Cups and Gretzky and all the other greats on the team, booed him. Gretzky, always highly sensitive to criticism, was soon reading reports that Mario would overtake him. "When I first came up," Gretzky told *USA Today*, "they said I was too small and too slow. Now they're saying I'm over the hill. It seems like only yesterday they were saying I couldn't play in this league. Now they're wondering who will take my place." Gretzky was leading Lemieux 147 points to 94 at the time. "Mario's a great asset to the game," he said. "He's a fine kid with a lot of heart. To push me in the scoring race, somebody will have to be up around 200 points. Right now there's a gap of, what, 50 points? He's young yet. Maybe he will give me a push one of these seasons."

"I think I have the talent to be near to Gretzky," Lemieux said. "If we ever have a Stanley Cup team with great players around me, I could get as many points as him. But it's too early now. It's too early for me in my second year." Without great wingers like someone else had, without a bodyguard like someone else had, without the experience in the league like someone else had, Mario knew it would take time.

In his first season Mario had suffered a knee injury, but he had been free of the back stresses that infrequently flared up in Laval. Now, however, Dr. Réal Lemieux's predictions about likely recurrence came true. He missed a practice because of back pain. A few days later, after scoring five points against Winnipeg, it was announced that he would take some days off because of strained back muscles. It was nothing serious, Mario told the media, and he appeared to be right. He missed only one game.

Beginning the final month of the season, the Penguins, who had enjoyed a good February, appeared on their way to making the playoffs. Playing in the best division in hockey, this was no small accomplishment, especially given their 16–58–6 record before Lemieux joined the club. But beginning with a 9–3 loss at home to Edmonton, the Penguins closed off their season horrendously. Gretzky rebounded from being outplayed in Edmonton and scored four points to Mario's one in the Oilers win. The Penguins lost twelve of their last sixteen games. Winning only five of those sixteen would have seen them finish ahead of the Rangers for the final playoff placing. But Mario couldn't lead the team to clutch wins.

"I could have done a lot better," he remarked. "The last two weeks I didn't play very well. I wasn't making good passes. I wasn't skating as well as I had been." It was the second year in succession that he and his team had finished badly.

"We need a good defenseman like Paul Coffey or Ray Bourque, and one of those players [enforcers] who can take care of everything that goes on out on the ice," Mario said. And maybe, he added, he could help more himself by taking on a greater leadership role. "This year I just stayed in my corner and said nothing."

TEN

THE ANTI-GRETZKY

MARIO'S BEST FRIEND IN PITTSBURGH WAS JIMMY MAGANELLO. Jimmy Maggs, as he was called, owned a string of bowling alleys and the bar-restaurants that went with them. He was worth a fortune, and was rumored on occasion to be interested in buying the Penguins. Maggs had darkish skin, a prominent nose, curly dark hair, and dark eyes, and he dressed well. He would dot virtually every sentence with a mumbly "you know." He'd say, "The coach has to, you know, prove himself to Mario that he's capable, you know, of running the team."

One of the Penguins' most ardent fans, Maggs had become close friends with Randy Carlyle, a defenseman who predated Mario. He knew Eddie Johnston well, went on some road trips with the team, and presented players with jackets from his bowling alleys.

Because of the age difference, it struck many as peculiar that Mario became such a close companion of Maggs. By the the end of his first season, Mario liked him so much that he moved into the Maggs' family home for a few weeks before taking possession of his new condominium. Maggs taught Mario to bowl and Mario taught Maggs to golf. "We were both, you know, quiet kind of people," Maggs explained. "And, you know, it just kind of gelled, you know."

Maggs was honest, loyal, didn't flaunt his money. He did everything he could to make life comfortable for Mario in Pittsburgh. Bob Perno thought very highly of him. Perno came to Pittsburgh one day for a routine visit and Maggs was waiting for him at the airport. "What'ya doing here, Jimmy?" Perno asked. "Just thought," Maggs said, "you might like, you know, a drive into town."

Mario hung around mainly with Mathews or Maggs, both old enough to be his parents. But it was obvious that the Mathews didn't like to see Mario spending so much time with the bowling-alley man. Maggs wondered what the problem was. "I don't know what they're worried about," he told a friend. "What do they think I'm going to do, harm him or something?"

Mario confided in Maggs, telling him what he thought was wrong with the hockey team. This was important because Maggs knew the owner, DeBartolo, and was also good friends with club vice-president Paul Martha, a tall, slim, calculating lawyer. Maggs acted as the go-between, relaying Mario's thoughts to them.

Through year two and especially year three, Maggs often found Mario depressed by the low quality of the team and the continuing losses. Mario was acutely aware, noted Maggs, that unless you got your team into the playoffs, you were forgotten; you could never be a big star. "If you don't make the playoffs," Mario told his friend, "they all forget about you."

Year two had closed down with Mario slowed badly by a long bout with bronchitis. "You had to play with him to understand how sick he was," said teammate Mike Bullard. "We used to sit there and watch him cough. The team went out and bought a special machine to help him breathe better and clear out his lungs." By the last week of the season, when the Penguins

Mario, with eleven goals and eleven assists, was named the MVP at an atom tournament in Sorel, Quebec.

Mario, aged nine, is shown *(far right)* with his Ville Emard teammates following their victory in the 1974 Tom Thumb hockey tournament. On the far left is Mario's high-scoring teammate, Stephan LePage. (HEINZ WEGNER)

Carl Parker *(left)* and Mario Lemieux *(right)* pal around in their days as peewees playing for the Black Machine.

In his third and final year as a junior, Lemieux *(far left)* led the Laval Voisins to the Quebec Major Junior Hockey League title.

Capping the most impressive season in the history of the QMJHL, Mario accepts the trophy as the league's MVP.

A nervous-looking Lemieux moments before his refusal to don a
Pittsburgh Penguins' jersey at the 1984 NHL entry draft at the
Montreal Forum. (CANAPRESS/IAN BARRETT)

Lemieux, picked first overall in the draft, poses with second
choice Kirk Muller *(left)* and third pick Ed Olczyk *(right)*.
(CANAPRESS/IAN BARRETT)

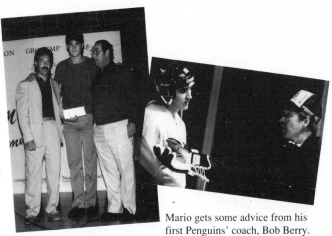

Lemieux and Bob Perno *(left)* in happier times.

Mario gets some advice from his first Penguins' coach, Bob Berry. (CANAPRESS)

Lemieux celebrates his first NHL goal, scored against the Bruins in Boston. (CANAPRESS/PAUL R. BENOIT)

After a 100-point inaugural season, it was no surprise when Mario was awarded the Calder Trophy as the rookie of the year.

(CANAPRESS/JOHN FELSTEAD)

Lemieux and Gretzky face off in the annual NHL all-star game.
(CANAPRESS/RAY GIGUERE)

Sidelined with a knee injury, Lemieux watches the Penguins take on the New York Rangers on a TV in Bob Berry's office. Despite the injury, Lemieux still beat Gretzky in the fan balloting for the 1986 Rendez-Vous tournament, which pitted NHL stars against the best from the Soviet Union. (CANAPRESS/FRED VUICH)

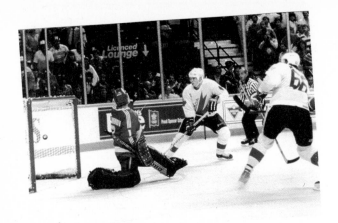

In an inspired performance, Mario scores the game-winning goal
against Soviet goaltender Sergei Mylnikov in the 1987 Canada Cup.
(CANAPRESS/SCOTT MACDONALD)

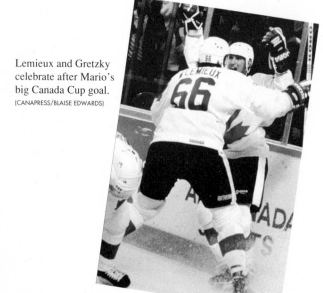

Lemieux and Gretzky
celebrate after Mario's
big Canada Cup goal.
(CANAPRESS/BLAISE EDWARDS)

Often criticized for spending too little time on charitable causes, here Mario signs an autograph for a boy with muscular dystrophy.

(SUE BRADNAM/
LONDON FREE PRESS)

The 1988 all-star game in St. Louis featured one of Lemieux's finest performances–three goals and three assists in a 6-5 Wales Conference victory. (CANAPRESS/JEFF ROBERSON)

After conquering the back infection that placed his hockey future in doubt, Mario, never one for the exercise bike, begins training again on December 21, 1990.

Lemieux loves golf almost as much as hockey. Here he is seen playing in the Canadian Open's pro-am event in 1992.

With a heat pack wrapped around his ever-ailing back, Mario watches teammates practice in Edmonton in 1992.

Mario celebrates his 1991
Stanley Cup triumph.

(CANAPRESS/JIM MONA)

In the dressing room after the 1991 Stanley Cup victory, Lemieux
poses with his mother and father *(foreground)* and long-time
girlfriend, Nathalie Asselin *(center front)*.

(BRUCE BENNETT/BRUCE BENNETT STUDIOS)

In January 1993 Lemieux, shown here with Dr. Ted Crandall, tells a crowded press conference that he has contracted Hodgkin's disease. (CANAPRESS/GENE J. PUSKAR)

Too sick to play, Mario still gets a standing ovation from the fans at the Montreal Forum for the 1993 all-star game.
(DOUG MACLELLAN/HHOF)

Mario is greeted warmly in Philadelphia as he returns to action on the day of his last radiation treatment for Hodgkin's disease.
(CANAPRESS/CAROL FRANCAVILLA)

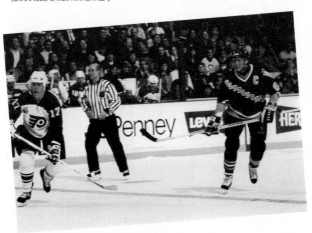

Although he just finished cancer therapy, Lemieux gets right back in the game. (SCOTT LEVY/BRUCE BENNETT STUDIOS)

Despite image problems elsewhere, Lemieux has always remained popular with the Pittsburgh fans. Here they cheer the return of "Mr. Courage." (JIM CUNNINGHAM)

Mario shows off his bounty from the 1993 NHL awards: the Bill Masterton Trophy, the Art Ross Trophy, and the Hart. It is the first time one player has collected all three.
(DOUG MACLELLAN/HHOF)

After all the trials and triumphs of the preceding months, Mario
and Nathalie wed in Montreal on June 26, 1993.

Mario the Magnificent.
(BRUCE BENNETT/BRUCE BENNETT STUDIOS)

bowed out of playoff contention and Mario received his invitation to play in the world championships in Moscow, he had almost regained normal health. But Lemieux didn't want to risk a resurgence of the illness, he was tired from the season, and he told Hockey Canada he wasn't going to Moscow. Bullard, who made the trip, could sympathize with his teammate's decision. "The guy just played thirty minutes a game for us, every game. We weren't a physical team and we used to get killed out there. I mean, we used to go into Philadelphia and they'd run Mario left and right." Others were less understanding. Wasn't this the Mario who had vowed a year earlier, following his success in Prague, to return? How could the legs be so tired at age twenty? Were there not players now embarking on two months of NHL playoff hockey, a game every second night? And was the bronchitis, the official reason for not going, so bad? It didn't seem so. One night during the playoffs Mario was spotted in a booth in the Montreal Forum dragging on a cigarette. He drew the hot smoke down into his lungs and exhaled smoothly.

This scene was reported in the media and didn't win him much favor. As usual, he handled the controversy poorly. There was no public-relations frontman, no one to help cushion the landing. His bronchitis condition was hardly reported.

Mario was getting used to the controversies. Saying no was sure to bring on bad press, and Mario was saying no a lot. He was saying no to playing for his country, saying no to hosting his charity golf tournament, saying no to interviews. After many games, he'd sequester himself in the trainer's quarters adjacent to the Penguins' dressing room to avoid the press. He was sick of answering the same questions, many of them stupid questions. Besides, he didn't like to be around crowds. He never liked crowds.

Mario even began saying no to endorsements. This shocked Perno, who had always thought of Mario as highly money-conscious and mindful of the balance sheet. A recent experience with Mario had driven the point home. In the latter part of his second season Mario signed his new half-million-a-year contract. Perno's five-percent fee was standard for hockey agents. He had by now split with Badali and was handling Lemieux on his own. Because he and Mario were so close, they operated on a handshake.

Perno was surprised when, after concluding the new contract, Mario called him to discuss the arrangement. He had been figuring things out. Wasn't the five-percent fee a bit steep, he asked? Some other players he had talked to paid a flat rate that was less, he said, than five percent.

Perno wondered just who else Mario had been talking to. He didn't consider his rate exorbitant, particularly given all the seeding time he had spent with Mario, all those years in junior when he didn't make a penny and all the time he had spent going back and forth to Pittsburgh to serve his needs. He asked what fee Mario considered fairer. You suggest a figure, Lemieux told him. Perno said he would settle for $16,000 a year, on the condition that Mario retain him to do the next contract. The proviso was very important because players frequently changed to any new agent with lower fees who came along. Mario quickly agreed to it. "You have my word on that," Perno recalled him saying.

Sensing some of the bond was loosening, Perno later suggested that instead of the informal handshake arrangement, they draw up a formal contract. Mario wasn't interested. He told Perno that they'd always been honest with each other and that Perno could trust him. He used the word family. "You're family," he told his agent.

Mario did a few endorsements, mainly for Canadian products. Hockey wasn't big in the United States, and the possibilities that did exist were snapped up by Gretzky. One of

Mario's Canadian contracts was with Gillette. As a part of the agreement he was scheduled to come to Montreal and sign autographs and hype the company. It would take only a day of his time. Mario, however, decided at the last minute not to go. He didn't feel like it. His brother and some friends were playing golf in Florida and Mario wanted to join them. He phoned Perno and had him tell the Gillette people he wouldn't be there.

Perno argued that it wasn't only money he was losing, but credibility as well. Gillette dealt with ad agencies throughout the United States. The word would get out that Lemieux was unreliable. Mario wasn't worried. He enjoyed his golf game.

His Gillette contract also committed him to doing a TV commercial. The company wanted him to come to Montreal to shoot it there, but Mario wouldn't do that. He preferred it be done in Pittsburgh. That was too much. An option year remained on his Gillette contract, and when it came time to exercise it, Perno was hardly surprised when the company didn't pick it up. For the sake of a round of golf, Mario had lost an endorsement contract. It wouldn't be the last time.

Mario's golf game was now down in the low seventies. He had all the shots and was thinking more about pursuing a pro career when hockey ended. Though he had dropped out of hosting his own charity golf tournament, he continued to play in those of others. At Denis Savard's Montreal tourney, he paired with Carl Parker, whose hockey career had ended at the junior level. As was customary when Parker came around, the unexpected came with him. Mario, so serious about his game, began the day badly, slipping a couple of strokes over par. He was putting poorly and becoming progressively more irritated. Midway through the round he missed another short one. In the time-honored tradition of hot-tempered golfers, Mario decided to see if putters fly. He leaned back and heaved his flat stick to the heavens. It flew far beyond the shoulder of the green and the sand traps until it met up with an oak tree. There it came to rest, high up in its limbs. The challenge was now to retrieve it. Parker, laughing uncontrollably, and Mario and the two others in the group, began throwing rocks and other projectiles to try and dislodge it. While the gawking group behind them waited, the hurling continued for ten minutes until the putter was struck and returned to earth. The incident did serve to break the tension. Mario played a relaxed, good-humored game from then on, shooting a seventy-six.

Golf still remained his primary source of off-season exercise. The first season weight-training session and other similar embarrassments did prompt the occasional spurt of effort. But it didn't amount to much. "Iron Man" Mario was still needled about his inability to bench press. One summer day, while Assistant Coach Doug McKenney was leading some veterans through a physical training session, he reported that he had just talked to the big guy.

"That was Mario on the phone," he said.

"How's his weight-training program going?" a sarcastic voice shot back.

"Well, he told me he's pumping irons every day."

"Yeah, right," muttered one of the disbelievers. "What other bullshit have you got for us?"

"No, it's true," said McKenney. "The two iron all the way to the nine and the wedge."

Mario's third season in the NHL began with an acknowledgment of past lapses in consistency. "It's just my concentration," he explained. "Sometimes, it just gets away. That's what I want to do—go out there and work hard every shift. I know that sometimes last year I didn't do it, because of many reasons." He didn't do it, but he knew that to be a great hockey player like Gretzky and Bobby Orr, he had to. "They went out and worked hard every shift and that's what I'm going to have to do to be as successful as those guys."

The statements represented a major change from his first season when, in an interview with the *Philadelphia Inquirer,* he was very candid. "I'm the type of player who will work when I have to work," he admitted. To those who knew him well, this statement summed him up precisely. In the interview he explained further that "in certain situations I'll wait until I see a guy is getting tired, and then I'll make my move. I always thought that was a smart way to play, but maybe it gave some people the wrong idea."

In their 1986–1987 season the Penguins won their first seven games in a row. They had brought in Dan Quinn and Randy Cunneyworth, two forwards who, while not top caliber, could score. Though goaltending remained inconsistent, the defense, led by Doug Bodger, was maturing.

But after the unprecedented beginning, the Penguins and Mario went into a slide, and on December 20, Lemieux sprained his knee in a game against the Flyers. The injury kept him out of play for a month. There had been knee problems the first year, bronchitis the second, hints of back troubles, and now more knee problems in the third. Though none of the setbacks was grave, a depressing pattern was setting in.

He returned to the line-up for a short while following the knee injury before being sent off to hospital again, this time by Bobby Gould, a fighter from Washington of no renown. Gould knocked Lemieux semiconscious in a battle along the boards at the Capital Center in Maryland. Mario had checked Gould and Gould had shoved back. The whistle blew and Mario said to the Capital, "What's the matter? Can't anybody hit you?"

Gould replied, "Yeah, anytime."

They trash-talked, then dropped their gloves. Lemieux lunged at Gould, but in grasping for his arms, Mario left his face fully exposed. Gould began beating him to a pulp before Craig Simpson finally arrived to help out. Lemieux was taken directly to George Washington University Hospital.

In Montreal Pierrette and Jean-Guy saw the TKO on television. They later woke up Perno with instructions to find out the condition of their son. Perno phoned every hospital in the District of Columbia until he hit on the right one. The hospital refused to release any information, but with Mario's parents frantic, Perno appealed to superiors, who told him Mario was going to be all right. He had regained consciousness and the jaw didn't appear to be broken.

Labeled "Rocky" by his agent, Lemieux was able to laugh off this clobbering, but he was more and more frustrated with the Penguins' inability to land him a bodyguard. He could understand, in part, the difficulties involved in finding him a talented winger. Eddie Johnston didn't have strong trade bait, nor did he want to deal away a first-round draft choice. For flankers, that left Mario with the likes of Dwight Mathiason, Mike Blaisdell, and Dan Frawley, a fourteen-goal scorer.

If that was understandable, though lamentable, there was no excusing Johnston's inability to find him a good goon. Any GM could do that. The Penguins had traded away Marty McSorley in 1985 before he became a reputed pugilist. That year they also dealt off a fearsome brawler named Bennett Wolf. But because of Mario's size, the coaching staff felt there was no need for a protector. He could handle himself. One day Lemieux's friend Bill Kelly approached Jimmy Roberts, the assistant coach, to take up the matter with him. "Jimmy, Mario's taking a beating every night," he said. "You're going to have to get some muscle to back him up." Roberts rebuffed him. "Billy, Mario's big enough. He's going to have to fight for himself." Mario finally had to tell Perno that since the team wasn't finding him anyone, "You try and get somebody." Perno came up with

Jimmy Mann, a former first-round draft pick of Winnipeg's coach, John Ferguson. Mann could never crack a line-up, but he could fight. Perno convinced the Penguins to give him a try, but he didn't last.

During his absence with the knee injury, Mario's team won only two of thirteen games. Unless Lemieux could revive them, the Penguins appeared destined to miss the playoffs one more time. Shortly after his return he played in a two-game series in Quebec City called Rendez-Vous. A brief hockey summit, it featured the NHL stars against the best from the Soviet Union. Primarily because Quebec hosted the series, Mario, the favorite son, drew many French-Canadian votes and finished first in the fan balloting for the center position. Gretzky, everyone realized, merited the starting position, so Mario graciously offered to cede his place in the starting five to him. Gretzky graciously declined. In the two-game set, which was split, Mario neither soared, though Gretzky did, nor did he fall. While he gathered three assists in the first match, one on the game winner, he was barely visible in the second.

Back in Pittsburgh he was needed to lead the drive to the playoffs. But despite his vow at the beginning of the season to change his ways, to be like Orr and Gretzky, he could not maintain a high intensity level. He had big nights and he had indifferent nights. His scoring statistics continued to be impressive—how could anyone criticize a player averaging almost two points a game?—but he was unable to rise up, as he had sometimes done in the past, in the critical games and steal them. During the season's final two months the Penguins played eight games against division rivals. These were games that would decide the playoff story. Lemieux scored one goal in the eight games.

People expected more by now. Old criticisms resurfaced. Even some in the Pittsburgh media now began to wonder. "If he ever decides to show up for work eighty nights a year, Lemieux could be the best—yes, the best—player in the NHL," wrote Dave Molinari of the *Pittsburgh Press*. "If not, he always will be a pale copy of Wayne Gretzky and the Penguins will remain mired in mediocrity."

Lemieux appeared to be courting the fate of another French-Canadian junior phenomenon, Marcel Dionne. After nearly matching Lafleur's fame in junior hockey, Dionne went on to post big numbers in the NHL, but he did it in a non-hockey town for a perennially weak team—the Los Angeles Kings. He could never extricate the team or himself from obscurity.

The Penguins finished their third season with Lemieux 30–38–12, four points behind the New York Rangers, who secured the final playoff position. As if he needed the aggravation, Lemieux brought more of it upon himself by refusing to make the trip to the world tournament, this one in Vienna. He didn't have bronchitis, he was injury-free, the site was more appealing than Moscow, and the pressure on him from Eagleson and others to sign up was concerted. But nothing could push him over there.

His refusal angered not just the hockey establishment, but also the players. The fourth installment of the Canada Cup tournament was to take place in September, and some thought that Mario should not be issued an invitation to the Team Canada camp. Because of his demonstrated lack of interest in playing for his country, he didn't deserve it, players said.

Among Mario's critics was Dionne. "I think he can push himself a little bit harder," said the former King, who was now with the New York Rangers and often made the trip to the world championship. The great players competed for their country even when hurt, Dionne said. "Those are the things that great players do. That's how you gain respect from your peers. That's how you can tell the great players." Bill Clement, the former

Philadelphia Flyer who was now broadcasting, said of Lemieux: "You never see him in a do-or-die situation where he seems to want to die for it. You don't visualize a picture of a soldier with a bloody bandage wrapped around his head, his arm in a sling, uniform torn off his body, struggling to get back into battle, do you?" Alan Eagleson attributed his attitude to the immaturity of age. "I don't think he's yet to understand the obligation that exists out there. It's disappointing when you have to beg him to play for his country. I hope that disappears when his youth disappears."

Mario calmly accepted the criticism for the Penguins' failure and for refusing to go abroad. He knew he hadn't had a great year, but evinced a stoic self-assurance, as was his custom, that all would be right. He had played only sixty-three games in the season, but had racked up fifty-four goals and fifty-three assists. Even with the disadvantages the Pittsburgh situation presented, Mario was leaving every other player in the game, except Gretzky, miles behind. His record was not one to be scoffed at, and he was only twenty-one. At twenty-one Terry Bradshaw was still in his final year at Louisiana Tech. Willie Stargell was still in minor-league ball. Roberto Clemente was batting a modest .255. Good things had happened. Mario, it could be said, had saved hockey in Pittsburgh. Attendance figures were five thousand per game higher than in the year before he arrived. They loved Mario in the steel town. Local polls voted him the most popular sports figure, the most eligible bachelor, the Dapper Dan Man of the Year. But elsewhere, most particularly in English Canada, his image flagged. English-Canadians had their hockey king in Gretzky and no one was in a hurry to see a dark prince from French Canada succeed him. Many suspected, in a hushed kind of way, that if Mario ever put all his skills to use, he could be better—especially considering his size advantage—than the Great One. This was known, but seldom said, because people didn't want it to be so. Mario didn't appear the worthy heir. He was too distant and uncaring. He didn't look hungry enough, he didn't look as though he had to work hard enough. He was listless.

There had been others like this. One was a great baseball hitter whose presence was somehow an absence, whose gloom off the field transcended his magnificence on it. His name was Roger Maris.

Would Lemieux become the Roger Maris of hockey? Paul Steigerwald, the Penguins' marketing director, who admired Lemieux so much, was concerned. He saw the bad turn Mario's image was taking because of his reluctance to do the public things a star athlete was supposed to do, and talked to him about it. Mario was simple and to the point. "I'm different from a lot of people," Mario told Steigerwald. "I'm a private person."

Mario was highly conscious of the way Gretzky's image sparkled in comparison to his own. He envied this and expressed his envy on more than one occasion. He wanted to be that popular. But instead, he was well on the way to becoming the "other superstar." Instead of being all the things Gretzky was, Lemieux was showing himself to be all the things Gretzky wasn't. He was becoming not the new Gretzky, but the Anti-Gretzky.

Gretzky was 99. Lemieux wore 66. Gretzky hustled and worked for every point. Lemieux looked lethargic and seldom broke stride and worked only when he wanted to work. Gretzky was the ambassador for the game, the player who symbolized national pride. Lemieux couldn't even be bothered playing for his country. Gretzky enthusiastically did charities and honored his commitments and made himself accessible to the media. Lemieux canceled his charity golf tournament, skipped out on endorsements, and hid from the media. Gretzky was slight and smallish and proactive and had to sweat. Lemieux was too big and he wore a black uniform and he was passive. Gretzky earned it. The Anti-Gretzky, who hardly even worked out, never earned it.

Though their personas were so different, the two players were very similar in terms of talent. In this respect, Mario was no Anti-Gretzky. In Gretzky's first two pro seasons with Edmonton, one of which was in the World Hockey Association, he had 241 points. Uncannily, in Mario's first two pro seasons he had the exact same total. Mario's came in seven fewer games. In his third pro season Gretzky earned 164 points in eighty games. Mario played seventeen fewer games in his third year, but managed 107 points.

Though Mario's marks by age twenty-one stood up well with the Gretzky of the same age, he was being compared not with Gretzky's early years, but with what the Edmonton star was doing concurrently. In the 1985–1986 season, for example, Mario's 141 points had to be stacked against the greatest scoring season in NHL history—Gretzky's astonishing 215 points. Mathematically, Mario's output was highly appropriate: his point total that year was two-thirds of Gretzky's, 66 compared to 99.

ELEVEN
MARIO'S CUP

THOUGH SOME PLAYERS MAY HAVE WISHED IT, TEAM CANADA authorities did not give serious thought to excluding Mario Lemieux from participation in the 1987 Canada Cup. Coach Mike Keenan had the same reservations as others about Lemieux, but he also realized that this player possessed a reservoir of talent far too deep to ignore.

Mario wanted to compete in the tournament. It had more meaning than the world championship, it didn't involve going overseas at the end of the season, and it featured the best NHL players, not the playoff leftovers. His arrival at training camp in Montreal brought with it a feeling of unpredictability. Would Mario whine or shine? Would he be motivated? How would he mix with the many brassy players from the Edmonton Oilers' dynasty who were there? How would he skate against the fleet crews from overseas?

He'd had the one fine game in Prague against the Russians and then had played them in the two-game Rendez-Vous set. Theoretically, he could look forward to more scoring opportunities against the Red Machine, as well as the Czechs and the Scandinavians. Russian coaches didn't key their defenses on one player, nor did they clog up the front of their net as effectively as

NHL teams. Lemieux could benefit from all this, as well as the Soviets' offensive-minded style of play, which left them vulnerable to counterattack.

With his subdued precision and artistry, his even-keel pace, Lemieux's game closely paralleled the Russian one. He was reminiscent in a few respects of Alexander Yakushev, the pterodactyl Russian forward. The lanky Muscovite with the bull's-eye aim dumbfounded Ken Dryden in the 1972 Canada–Russia series, running up scoring totals like Phil Esposito. Lemieux was a more supple and creative player, a better player than Yakushev, but he had many similarities, not the least of which was his low intensity level.

It was if Mario was reared by the father of Russian hockey himself, Anatoli Tarasov. Fittingly for the Communist system, Tarasov taught hockey players to play rationally, without emotion. He wanted mood control, cool efficiency, and imaginative yet practical players, ever mindful of their role within the collective. In Tarasovian thinking, playing with too much emotion diminished discipline. Mistakes would result. Tarasov wanted musicality on the ice, art as opposed to the Canadian power game. "Courage," Tarasov wrote, "means the ability to stay out of a fight." With his booming voice, Tarasov once denounced Valery Kharlamov. As evidenced by his solo, comet dashes into the enemy zone, Kharlamov's game was marked by a spirit of irrepressible individuality. Tarasov fought to keep him in sync with the others. The puck carrier, Tarasov once bellowed at Kharlamov during practice, is the servant of the other players.

The Soviets' loss in the 1972 series, and many of the team's subsequent defeats, demonstrated the folly of Tarasov's way. What won for the Canadians was emotional intensity. What lost for the Russians was lack of it. What Esposito had in the final games of 1972, and what Yakushev lacked, was the torrent of passion necessary to take one's game to a higher level. Yakushev, who scored seven goals and had four assists in the eight-game set, came out as stony-faced for the final period of the final game as for any other. While reflecting on the event years later, he recognized that the robotic approach, that mechanical perfection, could only carry a team so far. "There is something that is missing in Europeans in general and Soviet players in particular," said Yakushev. It was, he believed, the Canadian players' overdrive, their will to win.

Except on those occasions when he was terribly rankled, Lemieux, in keeping with his laconic personality, played in the unemotional Russian style and was criticized for it. The most serious flaw in his game had always been, as he recognized himself, his low intensity level. Ron Stevenson, the bantam coach he admired so much, used to go out to Laval at the behest of Pierrette Lemieux to watch him in the junior games and offer advice. Mario would come straight to Stevenson after the games and, without even saying hello, ask how he did. The only criticism Stevenson had, if he had any at all, was the occasional lack of intensity.

Those close to Mario saw the Canada Cup as a potentially marvelous educational experience for him. For the first time in his life he would be skating alongside the best in the game, winners, players who won on guts and desire. The passive types would be on the other side.

Mario opened training camp at his typically uninspired pace. Given the heated competition for spots on the club, there were murmurs around the camp and suggestions in the newspapers that Mario wasn't taking the event seriously enough, that, while it sounded ridiculous, he might not even survive the team's final cuts. Keenan, hockey people knew, did not let sleeping dogs lie. He was more inclined to cut them loose.

Lemieux soon quashed all such speculation. In a pre-tournament game against the Soviets, he found free ice and room to maneuver in front of the Soviet goal and no football linebackers opposing him. He also found wonderfully dextrous teammates with whom he could do things that he could not do with the Penguins. As a result, he served notice in this game of who he was. He scored four times.

At the rate Keenan switched lines, Mario was playing at one time or another with everyone on the club. He began showing as much enthusiasm as they did, surprising spectators who had become soured by his leisurely tempo. Mario cruised in low gear in the early stages of a game played in Hamilton against the United States, and a fan with a stage actor's voice stood up and denounced him. "Get that bum off the ice! He's the laziest player in hockey! Get him off!" The fan erupted every time Mario stepped out. "You're a floater, Mario! Go on vacation somewhere else!" Mario scored a goal, lowering the man's decibel range a notch or two. He scored another, which calmed down the protester some more. He scored a third, which shut the loudmouth up completely and prompted those around him to remark on his foolishness.

After a few games Keenan was revising an earlier opinion of Mario. "Mario's earned some of the criticism he's had in the past. It's been deserved because at times he looked like he wasn't playing with that much intensity. . . . [But] I'll tell you this: Mario is not a lazy hockey player."

Lemieux scored two goals and added an assist against the then world champion Swedes. Though Gretzky, with a barrage of assists, maintained an edge in total points, Mario took over the goal-scoring lead in the tournament. In the match against Czechoslovakia to qualify Canada for the final against the Russians, Canada won 5–3. Lemieux did the same to the Czechs as he had to the Swedes—two goals and an assist. He now had four against the Russians (though in an exhibition), three against the

Americans, and two against each of the other top teams. No contending country had stopped him.

Teammates like Mark Messier lauded Mario on not just his play, but his accompanying attitude. They seemed genuinely surprised at his drive. Mario had an explanation. Because many players saw him only about three times a year, he said, they didn't know what he was really like. "I think I've proved some things. A lot of people have changed their attitude toward me . . . especially the players." Of his impressive production, he made the point that he had made all along. "That goes with the team you've got around you. We have twenty great hockey players in this room. A lot of things can happen out there if you do your job, and that's what I've done in this tournament."

Mario played with Gretzky only intermittently until the last two games of the final three-game set against the Soviets. A reporter had asked Keenan earlier in the tournament why he wasn't playing them together all the time. The coach responded that it would be counterproductive. When he finally did pair them, it was obvious that he could hardly have been more wrong.

Since boyhood, Lemieux had always been as assist-conscious as goal-hungry. In bantam, in junior, coaches frequently criticized him for passing too much. In his early days in Pittsburgh he faced the same criticisms. Gretzky had a similar bent. A brilliant passer, he played unselfishly and enjoyed making the play as much as finishing it.

With two extraordinary passers skating together, who would take the goal-scoring responsibility? Mario might sometimes have provided instructions for his fellow Penguin linemates, but he wasn't about to skate over to Wayne Gretzky and say, "Just get me the puck and go to the net." As could be expected, Gretzky, the senior of the two, made the strategy call. "On two-on-ones," he told Mario, "you take the shots."

"I wanted him shooting because he's got those awesome

wrists," explained Gretzky. "He could snap a puck through a refrigerator door. The guy stands six-foot-four but he's got the touch of a five-six guy." Overlooking Mario's own impressive passing statistics, Gretzky said, "He likes to shoot the puck, and I like to pass it."

Beyond shooting and passing, these two players found that they had a shared sense of ice vision, of where they were and where they would be. They could see the ice and read the play better than any others. "He has a vision of the play," said Mario of number 99, "which is absolutely exceptional." Ironically, it had been Gretzky who, seeing the eighteen-year-old Mario play as a junior, had noted above all else his vision of the ice. Now Mario Lemieux was admiring the same quality in Wayne Gretzky.

"We found out we weren't just friends," remarked Gretzky, "we were ice-mates. We understood each other. We went to the same holes."

In the first of the three games against the Soviet Union, won by the Red Machine in overtime, Mario had two assists. In the classic second game he scored Canada's last three goals, including the winner in overtime. Gretzky assisted on every one, the prettiest of which was the first. For that score, the two best players in the world advanced on a break against a sole Soviet defenseman, Vasily Pervukhin, the very experienced Moscow Dynamo veteran. Gretzky timed his pass wonderfully to Mario, who snapped the puck high above Yevgeny Belosheikin's shoulder. After the goal Mario looked back toward Gretzky. But 99 did not skate over to congratulate him. Other players did, not Gretzky. Having set up Mario so well, perhaps he thought he deserved the congratulations himself.

The other goals they fashioned produced the expected embraces and euphoria, including game three's historic winner. This one featured another exquisitely timed Gretzky feed, but the beauty was in the unhurried precision of Mario's shot, a classic wrist shot that afforded the marksman more opportunity of finding the small opening on either side of the goalie than the howitzer blast favored by so many unthinking players.

The Canadians won the 1987 series, the best since 1972, in the same manner they had won the first historic showdown. They won it, said Gretzky, on guts and desire. In 1972 Phil Esposito led in that department. In 1987 it was Gretzky. In the first showdown Paul Henderson was the trigger man. In the second series Mario Lemieux filled that role. Neither Henderson nor Lemieux had shown a shortage of heart either. The grand irony of the series was that Lemieux, the Canadian player who best exemplified Soviet dispassion, had raised his intensity and emotional level enough to beat them. He surprised no one in this series with his skill level. That was, and always would be, a given. What was noteworthy, though, was his passion. With his consistent display of ardor, Lemieux had lifted the pall of suspicion that hung over his game.

Mario scored eighteen points in the tournament to Gretzky's twenty-one. He set a record for most goals ever in a Canada Cup—eleven. He quieted those who said that he wasn't a winner or that he didn't play with intensity or that he couldn't do it in the clutch. Despite all this, they denied him the big prize. They gave the most valuable player award to the player who set him up. Nothing less should have been expected. While everyone appreciated the skill in Mario's performance, no one loved him enough to want to see him dethrone the king.

Awards are, in part, popularity contests, and Gretzky was more popular than Mario Lemieux. No one could imagine Gretzky scoring three in a row to win game two, scoring the winner in the final game, scoring a tournament record number of goals, and not winning the MVP. But Mario experienced exactly that. Though the performance of 99 throughout the series was remarkable, the other great one was entitled to some disappointment at not being named the MVP. Gretzky's assists were quality set-ups, but they weren't ones in which the scorer was handed an empty net. The shooter fulfilled the critical role.

Though the public Mario was gracious and effusive about the Great One and the tournament, friends believed that being overlooked for the best player award stung him. "I think that was heartbreaking to him," said Jimmy Maggs. Paul Steigerwald got a similar feeling. "They said Mario was great all right," noted Steigerwald, "but only after they had put a disclaimer on it by saying Gretzky made him look great."

On his return to Pennsylvania following the Canada Cup triumph, Mario found an expectant gang of Penguins. They thought that their time perhaps had come, that this could be the season. The players had watched the games, said Eddie Johnston, and "they saw him just take over. It's the first time he'd ever been in a pressure situation like that because our club hadn't made the playoffs. You were interested how he'd react." Mario particularly astonished his teammates, Johnston noted, with his defense. "They were just as enthused about his backchecking as the goals. It was kind of like, 'Hey, look! Here he comes back again!'" Johnston hoped that the Canada Cup experience had turned Mario into a leader. Because of his withdrawn nature, the Penguins had yet to make him captain. They weren't convinced of the power of silence. Lemieux hadn't complained, but now he did think he was ready to take on the responsibility. "I got a lot of confidence from this [Canada Cup]," he said. "You learn a lot about what to say in the dressing room between periods if you're down two or three goals. We had a lot of guys there who'd won Stanley Cups. I listened to them."

A new coach arrived, a Quebecker named Pierre Creamer from the Montreal Canadiens' farm system. After three years of failing to make the playoffs, Berry, the hockey purist who was a poor motivator and was dismal at public relations, was fired from his third NHL head-coaching job. Creamer was a curious replacement. He had no NHL experience. He spoke very poor English. He was a rather odd-looking character, with a head so big, one wag observed, that if the rest of his body were in proportion to it, he'd be twelve feet tall. Creamer had coached Pat LaFontaine in Verdun for the season in which the little American left Mario sucking up his exhaust fumes. Creamer then proved a winner coaching in the Montreal organization and a recommendation from Habs' management secured him the Pittsburgh post.

The coaching change also meant changes for Lemieux. Under Creamer, Mario would play a more prominent role. One of his first moves was to make Mario a penalty-killer. Making big scorers kill penalties made them more conscious of defense. Creamer also felt that since Mario represented such an offensive threat, he would curb the daring of the power-play attackers while scoring some short-handed goals himself. By and large, he was right. Lemieux was effective in the role and scored an impressive ten short-handed goals that year.

Creamer also decided to move Mario to the point position on power plays. "I like the switch," Lemieux said. "Teams are aware now that I play the left side on the power play and things have gotten a little crowded over there. Defensively, I have a little more responsibility on the point, but I think you're okay if you're able to read the play. I'll try to read what happens."

More importantly, Creamer began giving Mario all the ice time he wanted, in the belief that you use your best player as much as humanly possible. Mario, like most skaters given more ice, relished the opportunity. He began playing half the game, not just on big nights, but all the time.

Given his Canada Cup performance, the hockey world now looked to Lemieux to mount a conspicuous challenge to the

Gretzky hegemony. He became depressed at the start of the season, however, when, even though he was playing well, the Pens again opened abysmally, winning only one of their first eight games. After a loss in Detroit, Creamer and his assistants, sensing Mario's gloom, took him out for a private dinner to try and cheer him up. They told him not to take the team's failings so personally. He didn't say much.

He had twenty-eight points in his first fourteen games, still behind Gretzky. In November Alan Kerr of the New York Islanders rammed him into the boards, sidelining him for three games with shoulder and back pains, and leaving Mario to wonder if he would ever play a full season. In the same month the Penguins traded for the most fluid skating defenseman in the world. Paul Coffey came to Pittsburgh from Edmonton with Dave Hunter and Wayne Van Dorp. In return, the Penguins dispatched forwards Craig Simpson and Dave Hannan and defensemen Moe Mantha and Chris Joseph to the Oilers. Eddie Johnston had three purposes in making the deal: to dramatically improve the Penguins' stagnant power play, to open up more free ice for Mario by giving opponents someone else to key on, and to infuse the club with the feel of a Stanley Cup winner. Coffey's skating, his ability to quarterback a blitz attack, and his self-confidence immediately lifted the team. "A guy like Coff opens up the ice so much for the other guys," Lemieux noted. "I found that out in the Canada Cup. What you try to do is find the open ice, get the pass from him, give it back to him—a lot of give and gos. On the power play he makes a big difference. You don't have to go back, get the puck, bring it up, and make the play. You can divide what you have to do."

With Coffey, Mario felt freer. Gretzky's loss was Mario's gain. He improved his scoring, and the distance to Gretzky narrowed. He had sixty-seven points in thirty games for a 2.23 average. Gretzky had seventy-eight points in thirty-four games for a 2.29 average. The Penguins shot forward. In the twelve games immediately following the trade, they went 8–3–1. But just as the skies opened, Coffey went on the shelf with a knee injury. Bodger was also hurt and the Penguins returned to their traditionally wretched ways. They played a stretch of ten games, winning only one.

Discontent soon focused on Creamer. Eddie Johnston, players grumbled, could at least have chosen someone who could speak English. Creamer had few ideas, they said, and what ones he did have he couldn't communicate. After another loss to the Red Wings in Detroit, a particularly blue spot for the Pens this season, the normally quiet Lemieux spoke out. Mario was captain now, but only by happenstance. Dan Frawley, who had the job, got hurt and Lemieux replaced him in the function. Creamer had considered making Mario captain to begin the season, but decided the increased responsibilities would take away from his concentration.

Now, as the official leader of the team, Lemieux listened to his teammates' complaints and, in a move that was rare for any NHL player, publicly upbraided the coach. "Everybody's on the edge," Lemieux said. "Nobody knows what to do on the ice . . . what his job is. That's why we have to sit down with the coach pretty soon. . . . It's just a matter of knowing before you go on the ice what you want to do." Creamer responded, explaining that the players did in fact know what to do. "But sometimes, with inexperience, with a lack of aggressiveness, they don't exactly understand their role. It's a matter of interpretation."

The meeting with Mario proceeded cordially, communications were set straight, and the Penguins gradually rebounded, staying in close range of playoff territory. Mario had a new winger in the diminutive Rob Brown. Brown scored so many goals that hockey people thought he might have a special talent of his own. Was this the case, they wondered, or was he like

Warren Young and Terry Ruskowski, whose totals ballooned only because of what Mario could do for them?

By setting up Brown and Randy Cunneyworth, and scoring himself, Mario turned the points battle with Gretzky into a splendid spectator sport. Just as he did, however, Gretzky, who had won seven scoring titles in succession, was felled with a knee injury that would keep him out for several weeks. The injury allowed Mario to overtake him in the points race. But by now, with or without such turns of fate, the ascendancy of the Anti-Gretzky was taking on more and more of an inevitable look. *Globe and Mail* hockey writer William Houston wrote: "Lemieux is on the threshold of becoming the greatest hockey player in the world. This season in fact might be remembered as a milestone, a sort of rearranging of the order, or at least the beginning of such."

Houston's view was validated by Mario's performance at the all-star game in St. Louis. He played startlingly, either scoring or fashioning every one of his team's goals. He scored three and assisted on three others in the 6–5 Wales Conference victory. "That was a scary performance by one individual," said Mike Keenan, who coached him. "I'd like to congratulate the rest of our team, but Mario was awesome tonight." Some called it the finest performance in all-star game history, outdoing what Gretzky or Orr or Howe or Lafleur or Hull had ever done. On his first goal Mario whirled majestically from behind the net and gracefully wristed the puck in off his backhand side. "There probably isn't another man in the world who can do that," said Glen Sather, the Campbell Conference coach. "He didn't even move his arms. He just moved his wrists." Lemieux scored a second goal on a severe-angle wrist shot and a third in overtime, when he maneuvered in front of Mike Vernon and, again on his backhand, poked the puck through the goalie's gaping legs.

Gilles Meloche, Pittsburgh's goaltender, described how

difficult Mario made it for netminders. "He comes across the crease and you aren't going to give him time to bury you. So you reach and he pulls the puck back a little farther, and then you can't reach anymore and he still has something left. When I'm watching from the other end of the ice, it seems like Mario, with that stride of his, is almost in the corner by now and I'm saying to myself, 'Shoot it Mario, dammit, shoot it.'" But Mario is too patient for that. "The speed he does it in seems slow-motion," said Kevin Dineen, then of Hartford. "He's always completely composed."

Lemieux had faded in the stretch in his first three NHL seasons, but in 1987–1988 he maintained a dominant pace until the end. In a six-game run through mid-March, he scored twenty points. He spent so much time on the ice that, by virtue of the law of averages, he would score many points. For all its statistics, the NHL didn't (because of the enormous difficulty involved) measure the most important factor in a player's points totals: ice time. Despite their unquestionable superiority, Gretzky's and Lemieux's totals would be far less if they saw the ice only as much as normal players. Playing thirty minutes a game meant playing twice as much as a normal quality forward. Logic dictated that Gretzky and Lemieux would score twice as many points.

Despite Mario's inspired play in the closing weeks, the season again ended in anguish for the Penguins. They won eight of their last eleven games. They finished 36–35–9, above .500 for the first time in nine years. They finished only seven points behind the first-place New York Islanders in their division. Still, they didn't make the playoffs. The Patrick division was of such high quality that .500 hockey got them only last place, albeit just two points from qualification for the post-season.

Though Pierre Creamer had taken them to their best season in nearly a decade, the Penguins had already had enough of him.

They felt he was in over his head, the most recent example being the second-last game of the season. Creamer, the players said, wanted the team to play for a tie thinking that would be good enough to get them in the playoffs. The players knew they needed a win to stay alive. Mario got them the victory in over-time, but as it turned out this triumph was still not enough.

A mini-revolt had been long simmering. The players wanted the coach out and they wanted Mario's support for the putsch. Lemieux was reluctant. He had enjoyed his best season under Creamer. While he had reservations about the coach's ability, he had good personal relations with him. But in the end, given the feeling of so many of the team members, he decided he couldn't support Creamer. Mario's power on the team was such that a strong vote of confidence from him would have saved Creamer's job. But Mario didn't come forward, nor did he get his friend Jimmy Maggs to work the back-channel to Paul Martha with good words about the coach.

Creamer had dinner with the team in the Igloo the day after the last game. He told the players he wanted to see them indi-vidually. He looked forward most to seeing Lemieux, his captain, his fellow Quebecker. He saw Coffey, who was one of his detractors, and he saw Hunter and others, but number 66 never showed. "He didn't come to shake my hand or say goodbye to me," said Creamer. "I'm a proud guy and I didn't wish to make the first step, going to him." The coach concluded that Mario was already privy to the decision that he would be fired and therefore wanted to avoid him. But he still wished Mario had had the fortitude to say goodbye. It remained the one black mark in Pierre Creamer's picture of Lemieux. He never spoke to Mario again.

After he had hung by a thread for a few weeks, the decision was finally taken to hand Creamer his hat. He didn't go quietly. "I wasn't going to play, excuse the expression, the shit game with them," he would say later. "I wasn't going to come out and smile and say I understand the decision and I respect you gentlemen for making it. I'm not like that." Instead, he was blunt about why he was dismissed. "The players wanted to find a big dummy for not making the playoffs and they chose me. Players are all the same. They want to find someone responsible, and it's much easier to say, 'That's the coach,' instead of saying, 'It's me.'"

The unfortunate ending to the season meant that Eddie Johnston had to go as well. He had had too many problems finding the team a strong goaltender, a policeman for Mario, a right winger for Mario, and a playoff position. Tony Esposito, the former Chicago Blackhawk goalie, took over as general manager, and began a coach hunt. Mario got an oar in on what Esposito might look for. "The next coach," said Lemieux, "has got to be a coach who can help the young guys. . . . He's got to talk to them. He's got to give them confidence."

Lemieux finished the season with 70 goals and 98 assists for 168 points. Gretzky, who played 13 fewer games, had 40 goals and 109 assists for 149 points. With a full slate of games, Gretzky likely would have won another scoring title. But that couldn't diminish the year Mario Lemieux had enjoyed. It had all begun with the inspired performance in the Canada Cup and continued that way through the regular season and the all-star game all the way to the scoring title. It took Mario, like Guy Lafleur, three NHL seasons before he began to realize his potential. Lafleur underwent three painful seasons scoring twenty-nine goals or less before his surge in year four. Lemieux did much better in his first three years, but just like the Flower, the fourth marked the great leap forward.

To cap it all off, he was voted the ultimate prize, the one Gretzky had won an astounding eight times in succession—the Hart Trophy as MVP.

Gretzky didn't come to the awards ceremony, though he

was nominated in two categories. "There was no reason to be there," he explained. "People will always say things and have their opinions, but the bottom line is there was no need to be there, so I didn't go. It was definitely his [Mario's] day. He had a tremendous season. There was no need to take anything away from Mario. He was a very deserving winner."

Mario was gracious and diplomatic as he accepted the prize. "I thought it was about time this year that I started to show my stuff," he said. "It started at the Canada Cup, playing with Wayne. I learned a lot from him. In my opinion, he's still the best player in the world. He had an injury this year and I took advantage of it." He seemed aware that he had image sins to atone for. In an interview he reflected back on some of his growing pains. His decision not to go to the Pittsburgh table on draft day, he said now, was inappropriate. "I didn't know much about the NHL then. I didn't realize how you had to earn respect. It took a while for the other players and the fans to get to know me better . . . to know I'm not that bad a guy." With these and other statements, he appeared to be demonstrating a maturity of age. But some, including the Great Gretzky himself, and including Bob Perno, the agent who had reared him, remained unconvinced.

TWELVE

SEVERING THE TIE

MARIO LEMIEUX HAD VERY FEW CLOSE FRIENDS, BUT IT WAS often said that he was extremely loyal to those he did have. That's why what happened with Bob Perno, and, more particularly, the way it happened, came as such a surprise.

In late January 1988 Pittsburgh played in Montreal against the Canadiens. Lemieux had a Coca-Cola commercial to tape during the stopover and, on the day of the shooting, Perno and Steigerwald, the Penguins' marketing director, drove out to the location together.

"Bob," Steigerwald asked Perno on the way, "is there something going on between you and Mario?"

"No. Why?"

"Because Albert Mandanici came up to me and said you're not going to be doing Mario's next contract."

Perno's face froze. He had heard nothing, but he could well imagine Mandanici doing this. He had not enjoyed a good relationship with the Penguins' Quebec scout since they had squared off on draft day in 1984. It annoyed him to see that, following the controversy, Mandanici had won back his favorable standing with Mario and the Lemieux clan. Mandanici, in fact, soon became a regular at the Lemieux household to watch the Pittsburgh games beamed via satellite through the big dish on the roof. Perno suspected Mandanici was using these occasions to stab him in the back. His suspicions were not without foundation.

Mandanici had heard stories about Perno's inability to keep his mouth shut on important client-agent matters. He had heard, for example, that Perno was telling people which players were slow or negligent in paying him his agent's fee. Mandanici gave the Lemieuxs his opinion on this and other matters. Pierrette Lemieux, still extremely close to her son, began to have second thoughts about his long-time agent. She wondered if Perno was right for him. Nathalie Asselin was even closer to Mario and she, of course, had entertained second thoughts about Bob Perno more than a few times.

While he already knew that sharks infested the waters, Perno was still alarmed at what Steigerwald reported. He couldn't wait to confront Mario on it and decided to bring it up right there, at the commercial shoot.

"I heard through the grapevine that Mandanici says I won't be doing your next contract."

"No, that's not true," said Mario.

"Well, look," said Perno, "I want you to tell me, because this spring I'm building an extension for my office and it's going to cost me about $40,000. Before investing the money I want to make sure everything's okay."

Mario, according to Perno, gave his assurance. "Why would I change agents?"

By this time, however, Lemieux was being advised that Perno might not have the necessary clout or expertise to get him endorsements in the United States. This required, Mario was told, a big-time agent, someone like Tom Reich, who represented the famous names of baseball. For all Perno's devotion to Mario, some felt that he couldn't carry the big load. They liked him, they liked his honesty and his loyalty to Mario, but they found him to be a notch below the top rung. He didn't turn heads when he walked into a room or command attention at the bargaining table.

Mario had no national endorsements in the United States, which, Perno realized, was a bone of contention. But as he explained to Mario, hockey wasn't big enough in the American market yet. It didn't even have a major TV contract. He also knew that, given Mario's withdrawn personality, his shyness, and his ethnicity, Madison Avenue viewed him as a deadhead. He didn't have the sparkle to sell products.

Mario's casual attitude to the whole marketing business also entered into this. If work on an endorsement conflicted, for example, with a golf outing, there was a good chance golf would get the nod. Soon after he backed out on the Gillette promotion, it happened again, this time with Micron Skates. Micron had a promotion scheduled for him in Buffalo. They went to some expense to advertise his appearance at a sporting-goods store on a Saturday afternoon. On the Friday, Mario phoned Perno to tell him he wasn't going. He had some friends who were playing golf in Florida and he was taking off to join them. Perno tried unsuccessfully to change his mind, then delivered the news to Micron. They were "absolutely steaming," he recalled.

Mario wasn't the first star athlete to back out of an engagement. Even Gretzky had done so. One time, returning dead tired from a trip to Moscow, he found his schedule jammed and felt he just couldn't face the cameras the next day. He was supposed to do a Mattel commercial in Toronto, but canceled it. "Boy, were they furious," Gretzky said, "but I just couldn't bring myself to smile for one more camera." He went to his grandmother's farm to fish that day. On canceling the appearance, he told Mattel to send him the bill for studio rentals, crew members, and all their troubles. It came to $15,000. "And you know what?" said Gretzky. "It was worth every penny."

For Gretzky, this cancellation was a once-in-a-career thing, or close to it. Mario, however, was doing it more and more often, and wasn't offering to give financial compensation to the jilted party. In fact, he wasn't making a big effort on charities or public relations of any kind. "He considered his time away from the game precious," explained Steigerwald, "and he wanted to be able to enjoy it. . . . He didn't like being shuffled around to do this and to do that. The money wasn't as important to him as the time."

Nothing wrong with that, said Steigerwald. "It's just what he thought. But he did get a negative image as a result of it. The people who wanted him to say yes to this money and to their offers are going to be insulted 'cause he says no, instead of respecting him for doing what he wants to do.

"Mario Lemieux has a tremendous amount of conviction. He does things the way he wants to do them and he really stands up for what he feels."

"Hey, that's Mario," said Penguins' VP Paul Martha, referring to the no-shows. "You have to ask yourself whether he is entitled to do things like that. Well, maybe he is, maybe he isn't. That's Mario. He wanted his own time. Maybe he overdid it."

Given his attitude, Perno wondered how Lemieux could be all that concerned about getting a new agent to chase American endorsements. Though Mario assured him he wasn't contemplating a change, Perno suspected something was in the works. He knew by now of the closeness between Tom Mathews and Tom Reich. He knew that the Mathews family had become friends with the Lemieux family. He believed that Pierrette Lemieux, even though she still preferred her small home, would have stars in her eyes at the thought of the numbers dangled by Tom Reich.

Shortly after the incident in Montreal, Perno journeyed to Pittsburgh. He had negotiated a local endorsement for Mario with a potato chip company and was to meet the parties concerned to finalize the arrangement. When he arrived, he noticed Mario had a new friend in tow—Steve Reich, nephew to Tom Reich and member of the Reich sports agency. Perno felt his shirt collar tighten. He could barely contain his outrage. It was obvious Mario had been slowly drawing the noose. Now he was yanking it.

When he got the chance, Perno took Mario aside. "Mario, what's this guy doing here?" he sputtered.

"Uh, he's just tagging along to have a look at things, Bob. He's a friend of the Mathews."

Perno flew home, feeling it was all over. He called Mario and said, "Come on, give me the truth here. What's going on?" Again, Mario assured him that he had nothing to worry about, that there were no changes planned. Perno didn't believe him, but continued in his agent's role.

He traveled to Chicoutimi, Quebec, for the Memorial Cup late that spring, 1988. There, he bumped into the newly appointed general manager of the Penguins, Tony Esposito. Esposito had no experience as a coach or GM, but he was a friend of the DeBartolos and that's all it took. His hiring depressed Paul Martha. Martha had met with Craig Patrick twice at LaGuardia airport in New York. Patrick had been let go by the New York Rangers, but Martha liked the foundation he had been building there. He wanted to hire him, but DeBartolo opted for a friend.

Mario's contract with the Penguins was up for renegotiation at this time. When Perno saw Esposito in the lobby of a Chicoutimi hotel, he thought he could make some progress right there. "Tony, when can we meet on Mario's new contract?" he asked.

Esposito paused. "I'm sorry, Bob, but I can't discuss that with you."

"What do you mean, you can't discuss it?"

"Well, I don't know how to tell you this, Bob, but I got a letter from Tom Reich saying he is now representing Mario Lemieux."

Perno mumbled, "What are you talking about?" But he

knew exactly what had happened. He went up to his room, incredulous that all this had gone on behind his back. He got on the phone to Mario and told him what Esposito had said. Now, after the months of dallying, Lemieux had to own up. He apologetically explained that yes, in fact, he had changed agents. He hadn't told Perno earlier, he said, because he didn't know how to do so.

They talked some more. Mario explained that he felt he needed a bigger office to represent him in the United States. A bigger office, he said, could get him endorsements. Perno replied that he would get only the local endorsements in Pittsburgh, which he was already getting, and that an American agent wouldn't get as many Canadian endorsements. At that time, according to Perno, Mario was making $200,000 a year in Canadian endorsements.

Mario began to soften up. He was coming to Montreal the following week, he said. Why didn't the three of them—himself, Reich, and Perno—get together and talk it out? They agreed, and met in Montreal at Thursday's, the brass-and-glass bar-restaurant that was once the haunt of Guy Lafleur. Mario admitted that Perno had been doing a good job for him in Canada and discussion centered on the possibility of the agent duties being split between Perno in Canada and Reich in the United States. Perno thought the arrangement was settled. He left with the understanding that Reich would get hold of him to work out the details. But he never heard from him. The Pittsburgh agent soon took over the Canadian account as well.

Perno was shattered. What about all Mario's promises, he wondered. What about all the things Mario said about Perno being family? What about Mario's insistence that the rumors of him going to another agent were nonsense? What about Mario's guarantee, after the agent had dropped his fee below five percent, that Perno would do his next contract? Perno had started work on the extension on his office. Now the money wouldn't be coming.

Though it was perhaps a cold-hearted move, many in the Pittsburgh organization thought Lemieux had made a good business decision. Reich was a hot shot. He knew the American market and got big contracts for his athletes. Perno, however, tended to view the decision as an act of disloyalty. After all he had done on Mario's behalf, after all the good times they had together, after such a close relationship had been built, how could Mario turn around and do this—and do it so furtively? He had said to Perno's face he wasn't changing agents.

In his office outside Montreal, Perno continued for years to keep Mario's Pittsburgh sweater on prominent display. He also kept a scrapbook and other memorabilia of their friendship. He had good memories of so many hours spent with the kid, a lot of laughs, a lot of golf, a lot of beer, a lot of hockey. Good times and, to be sure, bad times, but overarching both, a firm bond of friendship that would endure, or so Perno thought, forever. The agent had a difficult time getting over not only the financial setback of losing Mario, but also the perceived breach of trust. "I don't care how big Mario Lemieux is," Bob Perno said. "He's not bigger than the people who got him there."

Perno talked to Gretzky about what had happened. The two had maintained a close relationship, and Perno still thought of Gretzky as the epitome of class in sportsmen. When Gretzky came to Quebec, Perno would frequently act as his contact man, taking him to engagements or to Chez Paree or, until a bad evening soured Gretzky on the place, to Sean O'Donnell's Bourbon Street bar in the Laurentians. Bourbon Street was clean, as bars go, but one night Gretzky, who had been drinking there with Perno, came quickly out of the washroom and said he wanted to leave. He told Perno he'd seen some guys doing coke and he didn't feel like hanging around. Though it was hardly unusual to find coke users in a bar, Gretzky told Perno to warn Mario off the place as well.

Gretzky's attitude toward Mario may well have been colored by what happened between Perno and number 66. Gretzky, in fact, had split with Perno's former boss, Gus Badali. Among Gretzky's reasons for leaving was questionable advice he had received from a Badali partner on real-estate investments in Alberta. When the province went into a recession, the investments lost money. But though there was a change, Gretzky maintained a friendly relationship with Badali. He didn't forget who had helped him in the early days. That, in Perno's eyes, was the difference.

Perno knew that Gretzky had some reservations about the way Lemieux went about things. But he thought relations between the two players were cordial and, given the joint triumph at the Canada Cup, happy enough. They had lit up the hockey world then, confirming their status as the two best players in the game. They had embraced after it was all over and made all the politically correct comments about one another. That's why what happened the following spring shocked Perno. When Gretzky announced his plans to marry Janet Jones he left Mario off the invitation list. This was the wedding of the decade and Gretzky was inviting seven hundred guests—even *Playboy*'s Hugh Hefner made the cut. Yet his "friend" Mario, his "ice-mate" Mario, the marvelous player with whom he had just mesmerized Canada, was not among them.

Perno told Gretzky that he hoped his own problems with Mario were not among the reasons for the snub. Gretzky didn't spell it out, but Perno and others felt he was probably reacting to an accumulation of things: Mario's disloyalty to people, Mario's reluctance to give anything back to the game, Mario's laziness. Perhaps there was an element of pure ego involved, of Wayne not wanting his only rival in the sport sharing in his big day.

Gretzky would soon write his autobiography. Notably, in his first reference to Mario Lemieux, he would choose to knock him for lack of effort. He used a third party to do it, but the implication was clear. The "highest compliment you can pay me," wrote Gretzky, "is to say that I work hard every day, practice or game, and that I never dog it. Bobby Orr once said of Mario Lemieux: 'On sheer ability, Mario is good enough to win scoring titles with a broken stick. On pure talent, he's the best there is. But Wayne almost never disappoints you. He comes to work every night.'"

In Pittsburgh, when the subject of the wedding came up, Lemieux gave the impression that he was only too pleased not to be going. Jimmy Maggs talked to Mario frequently about Gretzky. "I think if he had a choice that day to play golf or go to Wayne's wedding," said Maggs, "he would have gone golfing." Maggs added that "it was probably best that Wayne didn't invite him. It was like two trains on a collision course." They respected one another on the ice and they were polite in their public comments about one another, but that's as far as it went, said Mario's friend. It wasn't easy for Mario to witness the degree of power Gretzky exercised over public opinion. "Gretzky kind of controlled the league," Maggs noted. "He said something and everything he said kind of went."

Both Lemieux and Gretzky had been tied to the Badali–Perno team. Now that they'd both left, there was no excuse to get together and, in mutual comfort, they drifted apart.

Mario's move from Bob Perno to Tom Reich worried the holders of the Penguin purse-strings at first. They feared that a big-time bargainer like Reich would significantly increase Mario's asking price and, in turn, that of the rest of the members of the hockey team. They feared that Mario was Reich's entree into hockey, that soon he would be representing most of the players on the team.

In that summer of 1988 Tom Lapointe, the Quebec

reporter who had befriended Gretzky and Lemieux, was finally rewarded for his efforts. Through sources in Los Angeles, he was able to announce to the hockey world the biggest trade in the sport's history: Gretzky to the Kings. Mario was in the middle of a round of golf when the news came to him. He was so stirred by it that he could no longer concentrate and didn't complete the round. He had heard the rumors before, but hadn't believed them.

The development, in a way, represented good news for Lemieux and he acknowledged it as such. The trade would be the great equalizer. Mario had always claimed that Gretzky, who played with superior wingers, enjoyed a distinct advantage over other scorers like himself. Now the advantage was stripped away. Gretzky was twenty-seven years old, still in his peak form, but Mario correctly anticipated that his astounding points production would diminish once he was in California. The playing field had been leveled, and Mario knew he could now overtake him. "It's definitely going to be tougher for Gretz to reach two hundred points," said Lemieux of the trade. "He realizes it's going to be difficult for him to get 140 or 150 assists. He's going to have to work a lot harder, even though he works hard every game. . . .

"It's going to be a lot tougher on his mind. The team is not as good. He's going to get tired of the traveling. And playing over there, it's not the same lifestyle. It's going to be tough for him to adjust."

Even from the point of view of public relations, Mario now thought that he might gain the advantage. L.A. was Hollywood, sure enough, but it was hardly hockey country. "It's hard to get good publicity out of L.A.," noted number 66. "The games are so far away, people have a tendency to forget about them. I think I'm going to get a little more publicity in Canada and the eastern United States. It's certainly going to be better for [me]."

THIRTEEN
"ACE"

UNLIKE GRETZKY, MARIO WASN'T UNDERTAKING A NEW HOCKEY life. Nevertheless, as he prepared for year five in Pittsburgh, the changes were significant. He had a new agent, a new coach, a new general manager.

He didn't know much about Tony Esposito, but he could hardly have been impressed by the early signals. One of Esposito's first moves was to fire Albert Mandanici. The decision no doubt pleased Bob Perno, but Mandanici, perhaps unbeknownst to Esposito, was a good friend of Mario's. Then the news flashed that Guy Lafleur was preparing a comeback bid. Mario was keen on having him in Pittsburgh and the Flower was excited about that prospect as well. Playing on a wing with Mario, what fine music they might make. But Tony Esposito didn't see it that way. Lafleur offered his services, but Esposito didn't return the call. He left it to his brother Phil in New York to grab Lafleur for the Rangers.

A more serious problem was Mario's dispute with the new GM over his contract. Asserting himself in a way that he hadn't in the past, Lemieux said at the September training camp that it was time for Pittsburgh to pay him and the team's top players "what they deserve." It was only fair, he said. In the past, maybe the players hadn't deserved very much. "But times change, and if you've got good players, you want to keep them." Lemieux, in fact, had two years remaining on a contract that paid him in excess of half a million a year. But the status he had won as the number-two player in the league entitled him to renegotiation. Gretzky was now reported to be receiving more than two millon dollars a year from Bruce McNall, the Kings' owner. Esposito's offer to Mario was worth less than half that. "I think the organization is smart enough to realize that some people are making big bucks in this league," Lemieux said. "I just want to be treated fairly."

The dispute dragged through the autumn and into November. On both sides of the table sat inexperience. Esposito was new at this game and it showed. Mario's new agent, Tom Reich, had no experience doing hockey contracts and it, said Paul Martha, also showed. A negotiating deadline of November 11 passed with Lemieux saying, "We might never talk again." While this may have sounded overly dramatic, Penguins' fans knew, given the Gretzky trade, that no one was sacred, that it was possible Lemieux could move on. Aroused, they got in on the act. In the last period of a game against the New York Rangers in which Mario got five points, they broke into several chants of "Sign Lemieux! Sign Lemieux! Sign Lemieux!"

A compromise came at the end of November. The parties could not agree to a long-term contract, but closed a one-year deal at an estimated base salary of $1.6 million. It satisfied Mario, whose threatening noises were more than just gamesmanship. He had been prepared, if a satisfactory arrangement could not be made, to leave Pittsburgh, even though he was deeply fond of the city, its people, and their support for him. His image problems elsewhere never seemed to touch down in the place he played. They loved him in Pittsburgh, in part for the very reason he was unpopular elsewhere: his quiet, self-effacing nature. Shortly after the superstar came to the city, Jimmy Maggs told Mario that to be loved by the "burghers" it was important that he never act the big shot, that he never expect to be waited on hand and foot. Follow this advice, he told Mario, "and you'll own this city one day."

While the salary controversy raged, Lemieux had surged to his finest start ever, scoring forty-one points in fourteen games, six ahead of Gretzky's total for sixteen games. This included a stunning eight-point performance against the St. Louis Blues. As rare as such an output was, for Mario it was a sign of things to come. He would have three eight-point nights this season.

He was twenty-three years old now and the experience of four years in the league was beginning to show. Self-confidence and self-assertion on and off the ice were more in evidence. The fiercely independent individual who tended to stay in the background became the fiercely independent individual who came forward. His public criticism of Pierre Creamer, his insistence that the club bring salaries into line, and, as would be soon witnessed, his growing opposition to the Esposito regime were examples of his emergence. In the dressing room the once quiet corner boy was now, with the experience of the Canada Cup, a leader. Wayne Van Dorp found out about it firsthand. Van Dorp was a Penguin enforcer who, in the view of his critics, was reluctant to fight anyone over five-foot-nine. The Penguins' new coach, Gene Ubriaco, hinted that Van Dorp might be sent down to the minors, to Muskegon of the International Hockey League. Tom McMillan, hockey writer for the *Pittsburgh Post-Gazette*, wrote the story and Van Dorp took great exception to it. If anyone was going down, he decided, it was McMillan. In the dressing room after a practice he began berating McMillan with the usual array of hockey-player expletives. The reporter was standing a few yards away from the much larger Van Dorp, taking it all in, not wanting to incite him further by responding.

But Van Dorp's tirade gained momentum. He hurled his sweater at McMillan, shouting, "Put that in the paper, asshole!"

In his rage, he started after the writer, who simultaneously made a beeline for the exit. Before Van Dorp could reach him, Mario jumped in to restrain him, allowing McMillan safe passage. Lemieux, who got on weil with the reporter, ordered Van Dorp to cool off. He told him that the team didn't need this kind of behavior. When McMillan phoned Mario that night to thank him for what he had done, Mario asked if he was okay, then said it should never have happened.

Mario could have benefited from such an intercession himself. He could not get through a season without being mugged. This time, the beginning of year five, he took a clubbing at the hands of David Shaw, the New York Ranger defenseman. In a third-period uprising in which the referees assessed 252 minutes in penalties, Shaw checked and highsticked Mario into the boards. Mario retaliated with a cross-check to the chest. With a two-fisted grip, Shaw swung his stick at Mario as if it were a medieval sword. It struck Mario heavily on the side of the face and upper chest, and he crumbled to the ice with a ringing in his ears. Skip Thayer, the Penguins' trainer, found Mario stunned, but still semiconscious. He had recovered by the next day, but he had escaped serious injury only narrowly. "He was going for my head, my face," Mario said. "The film shows it too."

Mario didn't miss any games on account of the blow, but sat out three in November as a result of a sprained wrist. Gene Ubriaco was asked the standard reporter's question about how the injury would affect the team. "How would you do without a typewriter?" the coach responded. Later in the year, Mario missed another two games with a pulled groin. For the average player, such absences meant little. For Mario, under pressure to post great stats and catch Gretzky, they were serious business.

The Penguins were gradually developing a better supporting cast for him, and with it, Mario's numbers were going up, just as he said they would. "I think," observed Martha, "that Mario always knew that 'Hey, give me a couple of good guys and I can do the whole thing.'" On defense, the team now had not only Coffey, but also the 1986 first-round draft pick, Zarley Zalapski, an all-round defenseman who did nothing spectacularly and everything proficiently. Tony Esposito, who could be expected to focus in on goaltending, saw it as the club's number-one weakness, and two months into his first season, wisely dealt for the Buffalo Sabre's Tom Barrasso. To get Barrasso, the NHL's 1983–1984 rookie of the year, he gave up two first-round draft picks, twenty-two-year-old defenseman Doug Bodger and eighteen-year-old left winger Darrin Shannon. Esposito equated the importance of netminding in hockey with pitching in baseball. DeBartolo supported Esposito's wishes, in a way he never had with Eddie Johnston. Johnston had had a deal arranged to send a first-round draft pick and goalie Steve Guenette to the Edmonton Oilers for Andy Moog. DeBartolo, who didn't know hockey, vetoed the trade.

The 1988–1989 season saw the Penguins contend for top place in their division. For much of the season, they played about ten games above .500. With his sensational beginning, Mario created crazy expectations of a 250-point season. When he slowed down later in the year to a mere 2 to 2.5 points a game, it was called a slump. For the average player, such figures were considered a tear; for Mario, they were a slump. In one stretch he had only 4 points in four games and spoke candidly of problems. "I know I'm not playing like I should. I don't have that zip I had . . . at the start of the season. Every time I stepped on the ice I felt I had a chance to score. I felt strong. Lately, I've felt sluggish."

Lemieux left this particular slump behind on New Year's

Eve when he stacked up 8 points in a game against New Jersey. He entered the record books by scoring the cycle, that is, scoring in every formation possible. He scored a power-play goal, a short-handed goal, a penalty-shot goal, an empty-net goal, and a regular-strength goal. No one had ever done this and the odds cried out against anyone ever doing it again. The chances of getting a penalty shot and scoring on one were rare enough, but for a player to do it in the same game in which he scored every other way imaginable was something not even to be contemplated. Until that night, no one had ever even talked of scoring the cycle. He had probably set the most secure record in hockey.

Though the Penguins and Mario were faring well, they felt it was in spite of, not because of, their new coach and GM. Gene Ubriaco had got the job simply because he was a friend of Esposito's, just as Esposito had been hired simply because of his friendship with DeBartolo. Ubriaco was part of the Italian connection in Esposito's home town of Sault St. Marie, Ontario. He had played for the Penguins in their inaugural year, quit playing in the early 1970s, and become a minor-league coach in Nashville, Birmingham, and Baltimore. The season before he was hired by Esposito, Ubriaco had guided the Penguins' farm club, the Baltimore Skipjacks of the American Hockey League, to a monstrous 13–58–9. "It's a strange game, hockey," observed Ubriaco. "I figured last season hurt my career and might have even killed it, but now I'm coaching in the NHL, which is always where I wanted to be and dreamed of being."

In hiring Ubriaco, the Penguins may well have made the same mistake they did with Pierre Creamer. They brought in someone with no NHL experience, not even as an assistant coach, and they soon discovered he wasn't the right man. Ubriaco brought minor-league tactics to major-league players. In the minors he could push players hard because they had another level to attain and were less inclined to talk back. In the

NHL of the late 1980s, however, the power was increasingly with the players and they had to be accorded more respect.

In the minors Ubriaco had a habit of giving players sophomoric nicknames. He carried the practice over to the NHL, even to the likes of Mario Lemieux. He started calling Mario "Ace." He'd say, "How ya doin', Ace?" or "Nice game, Ace." He'd urge Mario to greater heights: "Go get 'em, Ace!" Lemieux hated the nickname. But Ubriaco kept it up, and soon the players picked up on it and wouldn't let go. When Rick Tocchet eventually came to the club, he too got in on the act. By 1993 he was still calling Lemieux "Ace."

Ubriaco had little sense of how to give the superstars their due. His psychology in the minors had been to treat everyone equally. In Pittsburgh he wouldn't go out of his way to praise Mario. Asked questions about him, he was just as likely to start talking about Troy Loney, a routine player. Because of Mario's ongoing contract negotiations, the press suspected Ubriaco was under instructions from Esposito to keep the praise down.

Mario could tolerate slights such as the nickname and faint praise. Far more serious, however, was the attitude of the manager, Esposito, toward French-Canadians. Esposito was frequently overheard commenting condescendingly or insultingly on aspects of the French-Canadian character. He allegedly went so far as to refer to Mario and other Quebeckers as "frogs."

"You could tell there was a bias against French-Canadians," said Tom McMillan. "I took it as no different from what I saw between blacks and whites in the U.S." Since the matter involved the team's lead player, it became an explosive behind-the-scenes issue. Bob Perno had talked with Mario about the common perception outside of Quebec that Francophones were flashy but lazy players who wouldn't backcheck. They agreed that this prejudice would make life more difficult for him. They agreed that, as a general rule, it was more difficult for a French-

Canadian playing in the NHL than for an English-Canadian. But Mario never expected to be called "frog" to his face by the manager of his team. Mario told Jimmy Maggs that that was, in fact, what happened. "We discussed it," said Maggs. "I think it was the most souring point in his career. Mario couldn't understand how anybody could downgrade his nationality, especially when they were all hockey players. . . . [But] Esposito didn't like French-Canadians. He made sure Mario knew that."

The word quickly got to Paul Martha. "I knew all the time what was in Mario's head," said Martha, "either through conversations with him or Jimmy. Mario was very adept at sending the signal.

"At times," continued Martha, "I think Tony, in frustration, was not very discreet and, consequently, he paid for that because of the impressions the players got." The "frog" references were not just tasteless jokes either. "At times, it was said in a joking way," explained Martha. "At other times, the perception was that it was serious. That was the important thing, what perception the players developed about their GM."

Mario left no doubt he wanted Tony Esposito fired. But while the racism issue simmered, Lemieux had other problems. He and the Penguins entered into a winter of mild discontent, registering more losses than their talent should have allowed. Then Mario had his wrists slapped loudly by a high-profile TV analyst. Still not able to escape public-relations problems, still not able to play the game and smile and grant media interviews to all comers, Mario backed out of a couple of planned sessions with Canada's all-sports television network, TSN. Gary Green, the network's color commentator, lashed out. Lemieux was doing nothing to promote the game, he complained. Lemieux was giving nothing back. Lemieux's only public appearance for months, cried Green, had been for a potato chip company. "And he got ten grand for that!" He wasn't, said Green, deserving of the MVP award. "I figure he makes $2 million a year for more than just playing hockey." Mario had heard all this before, but coming from TSN, it was another image setback. Tom Reich, Lemieux's new agent, was having little success in improving Mario's public image.

Mario had a quiet all-star game that year, dipped through February, but came back in March to lead the club to a strong finish. He scored thirteen goals in his last six games, concluding the season the way he began it. Disappointingly, he fell just one point short of the 200-point plateau, the exclusive turf of Wayne Gretzky. His 85 goals and 114 assists easily topped his rival, however. Gretzky had a good year with 168 points, but this represented his lowest points-per-game average since 1980–1981. On the first test, Mario's predictions about Gretzky finding it tougher to score with a weaker team in California proved accurate. In the previous season Mario's scoring title had come with the aid of a Gretzky injury. This year, he had beaten him outright and by a wide margin, scoring 31 more goals. The margin, Mario thought, would likely ensure him a repeat of the MVP award, no matter what talking heads like Green thought.

Now in his fifth season, Mario finally got his first taste of the NHL playoffs. He had been hearing for so long about how he would never be considered great until he led his team to a Stanley Cup championship. Paul Coffey, who had three Stanley Cup rings, recalled that Edmonton coach Glen Sather had once said the same thing about Gretzky. It was unfair, said Coffey, to say it of Wayne and it was unfair to say it of Mario, because it took a strong surrounding cast to win the Cup, no matter who you were, and the surrounding cast was management's job.

"Mario's going to go out and play great hockey," said Coffey. "He's going to play the way he always does. It's tough for a player as great as Mario, a player as great as Wayne, to keep lifting it up to higher expectations all the time." Gretzky, he analyzed, hadn't played significantly better in the playoffs than he did during the season. "It's just that it means more. You do it during the season and it's like, 'Ho hum, Mario goes out and gets six or seven points.' But if he does it in the playoffs, all of a sudden everybody's figuring he picked up his game to a higher level, when all he's doing is just playing the great hockey he played all year."

Mario had a cautious and quiet debut in the playoffs. The Penguins smashed the New York Rangers, who had fired coach Michel Bergeron at the end of the season. They took them out in four straight games. Playing with a higher degree of defensive consciousness, Mario had only one two-point game, letting others light up the scoreboard.

They moved on to play the Philadelphia Flyers in round two. The teams split the first four games. Mario was still low key, and his fourth game was dismal. He missed on a breakaway. He was wobbled by the Flyers' monster defenseman Kjell Samuelsson, a player he considered almost impossible to beat one on one. Worst of all, he was struck by one of his own teammates. He and forward Randy Cunneyworth came from opposite sides toward Flyer Terry Carkner. Both missed him and collided with one another. Mario's head snapped back and he lay on the ice feeling a sharp pain at the base of his neck. The neck stiffened after the game and he looked doubtful for game five.

But game five produced from Mario what one scribe termed "a game for the ages." He had ten points in his first eight playoff games. In this one, he added eight more. He scored five times, four of them in the first period, in a 10–7 Penguin triumph. The coaches said it was the best they had ever seen him play. The pattern was familiar: Mario, down, hurt, coming off a horrid game, suffering from ego-depletion, snaps his internal control cord. Any and all feeling of lethargy is exorcised, and he plays as if the game were invented for him alone.

The Penguins now needed just one win to advance to the Stanley Cup semi-finals. But following his eight-point splurge, Mario's mood turned again. He was shut out in the next game, a 6–2 loss. He managed just two shots and was on the ice for three of the Flyers' goals. He dodged the media afterwards, and later gave his friend Tom Lapointe some quotes to share with the rest of the reporters. He played another quiet first period in game seven, as the Penguins fell behind 1–0. Rubbing his hands in the announcer's booth, Don Cherry, who would have preferred to see Mario rushing into the corners, banging people, harpooned him between periods. "He's floatin' out there," boomed Cherry. "If he doesn't wake up soon, they're gonzo."

Gonzo was the word. The Flyers, checking the Penguins tightly up ice in the incipient stages of their attacks, kept them disorganized. Mario scored early in the second period, but perhaps someone should have rolled the Cherry tape to incite him further. He wasn't heard from again. Flyers' goalie Ken Wregget, surprisingly inserted to replace Ron Hextall, performed admirably, stopping any other Lemieux bids during the Flyer win.

Summing up, Mario was disappointed but philosphical, pointing out that the team needed to go through such an experience to be ready the next time. "Hopefully, we can regroup next year and go as far as the finals. I think we have the potential to do that. It's just a matter of getting a couple more players and building from here." His unflappable inner confidence remained in place. "I know I'll drink from that Cup one day. I just know it." He was trying, unsuccessfully, to grow his first beard. There was lots of time.

The setback of the playoffs couldn't compare to the one he received a few weeks later, when he traveled to Toronto for the annual awards ceremonies. Because Mario had scored 31 more points than Gretzky, because he had helped his team improve its record over the previous season, because he had led it into the playoffs for the first time in so long, he was stung by the announcement of Wayne Gretzky as the Hart Trophy winner. But Gretzky had revitalized his team, moving it from just 70 points in the standings to 91. He had breathed life into hockey in California. He had improved Los Angeles more during the past season than Lemieux had Pittsburgh and that, technically, was the criteria for the MVP award—who helped his team the most.

Mario tried, but couldn't hide his bitterness. Before the ceremony, when the results were not yet known, he had stated his expectation: "In the past, it's always gone to the best player, the top scorer," he said. "I don't know why it should change."

After the presentation, after Gretzky had announced that "this one is special to me" and fought back tears, Mario left the room and was intercepted by reporters. "I don't want to comment," he said. "The facts are there." But he continued to comment and got more upset as he did. This was typical of Mario. In crisis moments he would initially say the right thing, but eventually the diplomacy would give way to what was really inside him.

"Nothing in this league makes sense," Mario complained. Maybe, it was suggested, he could use his defeat as incentive for next year. "I feel I proved I was there this year."

The truth was that he now thought he was a superior player to Gretzky and that it was about time the hockey world recognized it. To people close to him in Pittsburgh, people like Maggs and Martha, there was no doubt Mario felt this way. "The sense I got all along," said Martha, "was that Mario always thought or knew that he was better than Wayne Gretzky. Mario's size alone gave him so many advantages Wayne didn't have."

Gretzky was mum on Lemieux's post-awards comments, but at a later date acknowleged that 66 wasn't happy. "I think maybe Mario was misquoted a little," Gretzky said. "His English occasionally goes awry. But I didn't care. That Hart Trophy was the sweetest because of what I'd put on the line: my reputation."

Mario had had problems with his English before, but there had been no such problems that night. He knew exactly what he was saying. He was getting tired of Gretzky winning popularity contests. It didn't make sense to him anymore. He thought he was the better player.

FOURTEEN

A CHRISTMAS
PRESENT FOR TONY O

"I KNOW I PROBABLY LOST THE HART TROPHY BECAUSE OF MY relationship with the press," observed Mario, shaking off the disappointment a few weeks after the award presentation. "But that doesn't bother me so much . . . I don't go out of my way to be too nice to reporters. That's just the way I am." Smilingly, he added, "That's why I get a bad rap once in a while."

He made no inroads into image enhancement that summer when he journeyed to Florida for a meeting of the executive council of the NHL Players' Association. A rebel group was trying to oust Alan Eagleson, the executive director. It was a hot issue, but Mario showed maximum lack of interest. During the first day's meeting, he fell asleep. For the crucial session the next day, he didn't show up. He went where he normally went when he played hooky—to the first tee.

Questions about the league and how it was run didn't occupy his time. Some players made the effort, got involved, cared. Many didn't. Mario was one of the latter. Increasingly savoring his privacy, the Montreal native found himself more and more relaxed in the protected environment of Pittsburgh.

A transformation was taking place in the city. The once

blue-collar town, dominated by steel and its support industries, was reflecting a more affluent middle-class service economy. A modern, clean, progessive look replaced the smokestacks and grime. At the hockey games the once rough, boozer crowds became more upscale. Mario symbolized Pittsburgh's awakening and the advance of the city. Going to the Igloo to watch the Penguins became a social occasion, not just a jock pursuit. Large numbers of women, almost as many as men, attended the games. Mario had brought about the change, and just as he was becoming more identified as a family man, there appeared a long-locked, princely Czech whose stride and reach and creativity evoked visions of Mario himself. His first name, Jaromir, unscrambled perfectly into "Mario, Jr." Jaromir Jagr would carry the glamor torch forward.

Mario had joined one of the finest golf clubs in America, Pittsburgh's Oakmont. There, the steely-eyed Ben Hogan had walked to glory and Johnny Miller, with some of the purest iron play the game had ever seen, had won the U.S. Open. In the less rarefied atmosphere of Jimmy Maggs' place, Mario bowled, becoming reasonably proficient at it. He'd also taken up horse-back riding. Sitting tall in the saddle, he was initiated into its risks one day when his head banged square into a low-hanging branch of a tree. He emerged with a lump the size of a Titleist.

Penguins' management looked on happily at the evolution of Mario into a "burgher." So many athletes played in their cities with the attitude of borrowed species. At the sound of the season's final whistle, they were back on native soil. Mario had been so much the Montrealer when he arrived, so French-Canadian in tongue and look and longing, that few thought a substantial transfer of allegiance possible. But by 1989, in just five years, Americans had become his closest friends, an American had become his agent, Pittsburgh had become his summer home as well as his winter one. It was now his first city and he let it be known that following his retirement from hockey, he planned to stay in Pittsburgh, to make it his last city as well.

Beyond his fusion with his immediate family—and nothing could ever diminish that bond—the old ties with Montreal friends were falling victim to the gradual erosion that living apart inevitably brings. The plateau on which Mario was now elevated made the relationships, no matter how unpretentious or self-effacing a person he was, harder to sustain. Carl Parker was married, living in Gatineau, Quebec, just outside Ottawa, and working for Bell Telephone. He still played hockey in various amateur leagues and he often found himself having to defend his old friend. Parker's teammates granted that Mario was a special player, but wondered what was wrong with him. Why did they never hear anything about him? Why was he such a dud? Carl told them Mario liked to play great hockey and leave it at that. "And what is wrong with that?" he'd say. "That's the way he is."

Mario and Carl had been close friends from eight to eighteen. They'd played on the Black Machine together, they'd boxed in Mario's basement, they'd cruised the streets of Laval in junior. But Parker no longer felt that he could be a real friend. Mario had become too much of a god to be a friend. In his presence, Parker confessed to awe. The December Mario returned to Montreal for treatment of a bad knee, Carl and his wife went to the Lemieuxs' home. Thrilled to see Mario, thrilled to be given an audience, Parker asked him to autograph a hockey stick. Mario felt uncomfortable. He said he couldn't do such a thing for an old friend, but Carl insisted. "You're not my friend, you're my idol."

"Ah, come on," said Mario. "You're embarrassing me. Don't say those stupid things."

But Parker pressed, and Mario finally signed the stick. When Parker left the Lemieux household, he was so excited at having talked to Mario Lemieux that he was, in his own words, "jumping in the streets."

One of the old gang who had moved on to the big leagues was Marc Bergevin. He played first for the Chicago Blackhawks and later Tampa Bay. When their teams played against one another, Marc and Mario would get together for a couple of beers. Bergevin tried to keep the conversation off hockey. He'd joke around, tease Mario, get him in a light frame of mind, ease the pressure that he suspected Mario felt over having to keep everyone happy. "We never talked about hockey or how good he is," said Bergevin. "He knew that I knew that."

Once in a while, Mario saw Ron Stevenson, the old coach from bantam days. He turned up at a party celebrating Stevenson's retirement from the Montreal police department. When he saw Stevenson, he'd kid him about the grueling on-ice chase he would put the players through. Stevenson would send two players out first and two players following, then replace the two chasers with fresh bodies and kept on doing it until they caught the rabbits. The exercise was to build up endurance. Stevenson always believed in making the players practice when they were tired so they would know how to play tired during games.

Albert Mandanici's son Joey, who had played peewee against Mario, saw him occasionally. He found out about Lemieux's continuing attitude toward training one summer day when Mario, a few years in Pittsburgh under his belt, came home to Montreal. The two of them played golf. They weren't up to much afterward and Joey said, "I'm going over to the gym to work out. Why don't you come along?" Mario gave Mandanici a give-me-a-break look. "Come on, Joey, you know I don't train." Mandanici knew. He just wanted to see whether it was still the case.

Bob Perno, a strong tie for Mario to Montreal, had now faded from the picture. There was still Pierrette, of course. But in Pittsburgh, her influence over Mario was a bit of a sore spot. Paul Martha could see how she had spoiled him. "Oh, terrible. Oh, it was terrible," he said. "You know, we used to figure out how to keep his mom out of town for games. They are French, and when they'd win a game, she'd love to party and Mario would be up until 2:30 in the morning 'cause the Lemieuxs would all stay at his house." The problem was discussed with Mario and he understood management's point, Martha said. He too knew that it was sometimes better to have Mom in Montreal.

While Mario still maintained tight ties with his immediate family, a new group had come to exert considerable influence over his life. They included Martha, Jimmy Maggs, Tom Mathews, and Tom Reich. They were there when Mario fell into occasional folly, such as in the building of his new home in Mount Lebanon. In this, the area where the team practiced, the homes averaged between $300,000 and $500,000. Mario decided to have a behemoth constructed, at a price tag of about $1.5 million. Tom Mathews, who was in the construction business, got involved in the project, but a slew of problems came with it. Martha and Jimmy Maggs suspected that the architects and builders took advantage of the young big spender. The word got out that Mario's new home came with doorways so low that Mario would crack his forehead if he walked in without bending over. There were problems with the swimming pool and structural problems throughout the home. Maggs, feeling Mathews had made a mess of it, headed up a rescue operation with Paul Martha. A new contractor was brought in. "Mario built too much of a house for the neighborhood," said Martha. "He shouldn't have done that. But Mario being Mario, he was going to do it." There were "just a series of problems and we didn't want him to have problems. We wanted him to concentrate on playing hockey. So we got involved in trying to help him."

The difficulties of daily living, while bad enough, were

nothing compared to the problems with Esposito and Ubriaco. Each year had brought an increased measure of optimism about Penguin prospects. For the 1989–1990 season, there was talk of the Pens making the leap into the league's front-rank teams. Having gathered some playoff experience and brought in a good goaltender, and with a seasoned Lemieux leading a power attack, there could be no more excuses. "It is different for us all now," said Mario. "We've made a lot of progress as a team. Our goal is to finish in first place in our division, that's for sure. I think we have a lot of confidence in ourselves." He went even further. "Certainly, getting to the Stanley Cup final is the goal we have. That's all I'm working for now: to have a shot at the Cup this year. And to keep improving." Personal triumphs for Mario were just as important. He was confident of some day surpassing the league's two glorious records: 92 goals in a season and 215 points in a season. "They will come," he said, matter-of-factly. "One of these years, I'll score 216 points or something like that."

But any and all enthusiasm was tempered by Ubriaco and Esposito. The coach, sounding confident, was posting new goals for "Ace" this year. One was to see him in the running for the Frank Selke Trophy as the NHL's best defensive forward. "I don't want him to win it," Ubriaco said, "just get some votes. Gretzky never got any votes for that one. But Ace is capable because he can do the job all over the ice."

Mario had his goals, too. One of them was to terminate Ubriaco's NHL coaching career. He wanted him fired, along with his friend Tony Esposito. Many of the other Penguins also felt that the gruesome twosome was not the pair to lead them. At the beginning of the summer Mario had candidly told journalist Tom Lapointe how he felt. "He told me one night how pissed off he was about Tony Esposito," Lapointe said. "He said that 'One of these days, I'm going to have his head.'" Lapointe wrote the story, though not in words so harsh. When it appeared on the streets of Montreal, the word quickly got down to Lemieux in Pittsburgh. "Mario called me the day after from his house and gave me shit," recalled Lapointe. "He said, 'How come you wrote that? You put me in shit.'" Lapointe tried to explain himself. "I said, 'Mario, don't take it this way. You never told me it was off the record. I thought I could write it.'" Mario said he understood, but the timing was bad and maybe Lapointe should have been more careful.

That the season, before it began, looked to be headed for disaster was highly apropos for Mario Lemieux. Most every advance made in his career had been twinned with crisis or controversy, and this was only the beginning. For the quiet man who only wanted to play and, once away from the arena, be left in the shadows, there would be no peace. Whenever it looked as if all the hurdles had been cleared and the track opened, new, more imposing barriers blocked his way. Mario's talent came easily. Nothing else did.

As a junior he had faced national indignation for refusing to compete in the world championships. He had to go to court to win the right to play in league games. He did smash Guy Lafleur's all-time QMJHL goals' record, but no sooner had he done so than he faced a bitter confrontation with his coach and humiliation at the Memorial Cup. He couldn't get to the NHL without going through the biggest draft-day controversy the NHL had ever witnessed. He landed in a foreign culture with the league's most pitiful franchise. Even his good seasons were marred by his team's inability to make the playoffs. When the club did finally get going, the coaching went sour and the general manager used racial slurs to insult him. He scored in great bushels, but the Gretzky numbers always overshadowed him. Of all the times in its history that he was fated to enter the league, it was in the shadow of the most dominant player the game had ever seen. When he finally won something, the Canada Cup, the powers that be gave the big prize to the man who had set him up. When he finally conquered his rival on the scoring charts, they denied him the MVP award.

But if it had been difficult for Mario Lemieux until now, the worst was yet to come. If he thought the trials to this point had been daunting enough, he was deluding himself. It was as if the gods, having blessed him with talent more abundant than any other, had decided that he must pay for this fortune and pay dearly.

In the previous year, 1988, he had come to an interim agreement on contract terms. To begin the 1989–1990 campaign, he signed a new long-term pact. Summoned to Youngstown, Ohio, by Edward DeBartolo, he was handed a cheque for $100,000. This was the bonus money Mario would have received had he been named MVP. DeBartolo thought he was MVP, as did Mario. So, in a gesture that was appreciated, DeBartolo gave him the award money. He then signed Mario to a $12-million, five-year deal. Before Wayne Gretzky had signed with the Kings the previous summer, no pro hockey player had ever earned a million dollars for a single season. But Gretzky had set a new standard with his $2-million-plus contract and the Penguins had little choice but to match it. Mario, therefore, had Gretzky's move to L.A. to thank for a dramatic increase in income.

Having settled the contract matter, he had the coach and GM to take care of. He didn't wait long—one game into the season— before leveling his first broadside. In the opener Pittsburgh allowed five power-play goals in a 5–4 loss to Boston. Lemieux indelicately pointed out to the media that it might have helped if the club had spent some time practicing their special teams.

Dismal Penguin performances followed the Boston game. During a three-game home losing streak, the words heard most often from the players were, "We weren't ready." Translation:

the coach hasn't been doing his job. Lemieux got in another blast, pointing out that Ubriaco's constant line shuffling was disrupting the team. Penguin players who'd been traded away told reporters in other cities of the dissension in the club. Don Cherry picked up the story line and announced, correctly, that the Penguins were playing like a team trying to get their coach fired.

Ubriaco and Esposito had had a winning season their first time out. The Penguins had reached the playoffs under them and moved beyond the first round. Now, on the heels of one losing streak, a mutiny was under way. Esposito defended his coach. "We're not making any coaching changes," he vowed. "We just need to work harder." But Esposito may well have guessed that Mario was doing everything he could to finish off his tenure. Mario's stops at Jimmy Maggs' bowling alley and bar were more frequent. Maggs was on the line to Martha. Martha, who hadn't wanted Esposito running the team in the first place, was on the line to DeBartolo.

Lemieux had twenty-four points in fourteen games, compared to forty-one in the same number of outings the previous year. On October 31, Gretzky's Kings came to town and smothered the Penguins 8–4. Gretzky scored three goals and threw in three assists—a six-point night. Lemieux had two assists. He complained of not feeling well and submitted himself to a series of medical tests. He said he felt a loss of power in his body. Instead of skating around a defenseman one on one, now he would move off to the side, looking for a passing outlet. "I'm not skating as well as I did last year for some reason. I don't have my legs. I don't have the jump I had last year. Hopefully, that can come back."

The tests proved negative: no hepatitis, no viral infection, no thyroid condition, no mononucleosis. Perhaps yet another new linemate would cheer him up, suggested Ubriaco. Rob Brown's promise had begun to fade. He had become another example of a Lemieux-made scorer who, once on his own, deprived of the magical set-ups, became just an ordinary player. Now the Penguins moved American Olympian Kevin Stevens over to his unnatural position, the right side, to play with Mario. Stevens, a native of Brockton, Massachusetts, was a sixth-round L.A. Kings draft pick in 1983, who was then traded to Pittsburgh. He played four seasons for Boston College. In his last year there, 1986–1987, he scored seventy points. He played for Muskegon of the IHL much of Ubriaco's first year with Pittsburgh. But called up for the final seventeen games with the Penguins in 1988, he scored eleven goals, then was third in team scoring in the playoffs.

Not much was made of Stevens' temporary graduation to the Lemieux line. There had been so many, why would this one be any different? Few could see that he would become the long-sought, ideal winger to complement Mario. Stevens fit the mold of a basketball power forward, moving swiftly with cannon-fired strength toward the net. There was overdrive yet ease in his acceleration. He was a tall, noble-looking Marc Antony, with dark, radiant hair and handsome sculpted features. About his alert play, he was modest. "There aren't too many different ways I can play," he said. "I pretty much go up and down the wing, play my game, get some shots off."

Shortly after Ubriaco moved Stevens to Lemieux's wing, Ubriaco was gone. The fans in Pittsburgh, who had been quite patient through Mario's early years, were beginning to lose that patience. The coach, as was the custom in these situations, was the logical target, and in the case of Ubriaco, the burghers developed a particular dislike. In the Igloo the coaches had to walk across the ice surface to get to the dressing room. Such was the taunting by fans that shortly after coming to Pittsburgh, Ubriaco gave up on that practice. Instead, he crept down through a tunnel connected to the bench and walked under the dark stands. "It was amazing," said Lemieux's friend Bill Kelly. "You're supposed to lead your men into battle, not crawl underneath the stands."

The fans were in a particularly hostile mood the night of November 28. During a 6–3 loss to Philadelphia, the boos rained down on the players. Not even Mario Lemieux was spared. He heard the catcalls when his name was announced on an assist. He took note. "It does have an effect on human beings and I'm no exception to that," Lemieux said. "If I'm not playing well, they're allowed to boo me, which they did tonight."

But the worst treatment was reserved for Ubriaco. "Fire the coach!" the spectators chanted. "Fire the coach!" Others worked variations on the theme. "Pack your bags, Gene-o! Pack your bags!" Mario listened. He'd known for some time that their wishes were about to come true. During a recent road trip, the subject of the coach and GM had come up. Disparaging comments filled the cabin of the airplane, including a few choice remarks from Mario. Paul Steigerwald was on board. At one point, Lemieux turned to him and said, "Don't worry. We'll have a Christmas present for them."

"Mario knew then," said Steigerwald. "He was part of the reason it happened. He was party to it. And believe me, he did everyone a favor."

The Lemieux–Esposito conflict was grounded in more than racial slurs. Once, leaving Madison Square Garden in New York, the car Lemieux was in was assaulted by hoods who almost got to him. Mario asked Esposito for security protection following games, but was denied the request. Because of his chronic back problems, he asked that the team hire a masseur. It wasn't a major demand—other teams in the league had them— but Esposito also rejected that idea. There was little communication between the two men. Esposito had one of the world's top two players, but, inexplicably, could show him no respect.

Mario's views on Esposito and Ubriaco, whom he also

thought guilty of ethnic name-calling, registered resoundingly in the Penguin boardrooms. As Mario predicted, they got their Christmas presents—and well before the big day. On December 5 the Penguins announced that Craig Patrick, athletic director at the University of Denver, would replace the two of them.

Esposito took the news graciously. Not so Ubriaco, who smelled plotters in Coffey and Lemieux and declared that these two players had purposefully deserted him. Ubriaco saved his best shot for Lemieux. Trying to coach Mario, he declared, was "like trying to teach a shark table manners." In the end, "guys like Mario and Paul were awfully greedy," the coach said. "I've always been a team guy. I never liked catering to one or two guys on a team." He said he tried to reason with the players, but it didn't work. He would have preferred to be tougher as a coach, but if he tried that style, their power was such that he "wouldn't have lasted that first year."

Coffey and Lemieux responded. "All it does is reassure me and twenty-five guys on this team that Gene is and was the backstabber we thought he was," said Coffey. As could be expected after he'd been compared to a dinner-table shark, Mario's rejoinder had even less finesse. "He's been a backstabber since he got here," he declared. "The names he was calling me and my agent back then. . . . An intelligent human being doesn't do that. I'm just glad he's gone. We don't have to deal with him." Ubriaco, said Lemieux, "spent fifteen years in the minors when he was playing and when he was coaching and that's where he belongs." The vicious remarks didn't surprise Mario's friends. They knew that once crossed, he was not the type to turn the other cheek. He could carry a grudge. Get on his bad side, you remained there.

Patrick, forty-three, became the eighth general manager in the club's history. The division the Pens played in was named after his grandfather, Lester Patrick, who had coached and managed the New York Rangers to three Stanley Cup titles. Craig's father, Lynn, and uncle, Muzz, were also successful NHL players and coaches. Craig Patrick had played eight years in the NHL as a forward, then ran the Rangers from 1981–1986 before going to Denver.

He was low key, quiet—detractors would say "boring"— but knew how to command respect from a cast of egos who were not easy to manage. Patrick wanted to change the style of the team to a more defensive orientation. "The things I will stress are conditioning, hard work, and adherence to a defensive system. I believe that the innate offensive abilities that this team has can take care of the offensive part of the game. I will insist on adherence to a defensive system."

The Penguins didn't know it at the time, but therein lay the foundation for future triumphs. Patrick demanded that puck pursuit, defensive play in all three zones, become a priority. "Puck pursuit—that's the kind of system we played in Edmonton," said Coffey, whose brilliance as an offensive free spirit would be less welcome in the new system. "You can't give players a lot of time in this league." Patrick, he said, was talking the same kind of language as Edmonton coaches Glen Sather and John Muckler.

"It's been proven that it takes a good defense to win a Stanley Cup," observed Lemieux. "That's what we have to do here in Pittsburgh. We've got good players who can put the puck in the net. Now it's just a matter of getting a good system and following it."

Mario began to score in great numbers again. Happy with the new management, he had the spring back in his step. He put together a scoring streak—at least one point per game—that was beginning to rival Gretzky's record streak of fifty-one. He had the junior hockey record, a point or more in sixty-three straight games. Now the big one looked within his grasp. His incredible form was most evident in his performance at the annual all-star game in January 1990. This time, the big dance was held in Pittsburgh. The entire NHL was focused on Lemieux. A major American TV network was covering the game for the first time. Mario would be head to head against Gretzky. All-stars' coach Pat Burns asked him if he wanted to be put out when Gretzky was on. Mario said do it.

Seldom had Mario had more incentive to strut his stuff. He had won two MVP awards in his first five all-star game appearances. Few thought his performance in St. Louis, where he gathered the second MVP title, could be topped. But a tiny twenty-one seconds into the game, he looped out from behind the net to score his first goal. On his second shot of the period, he scored again. On his third shot, another. The arena was bedlam. Mario was turning the all-star game into a one-man extravaganza. In the last two periods he added a fourth goal.

In the 12–7 Wales Conference victory, Gretzky went scoreless. He was on the ice for all four of Mario's goals. Burns was asked if Mario was trying to tell Gretzky something. "I don't think Mario was trying to make any kind of statement," he replied, "but even Wayne smiled one time when he scored one of those goals."

"I could tell before the game he was pumped up," Gretzky said. "Then he scored the first goal on his first shift and he took his game up a few more notches in a hurry."

Jimmy Maggs looked on approvingly. His guy was doing just what he said he could do under fair and decent conditions. In the all-star games, Maggs noted, there wasn't a laying on of lumber. In the all-star games, Mario wasn't surrounded by duds. Was it any surprise that in such circumstances, Mario would show himself time and time again to be the finest in the land? No one had ever taken runs at number 99 when he was setting the records, said Maggs. He took the odd heavy hit, but you could count the number of times he got them on one hand. Maggs was right. Gretzky would never acknowledge it, but there was indeed an unwritten rule that you didn't run him. He was small, he was golden, he was the game. Number 66 was too big ever to be accorded that kind of respect. But in the all-star games he got it and, said Maggs, "Look what happened." Against the Russians he got that respect and, said Maggs, "Look what happened."

Pierrette Lemieux had come to Pittsburgh for the all-star game, so of course there was a big party. Mario invited some friends back. Tom Lapointe was one, Pat Burns another. Sean O'Donnell, the owner of the Bourbon Street bar, came along, as did some of Mario's golfing friends. Teammates weren't there. As was normally the case, Mario didn't socialize with team-mates, except on road trips. Teammates were another category.

At the party, Mario's aunt got on the piano and, with the star himself in full voice, the bacchanalia began. It lasted until four or five in the morning. "Some say this guy doesn't talk or laugh much," said Lapointe. "But he's a very happy man in situations like that with his own people, with people he trusts." Lapointe had rarely seen Mario as happy as he was that night. Everything now looked to be right. He was in his prime, with a new coach and GM, with a team full of talent. His scoring streak was bearing down on the record. His health was intact, his life good.

But it wasn't supposed to be so good. The Mario script wasn't written that way. And so, within days of those fabulous hours in Pittsburgh, the fates turned on him. The lower back began to ache and the pain was sharper this time and more enduring. It wouldn't go away. It had never been like this before. Before, it had always gone away.

As February began, he played hard through the pain. He took the lead in the scoring race and, with three goals and an assist against Edmonton, he extended his scoring streak to forty-one games. He was fitted for a brace, which was designed to relax the back muscles and the discs. "It's bad every day," he confessed, "but it's getting worse and worse." Normally, he would have sat out the odd game under these conditions, but he didn't want to give up the streak so easily. So he continued to play, aggravating the condition.

He stayed away from practices and decided to play only the power plays. He kept chalking up the points that way. By February 14, 1990, when he traveled to New York's Madison Square Garden, the streak was at forty-six games. Five to go to the Gretzky mark. Just a few more weeks and the record would be his.

The back was so bad he couldn't play much in the Garden. In the first period he didn't have a good chance to get a point. In the second, he started a play that led to a goal, but he didn't draw an assist. Two other Penguins touched the puck before the goal scorer did. By the end of the second period, he could play no more. The pain had become so wrenching that he couldn't hang around for the possibility of a power play in the final twenty minutes. When he left, he looked about as forlorn as anyone had ever seen him. The streak was over.

Following a few days of physical therapy, Mario, unable to touch below his knees, was sent—Jimmy Maggs accompanying him—to a spine specialist in Los Angeles. He had a herniated disc and an arthritic condition in his lower back. The doctors decided to put him through a therapy program, which would improve his condition, hopefully, to the point where surgery could be avoided. He was given cortisone shots and he began trunk-strengthening and isometric exercises. Similar programs had worked for baseball players, golfers, and other athletes.

If, after a month, no improvement was evident, team doctor Charles Burke said surgery would probably be required. There was always a possibility with this kind of surgery, he noted, that something terrible could happen. "There's a small chance that the surgery could be career-threatening," he said. Should Mario's back be destabilized, the doctor explained, severe back pain would continue, preventing him from playing hockey. Other athletes had had disks successfully removed, but the destabilization in the other areas of the back, he added, had made a return to action most difficult.

More currency was given to optimistic scenarios. The Penguins felt there was a very good chance Mario would be back and healthy and, if the team made the playoffs, leading the Penguins into them. Indeed, following six weeks of strengthening exercises on the lower back, abdomen, and legs, Mario reported considerable improvement and a desire to get back on the ice. On March 22, he resumed some light skating. On March 30 he was whisked back to Pittsburgh to suit up for the Penguins' final game of the season. Without Lemieux, the team had slumped miserably in the stretch run, winning only one of twelve games. Now they needed a win against Buffalo to make the playoffs. Mario hadn't played in almost two months. He'd sat out in California, rather bored, doing therapy every day, and not much else.

His back was far from healed, but the team considered it worth the risk to put him on the ice for the one critical game. "We'll see what happens in the warm-up," said Mario. "I feel I can help the team, especially on the power play. . . . There's always a risk involved, but I feel that it's a risk that I can deal with. I've been itching for a month and a half now. It was pretty tough over there, just watching the team."

Though a limited role was prescribed for him, no such limited role ensued. Mario played twenty-five minutes, more than any other forward in the game. In one stretch he played four minutes straight without leaving the ice. He scored a goal on a long slap shot that had to have used every back muscle imaginable. He added an assist. His effort helped propel the team into overtime. Now one goal in this, a meaningless game for the Sabres, would decide the Penguins' fate.

It was decided on a clearing pass that didn't get out of their zone. Uwe Krupp, the Sabres' big defenseman, stopped it at the blue line and shot from there. Barrasso didn't look ready. The puck went in and the Penguins, stunned, went on another early summer vacation. It was Mario's sixth season with the Penguins. They had made the playoffs only once.

Mario at least felt relieved that his back had held up. He said he wouldn't know for sure for a day or two, but the signs were positive. "It felt all right out there. It's just a matter of keeping with the [exercise] program now, every day for a couple of hours. It's going to be part of my life now."

When he left the Igloo that day, he felt he wouldn't need to have career-threatening surgery. Soon, he was repairing to the golf course and shooting low scores. The sport required much back muscle movement, but he wasn't deterred. He could still hit 300-yard drives, those beauties that zoom off on a low trajectory and, as if jet-propelled, then take to the skies and fall gently, somewhere beyond the range of eyesight.

Whether the tee shots had anything to do with it (unlikely, doctors said) was unknown, but by the end of June, the back pain had returned and it was piercing. It would recede for a while, then reassert itself. There was some second-guessing. Why on earth had they allowed him to play golf, to take those thrashing cuts at the ball every day? Penguins' management felt, however, that he had to be tested. If his back couldn't hold up playing golf, how would it hold up playing hockey? They wanted to know.

The final decision regarding surgery rested with Mario. "He called me on June 28," said Chip Burke, the team doctor. "His pain had worsened and the symptoms had returned to a level we had not seen for several months. I could sense that he himself had a change of feelings." Mario appeared in the Penguins' front office and told Martha, "I think I'm going to have an operation." The Penguins contacted a nationally renowned neurologist to find the best doctor to do the operation. While they had been clear about the dangers of surgery before, now they were sounding optimistic. "He'll be back skating and hopefully playing by the beginning of the season," said Dr. Burke. These operations, he said, in words that would return to haunt him, were a pretty sure thing. "The chances of complications are very small and very rare. I know that's sort of hard to understand, but this is a routine operation. There are many people who have had this operation and made a full and total recovery."

FIFTEEN
CAREER THREAT

A COUPLE OF MONTHS AFTER ALL THE ASSURANCES WERE GIVEN about it being a rather routine operation, Mario Lemieux was confined to a room in deep pain, wondering whether he would ever play the game again.

The doctor, Peter Sheptak, had performed the surgery on July 11, 1990. He labeled his work "technically, a success," said he was "optimistic about nothing going wrong," and anticipated "a fast recovery." There was one caveat. "He did have a mild crack in a supporting structure of the bone that was related to some old trauma, probably from hockey. That could make him more susceptible to some backaches and discomfort in the future."

Lemieux, at base an optimist, not one to second-guess himself for ignoring doctor's orders on back-strengthening exercises way back in his junior days, sounded relieved and delighted. A few days after the operation, he spoke of soon returning to peak form, perhaps even returning to a life in hockey entirely free of back pain. Entirely free of it!

He planned to be ready for the opening of training camp on September 7. If not then, certainly for the regular-season opener a month later. In late August he skated a relaxed fifteen minutes, fiddling with the puck, making it dance on his stick, flipping it into an empty goal. "It was definitely the right decision to have the surgery," he said after the skate. "I feel great pain-wise. My legs especially feel a lot stronger. There's no leg pain at all."

His enthusiasm shrank in mid-September. During a Penguins' exhibition swing through Texas, he woke up to pain. He hoped it was a false alarm, something temporary. Maybe he had slept at the wrong angle. But the pain continued and became so searing he had to fly back to Pittsburgh. At home it still wouldn't leave him, and there was something more distressing: it wasn't the usual hurt. These spears were deeper and sharper-edged. This was a new condition.

The doctors told him he had contracted an infection that, in layman's terms, was eating away at his spine. The infection likely hadn't done much damage, they told him, and it was very likely curable.

But Mario had heard these kinds of assurances before. If what they said was true, why could he barely even walk? He had been so confident that, with the surgery, his back problems had finally been cured. The whole point of going through the operation was to get the persistent disorder behind him. Now, for the first time, the steely, quiet confidence that characterized Lemieux had left him. For the first time, he felt uncertain about the future. He felt that his destiny was no longer in his own hands and it staggered him. He believed there was a good chance that his career would be over, finished at age twenty-five, before he could show Gretzky and the rest of the world that he was the very best.

Having less faith in doctors, Mario now turned to religion. He got hold of Father Michel Fortin, the priest in Quebec City who lived in the rectory where nine-year-old Mario had run the halls. Mario told the priest of his condition, laid it out in stark terms, suggesting that he might have played his last hockey game.

The sport was all he had, he told the priest. What kind of life would it be if he was deprived of what he had been put on the earth to do? "What if," Father Fortin recalled him saying, "you were in my position? Imagine if they told you that you had to stop being a priest tomorrow. What would you do?" He asked the priest to pray for him. "This is what I face. Hockey is what is in my heart. Pray for me so that I can get better again."

Fortin found Mario more depressed than he had ever been before. He had never talked this way. Dr. Burke had seen him distressed on many occasions over the back pain. He'd seen him standing in the dressing room, the tears in his eyes, bent by the frustration. But he had never seen Mario so low. "I thought this was over," he recalled Mario, in tears, saying. "I thought this would go away and not bother me."

"He was just so frustrated, so upset," said Burke. "He had been doing better. It was like it was almost too much for him." What people don't understand, the doctor added, is "the frustration factor that builds with the recurrence and the recurrence and the recurrence. That poor kid. Every time he thought that the problem had been solved, the answer found, something else popped up."

No one, not even the best surgeons, knew if, when, or how the trauma of the back would ever end. The doctors even disagreed among themselves. Before the summer's surgery there had been a difference of opinion on the nature of his back problem. The suspicion was that Mario suffered from a herniated disc. But he didn't have the classic symptoms of a herniated disc. When the pain came back in the fall, the debates started all over again. This time, whisper campaigns centered on the performance of the doctors themselves. What about the fantastically high success rate of these operations? Had something gone wrong during it? Had the doctor's work been sloppy, inferior? Had this led to the current problems that were threatening the career of one of the greatest hockey players in the world? If something had gone wrong during the operation, would the doctors ever admit it? Or would they, with the obvious advantage of their technical knowledge, be able to smother all dissent?

Initially, the doctors had said his California rehabilitation program could very well eliminate the need for surgery. This had not proved to be the case. After his West Coast rehabilitation, he was allowed to play golf. Shouldn't they have held off a few months before giving the go-ahead on that? Then came the surgery. They were so optimistic, so wrongly optimistic of its success.

It was serious business. One medical mistake could perhaps cost Mario his career. For precedents, some looked to the case of Bobby Orr twenty years earlier. Orr, the best of his time, had surgery on his knee and never recovered. An endless number of operations followed, but none could repair the condition that had resulted from the first. Orr's career ended ten years before it need have and it was never determined whether the injury itself or the doctor's treatment of it was chiefly responsible. He retired a resentful man, perhaps rightfully so.

In the case of Mario Lemieux, Dr. Chip Burke could find no fault in his performance or that of any of his colleagues. Any such speculation, he maintained, was the result of press reports, "just things written in the media which, we all know, are ninety-five percent wrong." In May 1993, he would say, "[Mario's] still playing and still playing well, so I must have done a pretty good job."

On October 25, 1990, the doctors called a press conference to tell the world what had gone wrong after the surgery. Lemieux had what they termed a disk space infection—an infection that could cause spine erosion. This infection, the doctors said, had not occurred as a result of Dr. Sheptak's surgery. Rather, it resulted from a sinus condition Mario picked up in early September. Bacteria got into his bloodstream. These bacteria circulated through the body and, before they were killed off by white cells, they had found their way to scar tissue formed from his surgery. The bacteria seeded the scar tissue and caused the infection.

How much damage had the infection rendered? Minimal, the doctors said. Heavy antibiotics could kill it off. Mario could be back on skates within three months, they insisted. On the other hand, chances did exist, as Dr. Burke acknowledged in the press conference, that the condition could be "career-threatening." It was a "real possibility," he stated.

This, the possibility that the end could be at hand, figured prominently in headlines that sped throughout the sporting world. Burke was furious at what he termed the sensationalism of the media, particularly a Pittsburgh newspaper report upon which many national and international stories were based. It described Mario as having contracted a rare bone disease, vertebral osteomyelitis. A medical specialist had been assigned to do the newspaper story and had drawn his conclusions from interviews with Burke and others. Burke was furious at the report, but in fact, he had left other journalists either confused or with the same impression.

Reports also said that doctors had initially wrongly diagnosed the postsurgical affliction as spondylolysis, the breaking down of bones in the vertebrae, and that they had started treatments on the basis of this faulty diagnosis. Burke later denied this as he denied every suggestion of doctors' wrongdoing.

On balance, noted Burke, the outlook was positive. "The things Mario has going in his favor are that the bone damage was not extensive, it was diagnosed quickly, treatment was started quickly, and he has responded to that treatment as fast—or faster—than we expected."

While the doctors' performance was said to be exemplary,

could the same be said for the patient's? When Burke was told that during his junior career, Mario had ignored Dr. Réal Lemieux's advice, Burke chuckled and interjected, "Nothing's changed."

Mario still smoked, he still didn't work out. While Burke, a great admirer of Mario's, didn't appreciate this, he understood it and was reluctant to fault him. "Mario Lemieux is so much better than everyone else as a hockey player that it's hard for people to understand. I've seen him play games at twenty-five percent and still be better than the others. . . . Say you were a golfer and you shot sixty-two every time you played and you won the tournaments. Would you go out and work on your game? Why? To shoot sixty-one when you're already beating everyone?"

Burke couldn't say for sure whether conditioning might have helped reduce Mario's chances of back torment. Through several years of treating him, Burke noticed that Mario particularly slacked off on his prescribed exercise programs when things were going well and the back wasn't bothering him. "But that is exactly the same as every other patient I take care of." The compliance rate for people following his rehabilitation programs, Burke said, was only twenty-five percent. He did not seem to think that in Mario's case, where his health was such a precious resource, more should have been expected.

The doctor believed that the problem stemmed from Mario being so tall and playing the center position. He suggested half-seriously one day that Mario should play defense. Mario looked at him as if he was crazy. Paul Coffey, Dr. Coff as some called him, thought that Mario's problem was likely in the lie of his skates. But Mario had heard that in junior and had tried different skates, to no avail.

So now he faced another period of grave uncertainty. With at least three months projected as the time for recovery from the infection, Mario could perhaps start playing again early in 1991. He had left the game in New York against the Rangers on

February 14, 1990, the back stress ending his magnificent run at Gretzky's fifty-one-game scoring streak. He had returned only for that one appalling loss to the Buffalo Sabres at season's end. He had not been able to start the new season. Thus, he was missing almost a full year of his career. It wasn't just any year. This absence came at twenty-five, the age when most hockey players were considered to be at their peak.

Mario took six weeks of antibiotic treatments, during which time he stayed far from the public eye. A more publicity-conscious athlete could have milked the story for public sympathy, but Mario just hid. The Penguins wanted it that way and Mario was only too happy to oblige. Even the medical staff, said Burke, was discouraged from speaking openly to the media. Though he wasn't a fan of the press, Burke thought this policy worked against Mario's best interests. He shared the view of many others that dismal public relations on the part of the Penguins over the years had had a serious impact on Mario's image.

The antibiotics did their work. They killed the infection leaving only, it seemed, marginal spinal damage. On December 21 Mario made his first public appearance in three months. Looking healthy, though slightly overweight, he greeted the media in a T-shirt, shorts, and sneakers, and rode a stationary bike for photographers. He described how frightening the experience had been. "I had some doubts that I would ever play the game again. . . . I think that was normal for anybody to think that way, with the way I was. But week after week, I started to get better." About the doctors' performances, he said, "I believe in our doctors. I believe I had some good doctors telling me what to do and what to expect in the future."

The year's layoff had left an impact on the way Mario saw life and the game. He had given the impression before that he took things for granted. Now he said he had a more mature perspective. "I see the game a lot differently now. Every time I have a chance to play the game I think I'll approach it a lot differently. It makes you think a lot and realize how lucky you are."

By late January, after a month of light workouts, he felt he could return to play. Though he had been away so long, this wasn't the type of athlete who easily retrogressed. No layoff could take away his hockey sense and vision. Regaining his flawless timing would require a stretch of games, but the main thing was that after all the trauma of not knowing whether his life's blood had been taken from him, he was returning.

He had missed fifty games of the new season, the 1990–1991 season. His hopes for the thirty that remained were unknown because General Manager Craig Patrick, who had an ogre's sense of public relations, had told Mario not to speak to the media until after his first game back. It came on the road, January 26, against the then dismal Quebec Nordiques. Skating sixteen shifts, totaling seventeen minutes of ice time, Mario scored three points, all on assists, in a 6–5 victory. He looked uncomfortable for the first few shifts but, quickly regaining his confidence and his deft sense with the puck, he began to maneuver splendidly, once slipping around defenseman Alexei Gusarov with majestic ease, leaving Gusarov lunging at him with both hands. Afterwards he said he wasn't sharp. "I made some plays that I don't normally make. It will take a while before I get back in the groove." The next morning he was relieved, and a bit surprised, to find no stiffness in his back.

Bob Johnson, the Penguins' new coach, put Lemieux on a line with Bob Errey and Mark Recchi. The cheery Johnson had been hired after the season-ending overtime loss to Buffalo, when Craig Patrick ceased filling the dual role of GM and coach. At the same time, Patrick brought in Scotty Bowman as director of player development and recruitment. Bowman had served as a color commentator for the Canadian Broadcasting

Corporation after his shining career as an NHL coach in St. Louis and Montreal had been diminished somewhat by his repeated failure to wrench the Buffalo Sabres from their bone-deep mediocrity.

Patrick called Johnson and Bowman "the best management team in the National Hockey League." Johnson had spent five years coaching in Calgary and had also coached many successful seasons with the University of Wisconsin. A high energy level marked this professor of the game, an energy level that was infectious. Many in the NHL felt he was the perfect candidate to exorcise the pall of despair that clung to the Penguin franchise.

But any optimism that Bob Johnson could bring was necessarily tempered by the long shadows of history. Lemieux had returned but, though his back felt well, for how long?

Pittsburgh fans got a look at their long-gone star when he returned from Quebec to play at home against the Washington Capitals. It was another festive occasion at the Igloo—the third in the past year, following on the heels of Mario's magnificent all-star game performance and his return for the last game of the season against Buffalo. Now the Igloo was festooned with bunting and signs that shouted "Mario! Mario! Mario!" and fans that cried the same.

So often a player for the occasion, Mario drew an assist early in the game and then, with only five minutes remaining, scored the tying goal. The Penguins won the game in overtime.

After two games, Mario had tallied five points. He pulled a groin muscle in Boston and had to sit out some more. When he came back, his play, while not at a peak, was good enough for a two-points-a-game average. "I'm still at the point where I'm testing myself and it's still in the back of my mind that I've got to be cautious," he said. "But I feel more confidence on the ice right now." The analysis was about as profound as Mario got on his condition and his play. He usually talked in clichés, giving only canned answers to the media. He gained a reputation as one of the most nondescript interviews in the league. Journalists found Mario frustrating because they suspected that he was a highly intelligent hockey player, capable, if he would only draw himself out, of insights far superior to the dross spewed out on a daily basis by unthinking athletes and coaches who could do no better than banal offerings like "He's got good work ethic."

When Mario rejoined the club after fifty games, the Penguins boasted a respectable 26–21–3 record. For the remaining games, with Lemieux in the line-up, they were at 15–12–3, roughly the same winning percentage. With or without Lemieux, this was becoming a fine hockey club. Under Craig Patrick, with input from Bowman, the Penguins had been dealing. They'd obtained Joey Mullen, a small but highly effective two-way player, from Calgary for a second-round draft choice. A bargain brought them Larry Murphy, the crafty defenseman, and Peter Taglianetti for Jim Johnson and Chris Dahlquist. And now, shortly after Mario's return, they bettered Hartford in a major exchange, gaining Ron Francis, Ulf Samuelsson, and Grant Jennings in return for John Cullen, Zarley Zalapski, and Jeff Parker. Francis, like Mullen, excelled both ways, while Cullen's talents were more offensively defined.

Murphy, Coffey, and Samuelsson provided strong, experienced, potent defense. Kevin Stevens had developed into a first-class winger. The talent of Jaromir Jagr was explosive and special. Mark Recchi was a sure-fire scorer and, for Stanley Cup experience, they had brought in Bryan Trottier of the New York Islanders. "There's less pressure on me," said Lemieux, "because we have a different team than we've had before."

Mario's back slowly strengthened through the remainder of the season. In the twenty-six regular-season games he played, he scored nineteen goals and added twenty-six assists for forty-five points. The Penguins captured the division title, their first in their twenty-four-year history. Mario didn't play in the clincher, March 27 in Detroit, this time sitting out with a wounded left eye that required fourteen stitches. But it was an important moment for him nevertheless. He had been with the team seven years, becoming one of the most senior players on the club. In all those years, this was the team's first real achievement. "I'm happy for all our guys, but especially guys like Mario Lemieux and Troy Loney and Bob Errey, guys who have been here the longest," said Bob Johnson. "Loney and Errey have been here eight years. Mario has been here seven. And they've never won anything. Never."

Lemieux stressed defense as the Penguins began the play-offs. If the defense was good, he said, the offense would take care of itself. Gone were the days when Mario was accused of playing the game only in the other team's end and when he scorned the critics by saying his job was just to score. Now he was a player who took pride in being able to stop the other team. Pierre Creamer, who had begun the practice of using him to kill penalties, could take some credit for developing his defensive consciousness.

Against New Jersey, the first playoff opponent, defense was the name of his game. He backchecked as much as anyone had ever seen him, content to let others help carry the attack. The Devils proved formidable, however, taking a 3–2 lead in games and giving themselves a chance to conclude the series at home. In a tight game six, Ron Francis scored the winner and the Penguins returned to the comfort of the Igloo. As luck, horrible Penguin luck, would have it, Mario went down before the decisive seventh game with back spasms. He couldn't play.

The recurrence itself didn't shock the team physician or Mario, just the timing of it. Burke knew and had advised Lemieux that the pain would periodically return. Fortunately, the Penguins were a team that had learned to play without Mario

Lemieux. They had played almost a full year without him. They had played better than .500 hockey without him, and in game seven, it showed. They played a disciplined game to beat the Devils 4–2, setting up a second-round confrontation with a woefully weak playoff team, the tinhearted Washington Capitals. The Pens lost the first game, but then obliterated the Caps in four straight. Kevin Stevens, his ascendancy to the ranks of the league's best wingers very apparent in these playoffs, scored the winning goal in three of the four victories. Ron Francis excelled, as he had against the Devils. Lemieux kept backchecking.

The Penguins had advanced to the Stanley Cup semifinals for the first time in their history. Now they would face a sterner test than in the first two rounds. Mike Milbury's Boston Bruins offered grit, power, and pride. They were capable of severely limiting Mario Lemieux's available space and did so. Bob Sweeney did the job in game one, holding Mario to a lone assist in a 6–3 Bruins' victory. To get more leg room in the cramped Boston Garden, Coach Johnson instructed Mario to stay in behind the rush, then pick up the opening and thread through it. The Professor, as Johnson was sometimes called because of his pensive demeanor, looked with scorn upon the diminutive ice surface, even measuring it to see if it was really as small as it looked. "You're in the neutral zone," he concluded, "and all of a sudden you're at the blue line." His criticism was specific to the Garden, but could have been said of all NHL arenas. The players in the NHL had gotten bigger, stronger, and faster, but the league had failed to take the trend into account. Rather than take out a couple of rows of seats to enlarge the ice surfaces and give the players more room, as they had on European ice, the NHL fathers remained tied to the status quo. Hockey played in crushed quarters meant more injuries, more fights, less room for skilled players, less art.

Mario was only too well aware of this. Since his first year

in the league, he had been complaining about how the game had been turned over to the clutch-and-grabbers. He escaped Sweeney's ensnarement enough to score two goals and an assist in the next game, but Boston still took a two-game lead in the series, winning 5–4 on an overtime marker by Vladimir Ruzicka. The Penguins had allowed six goals in the first game and absorbed five more in the second. They needed to tighten up in order to last. In game three, at the Igloo, Johnson assigned Lemieux to shadow the Bruins' star defenseman, Ray Bourque. Seven years earlier Mario had intercepted a Bourque pass to score his first goal on his first shift in the NHL. Now he spearheaded the Penguins' forechecking unit and counted a goal and an assist in a 4–1 victory to put his club back in the series. Mario is "coming back and stripping guys," observed the Pens' Mark Recchi, "checking low in our end. You can see the determination on his face, because he wants to win. He's a quiet kind of guy, but he's been more vocal on the bench and in the dressing room than I've ever seen him. He's excited. People say Mario doesn't concentrate on defense, but if that's all he worried about, he could probably be one of the top defensive players in the league."

Game three featured Ulf Samuelsson's open-ice "check" on Cam Neely. Samuelsson's knee figured prominently in the hit, slicing into Neely's thigh and felling him with what doctors labeled a "quad contusion." The assault enraged the Bruins. Milbury called Johnson "a professor of goonism," charging that he had instructed his players to make cheap hits. Milbury tried an assault strategy for game four, but its outcome was the same 4–1 score in favor of the Penguins. Tom Barrasso, who could be terribly hot and horribly cold, was all of the former in the two games in Pittsburgh. He continued in that vein when the series moved back to Boston, and Stevens and Lemieux lit up the Garden in a 7–2 Penguin victory. The Penguin attack, as Milbury acknowledged, was now as potent as any in the NHL.

"But their defense is where we didn't give them as much credit as they deserve."

Stevens, rocketing up and down the wing, had five points, but Lemieux, with four points on a goal and three assists, was taking charge of this series in both ends of the rink. He was playing, despite the fragile back, some of the most physical hockey of his life. The physical dimension was one that Gretzky, because of his lack of size, could never bring to the game. Mario could go through opponents as well as around them. Gretzky could only slither and circumnavigate. Mario was so big and heavy that he was almost impossible to move off the puck. His size and reach provided him with a greater defensive capability. His upper body had filled out since those first days in Pittsburgh when Paul Martha had gawked at his skinny top half, finding it rather freakish. He hadn't become muscular, but the proportions had improved.

Against the Bruins, the size was much needed. With a 3–2 lead the Penguins needed only a home-ice win to advance to the finals. They did it, 5–3, with five different players stepping forward to share in the scoring. Mario crowned the proceedings with a long empty-netter. At age twenty-five, he had reached the moment he had thought about since childhood, when hockey first began to consume his conscience.

Earlier in the season, in October, there had been the weeks when he could barely move and he thought it was over. Now his life had taken another improbable turn. He had recovered, his team had won its division, and he was leading the Penguins, a team that hadn't even made the playoffs a year earlier, into the Stanley Cup finals. "I didn't think," said Mario "that I'd be in this position at the end of the year, with all the problems I was having." His life had become a seesaw, alternating between highs and lows. There was no constancy to it, rarely times when the good stretched on and on, as it had for Wayne Gretzky.

Father Fortin's prayers must have worked. Lemieux's own prayers must have worked. It was somehow appropriate that in game six, when Mario sealed the Bruins' series with that empty-netter from 120 feet, he dropped to his knees. It was a show of ecstasy he had never made before. He had made it to the Cup and now he could drive a final spike into the coffin of those who said he wasn't a leader, wasn't a player who could take his team all the way.

Stanley Cups are often won partly on luck and now it was the good fortune of the Penguins to meet the Minnesota North Stars in the final. The North Stars, certainly on the basis of talent, offered only modest opposition. They finished the regular season with a meager sixty-eight points, far below .500 and twenty points fewer than the Penguins. They didn't belong in the playoffs with those numbers, much less at the finals of the big dance. With exceptional goalkeeping, they had suddenly caught fire in the playoffs, as any team can, and swept aside more talented clubs. But Pittsburgh, with its talent and a surging Lemieux (fifteen points against the Bruins), could not be expected to lose.

Mario had waited so long for the moment. Seven years. Yet, inexplicably, he failed to show up for the first game of the Stanley Cup final. His performance was reminiscent of occasional phantom games he had played in the past. He played, as one writer put it, "like a reluctant witness to a traffic accident." He scored one goal, but was on the ice for three from Minnesota. The Stars won 5–4. "I played badly," he admitted, sounding as mystified as everyone else. "I had no energy. I had no legs."

The Penguins had lost the first game of every series they had played in this Stanley Cup, but this loss came at home, which was worrisome. They more or less had to win the next home game before moving out to Minnesota. Lemieux advised a change of strategy. "One of the best ways I know to beat a good defense is with short, crisp passes. Almost all of our long cross-ice passes were intercepted in game one. It's something we'll definitely have to change."

Mario sealed a 4–1 victory in game two with one of the most exquisite goals of Stanley Cup history. It was a goal that had the Rocket's dash and Béliveau's panache. It was a goal only smaller players, those who can maintain their balance while making crazy shifts, are supposed to be able to execute.

Mario took a lead pass in the center zone from Phil Bourque and crossed the North Star blue line. Minnesota defensemen Shawn Chambers and Neil Wilkinson were back. They were positioned twelve feet inside the blue line and they slowly drew toward one another to close off a potential Lemieux burst through the middle. They wanted to force him to the outside. That, in fact, is what Chambers had done on a similar Lemieux rush earlier in the game. But Lemieux remembered. This time, he shifted strongly to the middle, as if he was going to split Chambers and Wilkinson in half. He then dramatically pulled the puck over to his left side, as if he was going to try again, as he had earlier, to beat Chambers to the outside. Chambers moved simultaneously with the shift. His momentum now heavily bound to his right, his outside, he could not defend against the next maneuver.

Sensing Chambers had now committed, Lemieux violently drew the puck back to the middle and, being so nimble of foot for someone of his size, he powered like a big dark tornado down that tunnel that wasn't supposed to be there. On Lemieux's first shift to the outside, the other defender, Wilkinson, had paused for a split second, leaving Lemieux to Chambers while protecting his own side. He was doing his job. But Mario's abrupt shift back in fooled him and he was left at a standstill as Mario knifed through. Now Lemieux, moving straight forward at a tremendous rate, had the puck in front of the goalie,

Jon Casey. He shifted to the right, drawing Casey with him. Then he pulled the puck back the other way and put it in the left corner.

The goal, deserving of the great many TV replays it would get, showed the majesty, agility, and power of Lemieux all at once. As a classic of Stanley Cup history, it ranked far above Bobby Orr's overtime goal against St. Louis in 1970 on the skills chart. The Orr goal took on legendary status, but in fact, it was not extraordinary. Orr had only to relay a perfect pass from Derek Sanderson behind the net that came right to his stick. That Orr jumped from his feet in celebration the split second after he hit it made the score look more sensational than it was. He had many better goals than that one, which came in a Cup final that was a mismatch.

The Penguins had been leading in the game 2–1 when Lemieux split the Minnesota defensemen in half to finish them off. "They played better than us the first half of the game," said Mario "and though we had a 2–1 lead, I thought we were in a lot of trouble. So it was a really big one." Pittsburgh now looked ready to bury the North Stars, but it would hardly have been appropriate if Lemieux had passed through his first Stanley Cup final without a health reversal. The back agony struck again. He felt pains before stepping out for warm-ups in game three. He was prepared to play, but as he bent over to lace up his skates, the pain got so bad he couldn't finish the job.

To some skepticism, the doctors explained that the new affliction wasn't related to his previous back infection or the surgery. Just a case of spasms that anyone could get, they said. Without Lemieux, the Penguins fell 3–1 to drop behind by a game in the series. They played hard, but Casey, the Minnesota goaltender, played better. "We're not going to make excuses or anything," said Kevin Stevens. "If we get twenty guys going at the same time, we can beat this team, even without Mario."

After the game, Penguins' management foolishly imposed

a news blackout on Lemieux. They deemed him not well enough to speak. The next day the press found Lemieux and some teammates working out at a health club in downtown St. Paul. John Welday, the Penguins' strength coach, tried to get the journalists to leave. They waited, however, and pursued Mario as he left the building. Not looking like a player in pain, Mario walked up a hill at full speed, ignoring the media. When a reporter asked if he'd been instructed not to do interviews, number 66 responded, "You got it."

The team, meanwhile, appointed someone to tie up his skates for him. They also started looking for a stiffer bed than the one in his hotel, where the mattress he slept on was soft. "There was a big sag," complained Dr. Burke. "He woke up feeling stiff." The doctor said these things were to be expected. "We've thought all along that if he was going to encounter any problems, it would be because of travel involved in hockey—being on airplanes, sleeping in different beds, not getting sleep." Boards were put under his mattress, and following a ramrod-straight night's sleep, Welday put him through therapy. It was a matter, said Welday, "of heating him up, followed by a lot of stretching and repeating that routine during the day and right up to game time."

He returned for game four. The Penguins popped in three goals in the first three minutes—from Stevens, Francis, and Lemieux—and played spottily the rest of the game, but held on, with Barrasso starring, to win 5–3. Although unable to move two days earlier, Mario skated fluidly, dished out checks, and berated opponents, including defenseman Mark Tinordi, whom he followed all the way to the Stars' bench. "My feeling is that I am normal again," Mario analyzed. "Just like I was after leaving game seven against New Jersey with the same problem."

The Penguins staked themselves to an early lead in game five and, after allowing two short-handed goals to make it close, held on to win 6–4. Lemieux created three of the Penguin goals.

Despite missing a couple of games, despite his concentration on defense, he had established a big lead on all playoff point-getters. "Dominating a Stanley Cup victory was the one thing left for Mario to achieve in establishing himself as one of the truly great players in the history of hockey," said Bob Johnson. "If there were any questions left, I think he has supplied the answers."

The Penguins had too many strikers for the Stars, which was never more evident than in the sixth game when, on Minnesota ice, they drubbed them 8–0. They thus completed the unlikely odyssey from a seemingly jinxed team to one that soared all the way to the Stanley Cup championship. In the final game, Mario had four points, a beautiful goal and three assists, to finish with forty-four in the playoffs. It was three short of the Gretzky record of forty-seven and quite possibly, given the two missed games, another instance of back pain depriving him of one.

"You dream of this," Mario said, "but it's even better in real life than it is in your dreams." In the dressing room he took his long-time girlfriend, Nathalie Asselin, in his arms and held her for interminable seconds. Then he turned to his mother and leaned forward so that she could hold him. Then he started to cry. Jimmy Maggs came over and Maggs and Nathalie and Mario all hugged, as the tears streamed from their eyes. "Jimbo," said Mario, "I finally did it."

To cap the victory he won the Conn Smythe Trophy as the MVP for the playoffs. He was modest in his assessment, saying the correct diplomatic things. "It's always nice to win an award . . . but Kevin Stevens played unbelievable hockey in the playoffs. Tommy Barrasso was great for us. Mark Recchi. I'd like to share the trophy with my teammates." Barrasso wasn't complaining about not getting the MVP award. "He's taken so much crap over the years," he said of Mario, "but he's a lot tougher than people give him credit for. Hopefully, this will get the critics off his back."

After it was over Mario took the Stanley Cup to Montreal, to his home in Ville Emard. It was time for the Lemieux clan to celebrate and that meant half the population of Ville Emard would wind their way through the house. Mario sat in the kitchen with the Cup beside him on the table and the procession began. It was steaming hot outside and just as hot in the kitchen, but Mario stayed there for four hours, signing autographs and posing for pictures with every person that came through. As a claimant on his time, the clan was still number one.

He'd won the Stanley Cup, but he still had more to shoot for. There was another prize, that of being recognized as the best player in the game. "I think the Stanley Cup is a big thing on his list," said Jimmy Maggs. But Maggs, who talked with Mario for hours about these things, added, "but I think the most important thing would be the MVP award for the season. I think when he sees how many Gretzky won, and knowing that he's so much the superior player to Gretzky, then that's [the one.]"

Mario was convinced that he was the best. He would say it a year later when he looked back on the Cup victory. "I think last year in the playoffs I was the best player in the world." But that was his assessment and many didn't share it. Wayne Gretzky had nine Hart Trophies. Mario, who had played five fewer NHL seasons, had one. Gretzky had four seasons of two hundred points or more. Mario had none. Gretzky had a healthy back. Mario had nothing of the kind.

There was still a way to go.

SIXTEEN

LORD STANLEY, LORD MARIO

MARIO RARELY TRIED TO DESCRIBE HIS TALENT. SKILLS THAT ARE learned are much easier to explain than those that are reflex and natural. Mario's were the latter. His talent had matured over time, of course, but it really hadn't changed that much since his days as an atom in Ville Emard. Those who had watched him compete as a boy saw it all played back over and over again as his NHL career unfolded and he skated to his first Stanley Cup win. What they found remarkable was how little he had changed, both as a player and as a person. Mario could be modified, but never changed.

Father Fortin watched the Penguins win the Stanley Cup. "People said to me, 'Father, did you see Mario yesterday, the way he passed that puck?' I said, 'Yes, I watched him do that in the minors. He was doing the same thing as a boy.'"

Roland Faubert, his atom coach, had such fond memories of Mario at age seven, eight, and nine. "I must have coached him for two hundred games and, everywhere we went, this kid brought so much joy to those who watched him. It was like ballet as he worked his way down the ice. It was slow-motion ballet. I look at Mario today. He's the same as he was at eight years old."

"He had that same style of motion then as he does now," noted Ron Stevenson, who took over Mario's coaching after Faubert. "He controlled the puck and beat the players more with fakes and dekes than with speed."

Mario spoke once about his magic, about what it felt like when he was performing at a high level. He talked about time control, about seeing the game and playing it as if it were all in slow motion. This gave him time to think and make the plays others only dreamed about. Like the ballet Faubert described.

"Everything seems to slow down," said Mario, "and I'm seeing everything on the ice. Everything seems to come easy. Every time I get the puck, I see the whole ice: who is open, who is not. It doesn't happen often, but if I'm playing real well, I can go four or five games like that." Sometimes, he said, he would look at the replays and find it hard to believe what he was seeing. What he did was so natural, so unmechanical, that he didn't know the source of it. Off the ice, he couldn't fathom the gifts he had on it. "When I'm on the ice," he said, "it feels natural. But when I look at the replay, sometimes I am amazed." His special hockey metabolism took over when he vaulted the boards to join the game. This fantastic intermeshing of hands, eyes, mind, and puck was and would remain his own unique mystery.

It would hardly be possible to make startling rushes like those against the Minnesota defensemen unless he could somehow mentally freeze-frame the play and slow down the hurtling bodies while the riotous action continued; slow them down enough to see how he could work his way through the thicket.

Ken Dryden, the insightful former Montreal Canadiens goaltender, concluded that this was what set Mario apart. "He has that wonderful luxury of time that no one else has. He has more time on the ice than anybody, more time to do what he wants to do." Lemieux said he treasured the sport of golf because it allowed him to be alone and within himself; it gave him time to reflect. That statement fit him well, said Dryden, because "at times, when playing hockey, he looks like he's out on the golf course." No other players could get away with such an approach. They'd be stripped of the puck and knocked over.

Analysts often spoke of his soft hands, his huge soft hands. "Soft hands," said Dryden, "means hands that don't panic, that don't tighten up, that allow you to adapt right up until the point where there's no longer time to adapt. For most of us, in everything we do, we tighten our hands too quickly. We don't have to. There really is a bit more time."

Wayne Gretzky could exercise time control too, but Dryden did not think that Gretzky could be put in the same skills class with Lemieux. "Lemieux looks different from everyone else," said Dryden. "Lemieux looks dominant. I don't think there is anyone that has the individual skills Lemieux has. To me, he's the only person in the league who can embarrass someone else. The others can beat you. He embarrasses you."

When Rick Salutin, the author of the play *Les Canadiens*, watched Lemieux, he saw "a hovercraft." He was fascinated by what a different plateau Lemieux appeared to be on as he skated up the ice. Mario cozied along, glancing over his shoulder while keeping one hand on the stick with the puck. At the same time, he drew out his other hand, instructing his disciples where they should move. Lemieux, Salutin analyzed, was directing his own play, his mind in fast forward, his body moving in such a way that he controlled the speed of the other actors.

Lemieux had wraparound vision and faultless hand-eye coordination. Just as he could seemingly freeze-frame the other players coming at him, he could do the same with a puck moving at flash speed. The number of times Lemieux raised his stick blade, stopped the speeding projectile in midair, and brought it softly to the ice stunned all around him. He used his stick blade almost like a baseball glove.

These God-given talents had been a constant with him. And just as his ability hadn't changed over time, neither had the character that came with it. The people who had known him well as a boy sometimes saw Mario on his return trips to Montreal. They saw the same private person they had known years before. They were not surprised that the hockey world's attempt to make a public person out of a private one had failed. Roland Faubert saw the same simplicity about him as a professional that he had seen in him as an atom. "Mario is still the type of guy who says, 'I want to play my game. I'm going to give you a good game, but then I want to go to my house. I want to be at home.'" He was so shy as a youth, said Ron Stevenson, that "when people tried to talk to him, he'd turn off. He was too shy to answer."

His teammates, the guys from Ville Emard, got angry whenever they saw criticism of him that was based on his quiet personality. People couldn't understand, they said, that this was the real Mario, that he was always like this, that he was only being true to himself. Mario was like his father. Jean-Guy couldn't crack a smile until one of his boys had notched a third or fourth goal. Carl Parker or one of Mario's other boyhood friends would go over to the Lemieux household, but they would never see Jean-Guy. He was there all right, but they would never see him. To be unobtrusive was his way, as it was his son's. But Jean-Guy's quiet demeanor gave way to a core that was as hard as steel. This inner strength would be manifest in Mario more and more as the hockey seasons progressed and the health setbacks mounted.

He had been brought up in a narrow, protected, spoiled environment and he had hardened, not broadened, in his ways. Socially, he had remained on narrow fields as well, tying himself to his family, the clan surrounding it, and a girl whose upbringing was no broader than his own.

Firmly rooted, stubborn, and supremely confident in his

sublime talent, Jean-Guy's son lacked a lot. But the qualities he did have were a blessing. Given the challenges and the trauma he had faced, and given the worsening crises he was about to face, only a young man of his inner strength and indomitability could make it through.

The fourth edition of the biggest and the best hockey tournament in the world, the Canada Cup, was scheduled to take place a few months after the Stanley Cup. Most everyone assumed Mario would participate. He appeared ready. His back seemed better. He was coming off the Stanley Cup victory. He was in his prime, and it was a prime-time show. Even Craig Patrick had ventured the opinion that Mario would play. The results of his first Canada Cup had been splendid. The 1987 version of the event had marked Mario Lemieux's ascendancy to the superstar plateau and provided him with a new level of confidence. Before the tournament, he *felt* he was the best. After it, he *knew* he was the best. The Canada Cup gave him a winner's look. None of the teams he had played on, going all the way back to the junior days, had ever won the big prize—until then. The Canada Cup also cleaned up his tarnished international hockey image. The old charges that he didn't care about playing for his country were given a rest.

The event had much to recommend it, but Mario decided not to go. He wasn't about to follow anyone else's script. For Wayne Gretzky, the script was written. He didn't really have much choice. He was seen as too much of a patriot, too much of a good guy, not to play in a Canada Cup. He had to go. In the case of the Anti-Gretzky, it was different. The public had no firm expectations. Mario was still a man in the gray zone—out there, but not one of them.

Mario had won the Stanley Cup and he wanted to savor it. He had come off the long year's layoff, the healing of his tender back was still in progress. He did not want to endanger it by starting the next hockey season several weeks earlier than he had to. Despite what Craig Patrick had said before, the hockey club also didn't want him risking his health in an intense series.

Playing on the 1991 Canada Cup team would have meant playing alongside Gretzky. Inevitably, the media would turn it into a personal rivalry between the two best players in the world. In 1987 relations between the two were good. By 1991 they had grown apart. There would be discomfort and intense, head-to-head pressure. Who needed it? Let Gretzky go. Let him get the glory again. Leave Mario where he liked to be: by himself, on the golf course, a 200-yard shot to the green, time to think.

Mario didn't feel entirely appreciated in Canada for his effort in the 1987 triumph. He felt he was the best player there, but his losing the MVP award showed where the fans' hearts lay. Had he sensed the affection, the love that Gretzky sensed, he would have shown up in 1991.

Pittsburgh journalists attributed a good deal of the lack of affection to his French-Canadian roots. They saw the English–French issue in the same context as the white–black issue in the United States. Paul Steigerwald, who left the Penguins' front office to do TV commentary, referred to it as "the French disease." Said Steigerwald, "I've been hearing about it since I came into hockey. I've heard coaches and hockey players refer to the laziness of French-Canadian players as the French disease. I heard it long before Tony Esposito came here."

Mario had some sensitivity to this problem, but did not appear to look upon it as seriously as the American writers did. He did, however, have a feeling of not being appreciated outside of Pittsburgh. "He feels like he's snubbed all the time," said Steigerwald. "But he's learned to accept it."

Instead of the Canada Cup, the challenge for him now, as it had been in Laval when international tournaments beckoned, was to set a scoring record, win another MVP award, and another Stanley Cup. He wanted to report to camp in the flush of good health and have that one big, full year that had eluded him for seven seasons. He wanted the health fates, just one time, to let him play all eighty games.

While Mario rested, Pittsburgh coach Bob Johnson made other plans. Badger Bob had finally made it to the top of the heap. He'd won the Stanley Cup for the first time. Now he saw a chance for even more. To him, the Canada Cup was the finest pure hockey tournament in the world. He'd been named coach of Team USA and looked upon the assignment with relish. Ranks of high-quality Americans had been filling the NHL for many years. Team USA was a legitimate contender. On a day of good bounces, they could beat the Canadians or the Russians.

For Johnson, age sixty, things couldn't get much better than this. He coached the U.S. team through an exhibition series in Saskatoon in August and when, on the flight back to Pittsburgh, he began to feel ill, he didn't worry about it. His notoriously bad teeth had caused this type of head pain before. A quick trip to the dentist would see to it.

The dentist could find nothing wrong. He advised Johnson to have some medical tests as a precaution. The coach arranged for them and was then feeling well enough to take his wife, Martha, to dinner. They could talk about the good turns life had taken in the last few months.

Dinner was barely underway when Johnson collapsed from an apparent stroke. Rushed to hospital, he was soon diagnosed as having multiple brain tumors. They were malignant. "I saw him about a week ago," Lemieux said, on hearing the devastating news. "He was the same old Badger everybody knows. It's scary, really sad." Mario had liked him. He liked the feeling he brought to the club. After all the Pittsburgh coaching problems, a guy who could soothe and energize and be respected all at the same time was most welcome. "What he's done for this city and this hockey club in one year is pretty incredible. Nobody thought we'd win the Cup, but with Bob Johnson, anything was possible."

Johnson, they said, enjoyed going to the rink. He loved the feel of the game, the smell, the rush of bodies, the sound of the puck against the stick and the boards. He was old school. One of his favorite expressions was "If you want to reap a harvest, you have to plow." Another one, the one that became his trademark, was "It's a great day for hockey."

With his death not far off, the Stanley Cup champions assembled for sad days of hockey at training camp. Other dark clouds now hung over the team. Three of its very best players— Kevin Stevens, Ron Francis, and Mark Recchi—were without contracts and negotiations had come to a thorny edge. Stevens was looking at a million-a-year deal from Boston. Recchi and Francis were also free agents with good possibilities elsewhere. Pittsburgh's offers weren't even close.

Sensing the impasse, one that could quickly destroy a Stanley Cup team it had taken so long to build, Mario came forward. "Everything they can get," Mario said, "they deserve." In the case of Kevin Stevens, who had played so prominently and so powerfully in the Cup run, he soon upped the ante. "I guess in a week or so, we're going to find out if the Penguins want to win another Stanley Cup," Mario said. "If they do, they have to sign him."

They did so, with manifest reluctance, and within a few weeks, all the holdouts were back in the fold. Through training camp, out of respect for Johnson, the Penguins had declined to name a new coach. On October 1, as the season was about to open, they named Scotty Bowman on an interim basis. Bowman was the opposite of Johnson in temperament and style. Aloof, cold, chippy, imperious, smart, he had accomplished two things in his career: he'd established a reputation for winning and he'd established a reputation for not being liked. He was too hard to like; he always seemed on the edge of paranoia. Despite having mellowed, Bowman still gave the impression of being authoritarian for the sake of being authoritarian. Though times had changed, he thought you could still yell at people to get them to do things. That hadn't worked in Buffalo. In Montreal he had won all the Cups, but his detractors said that with all the talent Montreal possessed in those years, the Canadiens could have won without a coach. The Penguins heard unpleasant stories of Bowman's treatment of players. Once, Sabre defenseman Richie Dunn was having trouble understanding a drill they were working on in practice. A frustrated Bowman came over to him and began tapping on his helmet with the knob of his stick. "Am I loosening any logs up there?" Bowman asked as he continued tapping. "Am I?"

In the initial weeks, even though the team didn't play like a champion, Bowman remained calm and won some grudging respect. DeBartolo's financial empire, meanwhile, was under siege in the recession and he reluctantly sold the team to the triumvirate of Howard Baldwin, Morris Belzberg, and Thomas Ruta.

Mario's hope that this would be the season of good health, the season when he'd top some of Gretzky's numbers, disappeared in January, when back spasms forced him to the sidelines again. If skipping the Canada Cup had helped his back, it hadn't helped a lot. This time the pain was intermittent and he entered into another one of those periods when he didn't know from one day to the next whether he would be playing. The slightest bend or twist could sometimes bring sharp spinal pain with it. Back from a western road trip on which he hardly played, he was examined to see if he had developed a new condition of any kind. Nothing unusual was found, but this did little to ease Mario's angst. The more mysterious the ailment, the worse it was for him. He was slowly resigning himself to the fact that the back condition would be there forever and that he would periodically be compelled to sit out games. "I've been fighting back pain for three or four years. I've got to take some time off from time to time. My back is not as strong as it used to be."

The frustration of not knowing what condition he would be in from day to day was added to by the battering he took when he did play. On January 26, 1992, skating against the Capitals in Washington, he was repeatedly mugged, repeatedly fought back, and was ultimately assessed a game misconduct by referee Ron Hoggarth. Jaromir Jagr received a ten-game suspension for running into Hoggarth. The controversy, which followed several others, prompted Lemieux to denounce the NHL as a "garage league." Some felt he meant "garbage league," but "garage" got the point across equally well. The way the referees worked the games, fumed Lemieux, clearly favored the junkyard dogs at the expense of the game's true artists. "It's a skating game, a passing game," he asserted, much to the dismay of crash-and-burn advocates like Don Cherry. "I think that's what the fans want to see. I think the advantage is to the marginal player now. . . . The good players can't do what they're supposed to do."

He wasn't finished. "There are so many rules that are stupid in this league, and instead of the good players, they protect the referees, which makes no sense at all."

While he was embittered by this, the neverending health trauma was far more disheartening. The pain in the lower back returned and he sat out yet again. Now, for the first time in his career, he broached the possibility of shutting it all down, of giving in to his crippled back condition and leaving the game. "If it's going to hurt me for the rest of my life, it's not worth it," Mario said. "I think everybody is frustrated because we can't figure out what's causing the pain." He had been feeling good early in the season and had actually forgotten about the back, but the recurrences had made him think of the long term. If he continued to play, he could be discomforted or badly postured for the remainder of his life. As teammates like Ron Francis pointed out, a few more years playing hockey wasn't worth it for the decades of pain that could follow.

Mario didn't normally make weighty pronouncements without considerable forethought. Friends said that while he had reacted emotionally in raising the prospect of retirement, he did actually think about it. He slowly got beyond the depression, however, feeling better when he began playing again. His back condition cost him a month of playing time, sixteen games, too many to allow for a run at any scoring marks. But he would still win the scoring title.

He returned to the game on February 15 in Minnesota, and immediately became embroiled in another dispute with the officials. The league had fined him a thousand dollars for the remarks he made in Washington. And though he subsequently discussed the comments with NHL president John Ziegler, the Minnesota game demonstrated to him that nothing was about to change. Minnesota linebackers mauled Mario while the officials, in his view, looked the other way. Lemieux blasted referee Bill McCreary, who promptly assessed him an unsportsman-like-conduct penalty. Shortly thereafter, the Penguins played in Philadelphia. Paul Stewart, with whom they'd had a running feud, officiated at the game. During an overtime brawl, Stewart made remarks to Lemieux that he and his teammates interpreted as threats. "Mario told me," said Kevin Stevens, "that he [Stewart] said he's going to get Mario or get the team in some way." Nothing came of it, but it was another example for Mario of how tough his NHL life was becoming. So much, it seemed, was working against him: his health, the referees, the media outside Pittsburgh.

This had been a year when, with a Cup triumph behind

him, he wanted to set new standards. But his beloved coach had died (Johnson passed away in November), the back condition felled him again, the league's goons got to him, and so did the officials. A Pittsburgh writer tried to imagine what Mario could do under circumstances that were ideal—no clutching and grabbing, perfect health, a full season. He came up with an estimate of four hundred points. Given Lemieux's incredible talents, perhaps the writer could be forgiven for the hyperbole.

With the Penguins plodding along without the look or the glow of a Stanley Cup champion, Craig Patrick, whose big trade the previous year for Ron Francis had proven wise, made another bold exchange. He traded Paul Coffey and Mark Recchi, the guts of the Penguins offense outside of Lemieux, for Rick Tocchet and defenseman Kjell Samuelsson of Philadelphia. Patrick wanted more physical presence. Tocchet skated as if he were on mud, but played meanly and could score. Samuelsson, a colossus, patrolled his zone like an oceanliner. Though Coffey was capable of scoring a hundred points more per season than Samuelsson, Patrick now had Larry Murphy to provide blitz from the blue line. Bowman had been experimenting with Coffey at forward, as he once had done with Phil Housley, another attack-minded rear guard, when he was in Buffalo.

The early hints of Coffey's pending departure upset Lemieux. They were good friends. Mario admired Coffey's ability to open up ice, feed the long passes, get things moving from back deep. He liked Recchi as well, and this being a trade that was generating controversy, Mario could have added immensely to it with the wrong word. Instead, showing a maturity concomitant with his position as team leader, Lemieux gave the deal his blessing. It was "probably time for a change," he said.

The trade failed to produce instant results. Hovering around the .500 mark, the defending champions found themselves in danger of not making the playoffs. The New York Islanders nipped at their fourth-place position and, looking for the source of the problem, the players blamed Scotty Bowman. Even a more relaxed Bowman was a distant, brittle figure for them compared to Badger Bob Johnson. Players like Recchi, before being traded, and Stevens openly criticized Bowman at the bench. Phil Bourque, who had enjoyed ample ice time under Johnson, had seen it substantially reduced and he too was bitter.

Patrick responded by calling a team meeting at the Skyline Plaza Hotel in Calgary on March 3. All grievances were to be aired, but the players only had one—Bowman, the winningest coach in NHL history. Player after player berated his lack of communication, his skipping out to his home in Buffalo on practice days, his failure to utilize players fairly. Mario viewed Bowman as a hockey legend who knew the game, but he shared in some of his teammates' criticisms. He did not come to Bowman's defense, nor, to any sustained degree, did Patrick. Bowman was flying into Calgary from Buffalo and was thus unable to rebut the mutineers himself. He was the third Pittsburgh coach of the last four to be subjected to a player uprising. First there was Creamer, then Ubriaco, now Bowman. Patrick told his team it was too late in the year to make a change, that the best thing to do was hold on for a few weeks, play hard, make the most of the season's end. After that, he said, coaching problems would be sorted out.

On the night following the day of the long knives, the Penguins beat Calgary. They began playing better, moving slowly beyond the reach of the Islanders. Mario averaged two points a game, a bit under his potential. A malfunctioning power play, he said, was part of the problem. "We just don't practice it. You've got to spend some time on it."

He scored his 1,000th career point on March 22 at Detroit. He did it in 513 regular-season games, the second fastest in league history. Gretzky needed just 424 games. In the eight seasons he took to reach the mark, Mario missed 121 games, the equivalent of a season and a half.

The Penguins finished the season 39–32–9. Though hardly exemplary, in the previous year, when they won the Stanley Cup, they had only two more wins, finishing 41–33–6. Having passed the New Jersey Devils and finished third in their division, they met the Washington Capitals in the first round of the playoffs. Before the regular season even ended, however, a players' strike halted proceedings, leaving the hockey world to wonder if there would be any Stanley Cup playoffs at all.

Common sense ultimately took hold. While Mario golfed, the two sides looked to Gretzky to help resolve the crisis. An intervention by him and Mark Messier added to the momentum that led to a settlement. Mario had been so doubtful that an agreement could be reached that he flew off to Florida for a golfing tour the day before it happened.

When action resumed, he injured his shoulder and couldn't participate in the playoff opener against the Capitals. But when he did skate out for game two, his back and legs were rested from the two-week players' strike and he had that look of intensity in his eyes. He could bend forward when he skated and stretch his body seemingly halfway across the ice. There was no sign of pain. When Mario played hurt, conscious of back pain, it was usually apparent. He skated upright, and instead of using his one-on-one skills to create opportunities, he would dish the puck off quickly to whichever teammate happened to be in the area. In these playoffs, there would be none of that.

Pittsburgh lost the first two games of the series. In game three, confronted with the proverbial "must win" scenario, Lemieux set up his team's first three goals. He scored the next three. Pittsburgh won 6–4. The Capitals then came back to pummel the Penguins at the Igloo. A high-alert defense, a factor in the previous year's Pittsburgh triumph, was absent.

Washington's 7–2 win uncorked the boo-birds in the Igloo. The fans went to bed thinking the reign of their Stanley Cup champions was over.

Terry Murray coached the Caps. He had been hired after his brother Bryan had coached them through one playoff collapse after another. The move amazed some. Terry had no more fire than Bryan. Weren't they just inviting the same problems? If Bryan couldn't inspire the troops, how could his decidedly low-key brother? With the series at three games to one, however, Terry Murray was smiling. He appeared to have an answer for the critics.

Lemieux wanted a re-emphasis on defense. He wanted the same commitment that the team had given the year before, when he announced that he would concentrate on prevention and the offense would take care of itself. Against Washington, Lemieux concluded, a new defensive formation was required.

Bowman had already endured a rough ride this season and Lemieux was reluctant to imply that the coach might like to step aside while he drew up a new system. He talked to the coach, however, and Bowman was receptive. To his credit, Scotty Bowman was man enough to realize that he didn't have all the answers, that a player with a genius for the game like Mario might have some better thoughts. Bowman knew that while the critics could rightly say Mario didn't physically train hard, mentally he prepared thoroughly. He spent hours with videotapes, studying the flow of the game, studying the weaknesses and the strengths, figuring out areas to exploit. His insight into the game was probably superior to that of most coaches. The NHL was not a league in which advanced intellects were to be found in abundance. A beer-hall mentality ran the sport and many coaches were former players. They taught what they had learned from their former teams, in many cases repeating the mistakes of their previous masters. The coaches got fired from one team and picked up by another, working their way through the system, taking their lack of insight with them, repeating their folly. There wasn't an advanced education system for coaching in North America, like that in the former Soviet Union. No one had taken the game into the lab and studied and dissected it. Unlike basketball, which was played with similar numbers of players on a similarly shaped floor, there were few variations in player sets. In hockey it was the two-three—two defensemen, three forwards—and that was it. Basketball had a diamond and one, a two-one-two, and various other possibilities. In Russia the father of hockey, Anatoli Tarasov, experimented with a one-two-two—one backstop defensemen, two rovers who could go anywhere they pleased, and two forwards. NHL coaches, outside of a few like Fred Shero and Dave King, rarely experimented. Their minds were welded to tradition. They learned one system, and thought of nothing else.

After the drubbing in Pittsburgh, Mario took the floor at a team meeting to explain the new defensive tactic he wanted deployed: one man in as a forechecker, four back to pick up the Caps in the neutral zone. On their return to the Capital Center, the Penguins employed the system effectively, cutting off every tunnel. The Caps had averaged almost thirty-three shots on goal in each of the first four games. They now were limited to twenty-three. The Penguins avoided elimination with a 5–2 win.

In game three Lemieux had tallied six points, figuring in on every Penguin score. Back in Pittsburgh for game six, he erupted for five more points as his team drove the series to a seventh game with a 6–4 win. Pittsburgh had taken a 2–0 lead in this contest, but the Caps scored four in a row and led 4–2 in the second period. Mario, playing almost two-thirds of the game, brought the Penguins back. In five games of this series, he now had fifteen points. Terry Murray could devise no successful formula to contain him. The only way to do that when he was at the top of his game was to foul him. But fouls risked penalties and the Penguin power play was an effective one.

For game seven, again in Washington, defense was the story. Lemieux scored a short-handed goal, Jagr scored on a power play, and that was all Pittsburgh needed to complete the improbable return from a 3–1 deficit in games and hurtle Murray and Washington hockey lovers into another long summer's depression.

"We were beaten by one man," said Terry Murray. "Number 66. Lemieux. Right now, he's the best there is . . . by far the best player in the NHL. He's on top of his game. He's a guy the puck just follows around the ice." Months afterwards, Murray could be found in a Pittsburgh hotel, his team in town, still talking about the series. Mario had shown something he hadn't demonstrated before, said Murray. "Mental toughness." He used to be a moodier player, Murray remembered, but he had grown hungry and become steely under pressure. "That series," he said, shaking his head, "we couldn't stop him. They'd clear the puck off the boards up into the middle and Mario would create something with it."

Mario had excelled in playoff series before, most often with his offensive output. The Washington series of 1992 would be remembered as the one in which he excelled in all facets of the game—offense, defense, team strategy, leadership. Bowman had coached Lafleur through his heroic days of the late 1970s and he had seen much of Gretzky in the 1980s. After this series against the Capitals, though, he was dazzled. "I have coached a lot of great players," he said, "but I have never seen a guy play so inspired." He admired Lemieux not only for his skill, but also for the way he handled himself—his quiet pride and power. No showboating, no head games, no sideshows, no piques. This was hockey at its sophisticated, intelligent best.

Gordie Howe had said once of Lemieux that in his early years in the NHL, he played a lot of five-minute games and that sometimes his five minutes would be enough to win. But Howe noticed, as did others, that five-minute games were no longer part of his repertoire.

The Penguins now faced the team with the best overall record in the NHL, the New York Rangers. They beat them 4–2 to start the series. Then, this being a season without enough mishap for Mario; this being a season when, merely, a coach died, the back ailment took him out, the garage league chewed him up, and his team rebelled against the new coach, another shot of adversity was due. It happened early in the second game, when Lemieux was knocked out for the remainder of the New York series and perhaps more.

The back anguish didn't return this time. Instead, the garage league struck. Adam Graves, using his stick like a tomahawk, smashed it so brutally against the padding on Lemieux's glove that the blow broke a small bone in the back of his hand. Graves, who later was assessed a four-game suspension, claimed he wasn't trying to hurt Lemieux. That's why, he said, he only aimed the stick at the glove.

The slash vindicated Mario's outburst of a few months earlier. It could hardly have been less timely, but he was getting used to it. "It's great not having to worry about Lemieux," Ranger coach Roger Neilson observed after the game. "You have a plan for him, obviously. If you don't need it, you can play a more straightforward game." Joe Mullen went down with torn ligaments in his knee in the same match, meaning he too was out. But the Pittsburgh team, reacting with passion and valor, and getting some extraordinary work from Ron Francis, Jaromir Jagr, and Tom Barrasso, went on to beat the Rangers in six games. Jagr's screaming horizontal strides and monstrous reach were capturing the imagination of the hockey public. "He's so strong," Lemieux said of the Czech. "He's one of the best in the league at holding onto the puck and making the play. He is a great player who is still learning. We have some similarities. I think he's got to learn to move the puck and get it back; sometimes he tries to beat the same guy three times. He's got to learn to shoot it at the same time. That's going to come with experience."

Lemieux remained out of action as the Penguins opened up the Stanley Cup semifinal with a win over the Boston Bruins. But he came back for game two, a week ahead of schedule. The hand was too immobile to shoot a backhand, but he was fine from his good side. In keeping with his average for these play-offs, he fashioned a three-point night—two goals and an assist—in a 5–2 victory over a Bruins team sadly missing Cam Neely. After trying to get it right all season, the Penguins and their megastar had hit their peak at the perfect time. They rolled through Boston in four straight, one highlight coming in the last game when Mario made a ghost of Ray Bourque. Attacking one on one, he slid the puck through Bourque, glided by, reclaimed it, then pierced the upper portion of the net with a wrist shot over Andy Moog's glove. "It's not how hard you shoot," Lemieux explained, "it's where you pick your spot." He preferred the wrist shot when bearing in on the goalie, normally utilizing the slap shot only from thirty feet out and beyond. He realized that, although slower, the chances of the wrist shot hitting the target were better and that its quicker release made up for any advantage lost in speed.

Gretzky watched from Los Angeles, where he had been unable to regain the luster he had in Edmonton and where his age (thirty) had become a factor. Mario now heard repeatedly that he, not Gretzky, was the best in the game. Bruins' coach Rick Bowness would echo Terry Murray. "He's in a class by himself," said Bowness. The coach of the Penguins' next opponent would eventually get around to saying it too.

Mike Keenan, the Chicago Blackhawks' coach, had intended on crowding Lemieux more than the Bruins had. But in the Stanley Cup opener, the Blackhawks inexplicably left Mario alone. There was no one within twelve feet of him, with the same number of seconds left to play. Mario's big wand deposited the puck behind Ed Belfour for the winning goal in a game in which they had been behind by three. Lemieux's winner followed his bizarre carom goal. He was standing to the side and slightly behind Belfour when the puck came to him. With no hope of shooting it directly in, he played a bank shot off the rear half of the goalie and watched its successful ricochet. He saved his praise, however, for an even more spectacular point, this one by Jagr. The Czech, coming out from the side of the net, took the puck around three Blackhawks in succession and drilled a low shot from the slot area into the net. "Probably the greatest goal I've ever seen," said Mario.

Keenan accused Lemieux of diving to draw a penalty in the game. Never a master of finesse, the Chicago coach impugned Mario as "an embarrassment to himself, to the game, and to the players he's playing with." Reporters asked number 66 for his response. "No comment," he replied. "At this point."

Had Keenan, who also feuded with his own star player, Jeremy Roenick, known Mario, had he had an idea of his hockey history, he would have known that the least advisable tactic was to goad him on, to snap his control cord. After his winner in the opener, Mario also laid the winning goal on Keenan in game two. The Penguins now gave their offense a rest, relying on some masterful play by Barrasso in posting a 1–0 win in game three. In game four, threatening to sweep, they moved in front and held a narrow 6–5 lead in the third period. Bowman feared the team was getting careless and so, apparently, did Lemieux. "Mario was on the bench as he saw what was happening," recalled Bowman. "He knew he was taking the next shift and he had to forecheck the Blackhawks deep to get back the momentum. Just before he went over the boards, Mario turned to Jagr and, like an uncle, said, 'Now just watch how I force them deep, and you do the same.'" To Bowman, it was an example of the command Mario had developed over the team.

The 6–5 triumph gave the Penguins a double sweep, the semis and the final, and their second straight Stanley Cup.

Mario scored seven points in the four-game final series. He missed seven games in the playoffs, but won the playoff scoring title by a wide margin. He had missed sixteen games in the regular season and still won the regular-season scoring race. He now had his second Stanley Cup and was honored with his second straight Conn Smythe Trophy as playoff MVP. Another year of crisis had been rewarded with the ultimate prizes.

The first person with whom he wanted to share the news was a family member. His brother Richard wasn't in Chicago. He had planned a trip to Pittsburgh, hoping to see the final there. After coming off the ice, Mario found a telephone and called him. Neither Richard nor Alain had ever shown a slice of jealousy toward Mario. For Mario, who loved them, the first priority was still his family.

He had a bit of squaring up to do with others, however. Having made no comment on Keenan's blistering attack following the opening game of the series, Mario now told reporters of his plans. "I'm just going to go into the locker room to dive into the Cup," he said.

SEVENTEEN
TRAGEDY AND TRIUMPH

FOLLOWING THE GLORIOUS DENOUEMENT OF THE 1991–1992 campaign, Mario's fortune turned and the fates once again dragged him through hell. Soon after the second straight Stanley Cup triumph, the question of why adversity stalked this great hockey player would resurface. Why couldn't the forces of darkness leave Mario Lemieux alone?

The first off-note to follow the Cup victory was his being spurned for the prize that meant so much to him, the Hart Trophy for the league MVP. Here was a player who had missed almost one-quarter of the season and had still won the league scoring title. Here was a player who had revived a team that had flattened out during his absence. Here was a player without whom, it was universally conceded, the Penguins could not have won the big prize.

Yet here was a player who, much less than receive the Hart Trophy, didn't even get one of three nominations for it. Sorry, Mario, the sports journalists' fraternity, in effect, told him. Winning the scoring title in only sixty-four games isn't enough. Had you missed half the season and still beaten everyone, you might have been a candidate.

Mark Messier of the New York Rangers won the Hart.

Mario, as Jimmy Maggs found out, was angry and bitter again. He registered his disdain by not showing up at the awards ceremony to collect his trophy for winning the scoring title.

Mario knew what was behind the slights. He had said it before. Put bluntly, Mario didn't kiss media ass. The press voted for these awards on the basis of popularity as well as talent, and if you hadn't cooperated with the press, if you had spurned a reporter who asked you for the 1,100th time about your back, you'd suffer the consequences.

What Gretzky realized and what Mario Lemieux overlooked, noted Ken Dryden, was that the great on-ice performer had to be effective off the ice as well. "I [Mario] may want to say to myself," analyzed Dryden, "that I am a hockey player, that my duty is performing in the game and that's where it begins and that's where it ends. But nobody else sees it that way. And Gretzky knew and understood this from the beginning, and Mario [did not]."

"The thing with Mario," said Bill Kelly, "is that he can't do something that isn't natural for him. He doesn't do something for the sake of making you pleased with him. He doesn't say, 'I'm going to do this. I'm going to be phony and, gee, it's going to make me look good in the public eye.' He can't do that kind of stuff. He's a behind-the-scenes guy."

Given all the other splendid features of the 1992 campaign, Mario could shake off the Hart disappointment and get set for another run at the two brass rings he really wanted now: Gretzky's record for goals in a season (92 in 1981–1982) and for total points in a season (215 in 1985–1986). "I think it's possible to score one hundred," Lemieux said. "For sure, you have to be on a roll. You can't go three or four games without scoring. You have to be consistent and get your goal every game and get four or five goals a couple of times."

One of the two records would do for now. But the way

Mario started the season, both looked possible. The team was scoring in piles. It was running on the arrogance of back-to-back championship rings. The Penguins were like the Edmonton Oilers of old. The more they scored, the more Mario scored. They were so strong they thought they didn't need a coach. They felt as if they could win without one. In the previous season Craig Patrick had indicated to the players that they would have a new coach, but then Bowman had taken them to the Stanley Cup. So, after waiting until the last possible moment, the day of the season opener, they hired him again. An arrangement was made whereby Bowman would be the game coach and the assistants would handle the practices. While the public was led to believe that this was the way Bowman wanted it, it was actually the way the players wanted it. They didn't like the way Bowman ran the practices, so Bowman didn't run the practices.

Mario just needed someone to let him play as many minutes as he wanted to play, and Scotty Bowman granted him that wish. Mario scored thirty-two points in his first ten games. Everything was perfect. The back, he said, felt better than at any time in years. New rules against highsticking and other fouls gave him more room to maneuver. More official time-outs during a period meant more rest and more ice time. He'd finally found permanent and stellar linemates in Rick Tocchet and Kevin Stevens. "Right now, I'm at my peak," he said, "especially with the team and the nucleus we have right now. It's a lot easier to come to work when you're pain-free." Of the new rules, which the referees would gradually forget about, he observed, "There's a little bit more flow to the game and there's not as much grabbing and holding and interference. That's good for the great players. And I think it's good for the game in the long run."

Goalie Tom Barrasso, who had gone on a golfing trip with Lemieux to Scotland in the off-season, said, "There's a definite correlation between his health and his desire. When he feels healthy, he feels he could accomplish just about anything." Bowman, having seen him up close for a year, was coming to appreciate how he used his size. "It's Mario's ability to take advantage of his reach that makes him really great. He is virtually impossible to check because he is so huge. You can take the body here, but he's still making the great play away over there." Boston Bruins general manager Harry Sinden, who had had Orr on his teams, was saying now that Mario Lemieux was "the most dominating player the game has ever seen."

So frenzied was his early productivity in the 1992–1993 season that the media started keeping game-by-game progress charts on how his numbers compared to Gretzky's pace for the seasons he set his two marks. After 16 games, Mario had 21 goals and 25 assists for 46 points. Extended over an 80-game schedule, such a rate of production would give him 105 goals and 225 points, easily surpassing each record. In this season, another factor was working in Mario's favor. The schedule had been expanded to 84 games.

He had a great distance to make up. The NHL record book was still, by and large, a one-man show. For regular season and playoff records, Mario was listed second to Gretzky seventeen times. Some of the records were due simply to Gretzky's having played more seasons, but not all. Gretzky, for example, had his four seasons of two hundred points or more by age twenty-seven. Mario, twenty-seven, had none.

Gretzky had missed only eight games in his first eight NHL seasons. For the 1992–1993 season, however, he was out indefinitely with a career-threatening fractured disc. For the first time, the hockey universe was Mario's and, realizing this, Pittsburgh signed him to a new seven-year contract, putting up out-of-galaxy numbers to do so. Mario's negotiator, Tom Reich, true to his super-agent reputation, nailed down a $42-million deal. At $6 million a season, Mario had suddenly doubled Gretzky's salary.

For a small-market team, the Penguins, trying not to fall victim to the miserly folly of the Edmonton Oilers, who lost their superior players in contract disputes, were paying gigantic sums of money to keep a winner together. Pittsburgh had the highest payroll in the league, higher even than the New York Rangers. Six of their players—Lemieux, Stevens, Barrasso, Jagr, Tocchet, and Ulf Samuelsson—made over a million a year or just shy of it.

In the Lemieux contract the Penguins were ceded the rights to use Mario as a marketing property. Mario talked about becoming more of a spokesman for hockey, an ambassador of the game like the Great Gretzky himself. Howard Baldwin brought in a marketing specialist, Richard Chmura, to attempt an image turnaround. One of Chmura's early initatives was the old chocolate bar gambit—the Mario Bun Bar. While Chmura hoped it would meet a better fate than other superstar bars, there was scant evidence that Mario could become a hot Madison Avenue property. A New York firm, Steiner Sports Marketing, ranked Lemieux near the bottom among superstar performers in terms of advertising and endorsement prospects. "Lemieux has been a marketing flop," the Steiner agency noted. "His looks, his attitude, his demeanor. He's just too low key."

Intensely private off the ice, Mario also lacked—despite his undeniable brilliance—charismatic flash on it. He made the game look too easy. On a night in Ottawa when he scored a routine two goals against the Senators, the *Ottawa Sun*'s Jane O'Hara wrote that "for the most part, he looked disinterested in the proceedings. . . . He tended to swoop like a swallow, gracefully, effortlessly, but always well out of traffic. Indeed, if he were any less the god of hockey he is, you'd be tempted to call him a goal suck. If he had spent any more time hanging around the Senators' blue line—even when the Penguins were killing penalties—I'd have sworn he was waiting for a bus."

Mario's back began to bother him in small ways in November, but then he got caught up in a different drama. This one, the first of no less than three crises that would plague him that season, was different from all the other controversies he had faced.

Mario had closely befriended Dan Quinn during Quinn's years with the Penguins. Profiting from being on a line with Mario much of the time, Quinn had 111 goals and 162 assists in 254 games from 1986 to 1990. He was a good hockey player, and an excellent golfer. As such, he became a close companion of Mario's away from the arena.

Quinn went on to play with the Vancouver Canucks, then the Minnesota North Stars. He and Mario kept in close touch, and when the Penguins played in Minnesota on November 9, the two hooked up at Hooter's Restaurant and Bar with some other players. The group started talking to a table of women who were also there that evening, and after a few hours, they all went to the Marriott Hotel in Bloomington, where the Penguins were staying. Some partying followed, whereupon the groups split up. Mario and Dan Quinn adjourned to Mario's room, room 1001, with female accompaniment. According to an affidavit filed by Bloomington police detective Ross Swanson, Quinn turned down the lights in the room and began fondling one of the women, despite her resistance and repeated assertions that she didn't want to have sex. The affidavit said Quinn removed her clothes and had intercourse with her.

Quinn maintained the sex was consensual. He was arrested, but freed on a $30,000 bond. Lemieux's involvement was peripheral, though he was still subject to false allegations. Tom Bauer, the alleged victim's lawyer, was quoted in press reports as saying Lemieux's behavior was suspect. The girl with

Mario was restrained in her attempts to help her friend while Quinn was molesting her, Bauer said. "[Lemieux] told her, 'You're staying here. Just leave them alone.'" said Bauer. Other reports disputed this, saying the girl with Mario did help the alleged victim.

The Penguins club was typically silent on the controversy. Tom Reich, Mario's agent, said that "the alleged victim has a vivid imagination." The incident took place at a time when Mario's common-law wife, Nathalie Asselin, was home in Pittsburgh, three months pregnant. Mario said nothing publicly. He suited up against the North Stars the next night and played soundly, enjoying a typical three-point evening. He sneaked out of the dressing room without seeing reporters.

The alleged rape story made headlines and Mario's image took a pounding in his home province of Quebec and elsewhere. The major Pittsburgh newspaper was on strike and not publishing at the time, which helped lessen the case's profile. But Pittsburgh TV and radio picked up the stories as they came in from Minnesota.

Mario's mother, Pierrette, flew into town and saw her friend Jimmy Maggs. Maggs tried to calm her down. "Everybody was upset, his family and everybody," recalled Maggs. "I told her everything was going to be fine." Mario met with Maggs. He obviously wanted to talk about the incident and explain what had happened, but Maggs dissuaded him. "I said to him, 'It's none of my business. Let's worry about playing hockey.'"

Mario had trouble keeping his mind on hockey. He was in the locker room during a road trip and spotted Paul Steigerwald, with whom he enjoyed a trusting rapport. He asked Steigerwald if he had heard anything. "He wanted to know what was happening in the news back in Pittsburgh about it," said Steigerwald. "He was obviously very sensitive to it and he was not at all happy with what was going on." The case closed when the county attorney's office decided not to bring charges against Quinn. It determined it would be unable to prove beyond a reasonable doubt that Quinn knew the victim did not consent to sexual intercourse. Lemieux was never under consideration for charges. Quinn felt victimized. "It has been two weeks of hell," he said. "It seems that everyone but the prosecuting attorney has forgotten about the presumption of innocence. The media continually focused, almost exclusively, on allegations that were obviously fabricated."

Mario's circle, those who knew him well, came to his defense, saying that compared to most superstar athletes and their relations with women, Mario could hardly be seen as a bad guy. "Mario could have been with millions of girls," said Steigerwald, drawing an obvious analogy to basketball's Magic Johnson. "I don't think he pursues it that much." Mario was basically a good person, his friends said. Sure, he was human and might have steered foul on occasion, but nobody was perfect. "I challenge anyone to come up with an example of Mario mistreating someone or doing something bad to someone," said Dr. Burke. On the Quinn case, he said, "No one knows the details. Let's take the worst-case scenario. Girls in the room and stuff going on. We all know from cases like this that who's to say who is to blame? Who is to say the girl wasn't secondarily looking for something? Once again, even there I challenge you to find where that kid did something wrong."

Car dealer Bill Kelly had seen Mario say no to all those "perfect tens" who passed through his showroom. He said the allegations about Mario made no sense.

Mario's former agent, Bob Perno, had a different view. He said he wasn't terribly surprised to hear about the episode and he really felt sorry for Nathalie Asselin. Nobody proved Mario did anything in that room, Perno pointed out, but "I think Mario owes it to himself, Nathalie, and the public not to even get close to this type of incident. I can't fathom that an intelligent person like Mario would even risk anything like this, especially with Nathalie being pregnant."

The Sun newspaper chain assigned a team of three investigative journalists to probe Lemieux's behavior in the matter. They found that attorneys representing the hockey players had gone to unique and extraordinary lengths to keep the case file sealed, but no new damaging evidence concerning Lemieux's behavior was turned up.

Subsequent events would quickly make the hockey world forget the Quinn affair. In the life of a young man who wanted just to play the game and be left alone, a disaster of a far different kind now stole the spotlight.

It was in December 1992, three or four days before Christmas, when Mario mentioned to Dr. Burke that he had a lump on his neck. It had been there for a year and a half, Mario told Burke, and it was beginning to bother him. Mario had mentioned the swelling to another doctor, a friend, when it had first appeared. This doctor simply recommended keeping an eye on it. After that, nothing had happened until Mario informed Burke. Through all the physical examinations he received, through all the rubdowns, through all the inquiries about his health, no one had spotted the lump.

Burke wasn't surprised. The normal time for the average person to detect and report such a protrusion, he said, was almost two years. But Mario, no normal person, was one of the world's premier athletes. His health needed round-the-clock monitoring. Still, said Burke, the delay was not unusual. "He may mention it to a trainer. But there's not many people who are standing in the presence of a doctor when they think of the lump. You know what finally brought him to say something about it? When he was shaving, it began to become more of a problem to shave around it. When he would extend his neck up, it would be prominent."

When Mario finally brought it to his attention, Burke was not terribly concerned. He told Mario that he didn't "think it [was] anything bad," and held to this viewpoint for some time, believing it was probably a harmless cyst. He advised Mario to have it looked at, but wasn't convinced that it had to be excised and a biopsy performed to test for malignancy. After a closer check-up, a scanning, the doctors still felt it seemed innocent enough. Recalled Burke: "We said to him, 'It doesn't look like it's anything bad, but if it concerns you, we ought to take it out.'"

Fortunately, it did concern Mario. It so happened that by this time, early January 1993, he was sidelined yet again with the recurring back ailment, just when he was mounting the charge at Gretzky's records. Because he was out of action anyway, they all decided it was a good time to remove the lump and diagnose it. Dr. Steve Jones did the operation on Friday, January 8, and on Saturday they had the results. The doctors had hardly even thought of Hodgkin's disease, cancer of the lymph nodes, as a possibility. "It was way down the list," Burke confessed. When he got the results and it was indeed Hodgkin's, Burke thought, "My God, what else can go wrong with this poor kid?"

In the space of two months, Mario had been peripherally caught up in an alleged rape case, sidelined again with back problems, and diagnosed with cancer.

Burke decided to wait until Monday to inform Mario of the latest disaster. He'd have the tests verified in the meantime and give himself some time to think of how he should put the news. "The way you tell him is a heck of a lot more important than telling him two days earlier." His strategy was to avoid using the word cancer for as long as possible. "If you walk into a room and tell someone that they have cancer, that is the end of the conversation."

Burke told Mario, "There's a problem with your biopsy,

but what you need to know is that the problem is treatable, curable, and should not interfere with your career. We know what it is, we can take care of it, there's a very good recovery rate, and you should be very positive."

Burke went on in that vein for a while, then dropped the bomb. Dr. Jones, who removed the lump and performed the biopsy, was also in the room for the meeting, which lasted fifteen or twenty minutes. Mario showed no emotion. He sat stoically throughout. He asked questions about how it might interfere with his career, with his life. He showed no signs nor made any statement of self-pity.

Burke and Jones talked about some of the misperceptions people had of cancer. Mario heard them out and said, as Burke recalled, "'All right, what do we do next?' We said, 'You [have] to go and get these tests done.' He said, 'Fine, set them up, tell me where to be.' That was it."

Mario left the downtown office, got in his gray BMW to drive out to his new home in Sewickley Heights. His parents hadn't been informed by the doctors, nor had his pregnant girl-friend, Nathalie. The doctors decided he should be the one to let them know. In the car Mario's emotions welled up and he began to cry. He found it difficult to drive through the busy, late after-noon traffic. He knew something about Hodgkin's disease. One of his cousins, a beautiful young woman in her twenties, had contracted it in the 1970s. She was the daughter of Pierrette Lemieux's sister. She died from the disease. Two uncles had also died of cancer, though not of Hodgkin's. Mario had become honorary fundraising chairman of the Pittsburgh Cancer Insti-tute a few years earlier. It was mainly a ceremonial title. Mario spent some time on it initially, but his interest waned.

Trying to gain control of himself in the car, Mario decided to phone Jimmy Maggs. Maggs was surprised to receive the call. Mario didn't usually phone at that time of day.

"Jimmy, what are you doing?"

"I'm just getting ready to eat supper."

"Have you heard on the news yet?" asked Mario.

"No, what do you mean?"

Maggs couldn't have heard anything—no news was out, nor would there be any for some time.

"I've got Hodgkin's disease." A long silence followed. "I just thought I'd call and tell you," Mario said, "if you hadn't heard it on the news."

There was another reason for breaking the news to Jimmy Maggs before anyone else. Maggs had been diagnosed with colon cancer three years earlier. He had kept it quiet, but Mario knew. The doctors successfully operated and Maggs, by this time, was gaining more confidence that he was in the clear. Now, the silence on the line was becoming more and more painful. Maggs didn't know what to say. Finally, he expressed his sorrow and asked if there was anything he could do. Mario said no, that he was going home to tell Nathalie.

Mario cried as soon as he got home. He was unable to tell Nathalie the news. Finally, after an hour, still in tears, he did so. Later, he telephoned his mother and tried to use soft words to describe his condition. He knew the term Hodgkin's disease carried too painful a meaning for her, so he didn't tell her of it. "I just told her, 'They found a tumor. It's cancer.' Before I told her that, I said, 'The cure rate is ninety-five percent.'"

The next day Mario and Nathalie visited a cancer specialist, Dr. Ted Crandall. Crandall found Mario calm, but Nathalie in distress, wondering if he was going to die. A great many tests followed. One, a scan of the lungs, turned up some potentially devastating news. There was a cloudy area on the lungs, a sign the cancer might have spread there. Another possibility existed, however. Lemieux had a touch of pneumonia. That too could have induced such a test result. They would have to wait to find out if, in fact, the cancer was far graver than what Burke had described in his office.

Doctors and friends began calling to reassure him; Paul Coffey was among them. Coffey didn't want to mention the disease, so he talked about everything but what had happened. "We talked about Nathalie being pregnant, we talked about his wedding . . . lots of little things." Coffey noticed that Mario was in a positive state of mind. Nothing new about that, his former teammate thought. It was typical of Mario to handle it this way. He had inner strength.

That inner strength, however, was now being tested in a way Mario had not felt before; in a crueler way than when he was laid out with the back infection, his future on the line. Mario went to Jimmy Maggs' restaurant for lunch. Because of Maggs' experience with cancer, he could now tell Mario a lot of what to expect. He did so at the lunch, answering many questions Lemieux put to him in a straightforward manner. But the answers weren't easy for Mario to hear.

When he left the restaurant, Mario was tense. "There were so many things on his mind," said Maggs. "He wasn't paying attention to what he was doing." As Mario was pulling out of the parking lot, he almost ran over Maggs' wife. Then he plowed into a car passing through the alley way, damaging it substantially. In such situations, it helps to be famous. The man in the smashed car, hopping mad, jumped out and looked as if he wanted to do some damage of his own. But then he was confronted with a real-live magazine cover: it was Mario Lemieux. The man's temperament quickly changed. He asked Mario for an autograph.

Lemieux saw his teammates. When he walked into the dressing room before a practice it fell as silent as a graveyard. Usually, as Mario well knew, it was a noisy place. Kevin Stevens was always going on about something and motor mouth Ulfie

Samuelsson couldn't shut up. That day, Kevin didn't know what to say, Ulfie didn't know what to say, no one else knew what to say. "There was dead silence," said Kevin Stevens. "It was an awful silence."

Mario had a press conference to prepare for on the Friday, four days after Burke had informed him of the cancer. Pierrette Lemieux, who was finding it difficult to cope, had come to her son's home. "This is the worst thing that could have happened to me," she told a friend. "[But] he's going to beat this because he's a winner."

As Mario prepared to leave for the press conference, he broke down and cried at his mother's side. He eventually regained his composure, however, and was able to get through it in noble fashion. In a dark blue sports jacket with light blue shirt done up at the collar and no tie, he looked pale and tired. He was reflective, smiled on occasion, got better as the conference wore on. He spoke as though he could see life in the broad perspective. "I'm very positive . . . I'm a positive person by nature and that's not going to change in the future even though I have Hodgkin's. That's not going to change my life and the way I live my life. Certainly it's going to make it tougher for the next couple of months but that's life sometimes . . . Sometimes in life you have to go through some tough periods and certainly I haven't been too fortunate the last few years with my back surgery, back infection, recurrence of back problems, and my hand broken in the playoffs last year. But it's a tough sport and sometimes you have to go through some injuries and climb the mountain. This is certainly another mountain that I have to climb."

The press was told a lot about Hodgkin's disease, but neither the doctors nor Mario brought up the dire possibility that the cancer had spread to his lungs.

Hodgkin's is one of the mildest forms of cancer. It has a ninety percent-plus cure rate. But even if they found it was localized only in the neck, not the lungs, the statistic was less comforting for someone who had lost a cousin to the disease. And there was the shadow that came with cancer, that would hang over Mario's life forever. As the doctors said, there was no foolproof cure. There was always a chance it would return. Mario could say, as he soon would, that the disease was behind him. But in fact, it would be five years before he would know if he had passed the major hurdle. If, in five years, there was no recurrence, he could be reasonably certain, though not completely certain, that it had been killed off and would not reappear in other parts of the body at a later date.

After the press conference, Dr. Crandall watched as Mario made his way through the klieg lights, the cameras, and the onlookers. He was asked if, given the high rate of recovery from Hodgkin's, perhaps too big a deal was being made of this story. Dr. Crandall paused for a second. "It's Mario Lemieux," he said. Then his voice fell a notch. "And cancer is cancer."

While Mario waited for the first radiation treatments to begin, still in doubt about the lung condition, he traveled with his brothers and their wives and Jimmy Maggs to Maggs' winter home in West Palm Beach, Florida. For a week, they played some golf, talked about sports, and rarely, though Mario was reading materials about Hodgkin's disease, did the subject of cancer come up. "Mario showed no signs of depression," said Maggs. "He was with his family members, whom he loves so much."

Soon the wonderful news arrived that the shadows had cleared from Mario's lung scan. They had indeed been caused by his mild pneumonia.

Now he would undergo weeks of radiation treatment to kill any other abnormal nodes in the area. He would go to the hospital each day for a month, be strapped into an immobile shell, and receive blasts from a radiation machine for three to five minutes. He expected to be out of action until the end of the regular season. He hoped to make it back in time for the play-offs, but no assurances were uttered. Father Fortin, who was scheduled to marry Mario and Nathalie in late June, telephoned to wish him well. Mario told him he didn't have to call, adding jokingly that he knew he was praying for him every day. A priest Mario didn't know called from Boston, home of the Bruins, to say he was having masses said for Mario. From highly Catholic Quebec, religious medals by the dozen were being sent to him with promises of prayer.

The radiation dosages progressed routinely. He was the first patient scheduled at the Beaver County Medical Center in Pittsburgh each morning at nine, five mornings a week. He was shot through the neck from three sides. He had to wear a mask for all these shots, which was a grim reminder of what was happening to him. "When I had the mask on, I thought, 'This is why I'm here, because of the cancer.' That's when I really thought about it. But as soon as I got out of there and got in my car, I let it go. I was just able to do that. It didn't really bother me that I had it, after a while."

He called his mother most every day with progress reports. Within two weeks of his first radiation treatments, he was skating with the team at the morning practices. On February 10, which was a warm day in Pittsburgh, he called Pierrette to say he'd finished his dosage and was on his way to the golf course to tee it up. That day, Mrs. Lemieux sounded very upbeat, remembering young Mario playing hockey in the living room after she had brought in snow and packed it on the carpet. She laughed gaily at the memories and expressed her confidence that everything would be well, despite all the bad luck that had come her son's way in recent years.

For the city of Pittsburgh, Mario's story was a continuation of the bad luck, heartache, tragedy, that had afflicted its sporting life. Preceding Lemieux's cancer was Coach Johnson's death from brain cancer. Before that, Ashley Barrasso, the infant daughter of the goalie, had contracted cancer. Penguins' GM Baz Bastien died in a car accident, the promising rookie Michel Brière was victim of the same fate, and winger Stan Gilbertson severed a leg in an automobile wreck in 1977. One of the last great baseball superstars, Roberto Clemente of the Pittsburgh Pirates, died in an airplane crash on the last day of 1972. Pitcher Bob Moose died in a car accident in 1976.

In a town with a track record like this, who could say for sure if Mario would not be among the very small percentage of Hodgkin's cases who didn't beat the disease?

Mario appeared to respond to the treatments well, but friends wondered about the emotional and psychological impact as much as the physical one. Would the game of hockey mean as much to him now that he had cancer, now that he was financially set for life, now that he had won two Stanley Cups and scoring titles and Hart Trophies and the Canada Cup, now that he had done most everything that an antihero could do?

He had been confronted with end-game before, in the autumn of 1990. "I had a chance a couple of years ago with the back infection," Mario said, "to change my perspective. And this disease certainly reassured me . . . that the most important thing in life is health and everything after that is secondary."

With a badly damaged back, with Hodgkin's disease, with so much accomplished, where would the motivation come from? What would the driving imperative be? Why not forget hockey and relax with the millions and pursue the golf career he so often talked about?

Such thoughts didn't weigh heavily with Mario, however. After only two weeks of radiation blasts, he was coltish and keen and anxious to play hockey. He began skating with the team in practices. Then, before the sessions were even complete, he asked if he could start playing in games. The club and the doctors wouldn't allow it. Yes, they wanted him back quickly. The team had initially played well in his absence, but now the Penguins were leveling off and losing their number-one ranking in the overall league standings. But they decided they could at least wait until the treatments were over.

On March 2, he got a last extra dose of radiation, a flare so hot it almost brought smoke from his neck. It left quite a burn. He went over to Jimmy Maggs, showed him the big red mark, and indicated his displeasure. But the shots were over and now it was time, that very day, to play hockey again. Maggs drove him out to the airport so he could catch a plane to Philadelphia, where the Penguins were playing that night. As they drove, they talked about the scoring title. It was clear this was uppermost in Mario's mind. He had now missed twenty-three games in the schedule and Buffalo's Pat LaFontaine, scootering from point to point, a pinball with eyes, had bolted ahead of him by twelve points on the scoring charts. Mario still thought he could catch him, even though only twenty games remained. He'd been thinking of catching LaFontaine, his foe from junior, ever since being sidelined. He even thought of it, he said, while lying in the encasing, getting the radiation shots.

In February, while still receiving treatments, he had gone to the all-star game in Montreal, where he met LaFontaine and told him, in a lighthearted way, that he would be coming back and coming after him. The new, bright young NHL commissioner, Gary Bettman, had phoned Mario to invite him to the game as a special guest of honor. Bettman knew that Mario was his superstar ticket to sell the sport. He was dominating hockey almost as much as Michael Jordan was dominating basketball. Gretzky had returned from his injury, but he was a non-presence at this all-star game and the writers, too early as it turned out, were burying him.

In Montreal a restaurant was reserved for a special luncheon for Mario, a luncheon not with writers or players or league executives, but the people who meant the most to him—the Lemieux clan, his family and relatives and friends from Ville Emard. After the lunch, Mario went to the Forum, where his very first coach, the one who put him on the ice before he turned four, Fernand Fichaud, led the security phalanx that took him around. He took Mario to a room to be greeted by the legends of the Canadiens: Rocket Richard, Jean Béliveau, Guy Lafleur. They embraced him and wished him well. After a few minutes, he was taken to the all-stars' dressing room, where the scene was repeated. Then he was introduced to the crowd at the Forum, who stood and applauded emotionally for the longest time.

On the day of his return to action, during the drive to the airport, Maggs made reference to LaFontaine. As he pulled into the parking lot, he said, "Move over boy. We're coming right through. You've had enough of a head start." To Maggs, Mario looked pumped that day, very pumped for a guy coming off cancer treatments, about as pumped as Maggs had ever seen him.

That night in Philly the normally hostile Flyer fans saluted Mario's return with a ninety-second standing ovation. At the beginning of period two he took the puck deep in the face-off circle and snapped a sharp-angle wrist shot into the goal. He played twenty minutes and added an assist. The legs felt weak and the mouth dry. He hadn't been able to taste anything for several days, and with the appetite so withered, hadn't eaten much. These were less significant problems, however, than what he experienced a few nights later in New York, when the wrenching back muscles made it difficult for him to get out of bed and limited him to five minutes' playing time against the Rangers.

As anticipated, the reception was thunderous for his first game back at the Igloo. He scored an assist in a 3–2 victory, but the burghers had to wait a couple of nights more until the Kings and Wayne Gretzky came to town to see the Mario they knew and loved. Mario and Wayne had met face to face nineteen times over the years. With forty-six points in these meetings, Gretzky was the clear winner. By comparison, Super Mario had only twenty-eight. That night the Penguins scored four goals in a 4–3 win. Gretzky had two points, but Mario was in on all four of his team's tallies, with a goal and three assists. This was the beginning of his great blitz. Lemieux began to produce at an astonishing rate. In a stretch of sixteen games in March and early April, he exploded for twenty-seven goals, twenty-four assists, and fifty-one points—an average of more than three points a game. He had back-to-back four-goal games against Washington and Philadelphia. In one four-game span, he had seventeen points. On April 10, he came to Madison Square Garden and popped in five against the Rangers, leaving the fans dizzy with appreciation. They cheered him wildly and when it was over, Lemieux paused at his dressing-room door and, lit up by the reverence accorded him, said with a smile, "Usually, I get booed up here."

Following this performance, Mario made a remark that harked back to those peewee and bantam days when he had left Coach Stevenson so puzzled. Asked by reporters how he could do so well, given the obvious fatigue that came with his condition, Lemieux summed up the illogical nature of his game. "Sometimes the more tired I feel," he observed, "the better I play." As could be expected, the remark left reporters scratching their heads. They'd never heard that one before. But some who had watched him since peewee, like Stevenson, knew that Mario wasn't making a throwaway comment. He was serious.

What everyone thought would be a tight race with LaFontaine turned into a rout in the final days. Having spotted LaFontaine an even dozen, Mario ended up beating him by an even dozen. And he still wasn't at his peak. "I'm not able to take long shifts like before," he said. "It's coming though. Hopefully, it will get better as we go into the playoffs." His motivation? "I have a strong will to be the best in the world. I draw a lot of strength from that."

He finished the season with 69 goals and 91 assists for 160 points. He did it in sixty games. It was the highest goals-per-game average and total-points-per-game average in his career. Spread over an eighty-game schedule, the totals would have equaled Gretzky's goals and total points records. Spread over 84 games, he would have smashed both marks in one season. These numbers would have represented the greatest output the sport of hockey had seen in the postwar era. Lemieux had fashioned one of the greatest scoring seasons in NHL history, and it was done with cancer, a disabled back, and the cloud of a sex scandal hanging over him.

Watching Lemieux, observed Ottawa coach Rick Bowness, was like watching "a man playing pond hockey with kids." "I'm still amazed," said Karl Nelson, a former lineman with the New York Giants, who played a season in 1987 after being diagnosed with Hodgkin's, "that he didn't have as much overall fatigue. I thought the radiation would have longer-term effects as far as being tired."

Because of the circumstances of his achievement, the recognition that had long been denied Mario Lemieux finally came to him in gushers. It took the cancer to do it. The cancer made his a story that transcended sport, a human drama of quiet courage and conquest. The *New York Times* headlined their feature article on Lemieux "Man and Superman." *Sports Illustrated*'s cover shouted, "Miracle on Ice." Mario appeared on "Wide World of Sports," "Sunday Today," every U.S. network. He pulled himself out of bed at six a.m. on a Monday to be on "Good Morning, America." "You get a lot more attention when something happens to you like cancer," he remarked. "I certainly didn't ask for that."

Nathalie Asselin was having a baby and it was typical of Mario that he would go to the hospital, but not the delivery room. "I'll be on the backstage," he said. "That's where I feel more comfortable." It was typical too that if a playoff game was on the night she was scheduled to give birth, Mario wouldn't, he told the press, be by her side. In such a situation, the priority had to be the game.

Through all the hype and tumult surrounding his illness and his feat, he carried himself with a calm, soft dignity. There were no boastful words, no effort to exaggerate his cancer. "You have to be around him a while to know him," said Craig Patrick. "That's when you find out about him, about his great inner strength and his great inner drive." Mario sometimes described in his interviews why he had been so hidden. "My privacy is very important to me. That's why I don't let people get close to me. It's difficult for me sometimes to talk to people in public. I'm not really good at it." What was important, he said, was that "the people who are close to me know my character and what I'm all about."

Nothing would change this aspect of him. He was still an intensely private star, a backstage French-Canadian thrust to the forefront of an English-American culture. He appeared to be maturing. Those who knew him well said the back infection and the cancer, particularly the cancer, had matured him ten years in the space of two. Cancer made you grow up fast, Mario acknowledged. Such an experience "makes you a better person." It was less likely now, his friends pointed out, that he would shirk the responsibilities that came with stardom. If he had sometimes been selfish in the past, they thought, he would be less inclined to be that way in the future. If he had not given much of his time to charity in the past, they thought, he would perhaps give more now. If he had overstepped the bounds of moral decency in Minnesota, it was probably less likely to be repeated. In the beginning everything had come too easy for him. But he had been hit by too many searing reality checks to go on taking everything for granted. Mario would be good now, they said. The class that marked him on the ice would be mirrored off it.

His wondrous spring of 1993 had reached beyond normal athletic perimeters. As he suffered, as he performed, as his rare blend of quiet strength and supreme talent prevailed over trying conditions, there was an eternal calmness about him that left many who watched him heartened and inspired.

His teammates spoke of how they drew strength from his performance. They and others compared him to basketball's Larry Bird or baseball's Lou Gehrig. They watched him in his phenomenal late-season surge, knowing that he was handicapped, not at his peak, but still doing it better than anyone else. They knew that if the fates would only let him, Mario could take the sport to levels higher than anyone ever had—as high as only he could imagine.

EPILOGUE

THE SEASON WOULDN'T END RIGHT. IT WASN'T SUPPOSED TO. IT would be too much of a fairy tale, altogether unbefitting the antihero, if on top of all he'd done, he led his team to a third straight Stanley Cup as well. The fates had to punish him more and try again to break his will. And so, the cancer having failed to arrest him, they had to hobble him in another way, and they chose the perfect time to do so.

When he returned from the radiation dosages, Mario had taken his stumbling team on a run of sixteen straight wins. It was an NHL record. The Penguins then tied the New Jersey Devils to finish the season with the unbeaten string intact. They were the grand favorites to win a third straight Stanley Cup. They were peaking at the best of times. After Lauren Rachel Lemieux was born on April 29 (with Dad far off in the waiting room), they predictably vanquished the Devils in five games in the first playoff round. The new father started the series in the same way he had finished the season—on another hockey planet, a man playing pond hockey among the kids. But his performance diminished in the later games and the whispers began. Mario wasn't Mario. Something was wrong. Something in the way he moved.

Two minutes into game one of the next series against the

New York Islanders, Mario skated off the ice toward the dressing room. The back muscles had flared up again, immobilizing him. He was out for game one and possibly more.

The Penguins were rocked, but they had come to anticipate this. It had happened too often not to be expected now. Team members felt they could still beat the Islanders, an average club. Without Mario, they won game two. With Mario appearing sporadically, they won game three. For the next encounter, a Saturday night on the Island, Mario couldn't get himself up from the locker-room bench. He had to be helped. He played sparingly and stiffly and New York tied the series.

The contrast to a few weeks earlier was sad. In his stunning regular-season stretch run, Mario had been ebullient when he faced the Islanders. In a game in New York he ran into defenseman Vladimir Malakhov so hard he separated Malakhov's shoulder. Steigerwald saw Mario after the game, getting on the bus. "You're a goon, Mario," he said, jokingly. "Who are you going to get next?" Mario laughed and responded in a gruff, exaggerated voice. "Whoever's in my path."

Many times in the past the doctors had given him anti-inflammatories to reduce the swelling in the affected back area. Now they wanted to do it for the crucial playoff games. But the anti-inflammatories had brought Mario stomach pain and diarrhea and he wouldn't take them. After game four, they tried something else. They put him in traction. They laid him out, arms and ankles tied down on a special table that stretched his muscles. Suddenly he felt great. He ran out onto the ice for the next game and scored right away and led his team to victory.

All the Penguins had to do was win either the sixth or the seventh game. The back plagued him again in game six, however, and New York won it to force the series to the limit. As Mario's problems mounted, the Penguins lost their edge. Goalie Tom Barrasso, who had excelled early in the series, now played poorly. Kevin Stevens, brilliant at power forward in previous playoffs, had turned invisible in these ones. Scotty Bowman normally would have made adjustments, but the team was never in enough trouble in the series for his red alert to go off.

Mario remained quiet about how his back had crippled him in game six. In preparation for the decisive encounter, he decided he'd risk traction again. The night before the game, no one except Pittsburgh management aware, he drove out quietly to the south hills of Pittsburgh to visit his trusted physiotherapist, Dr. Jim Kittelberger. He underwent the traction, but this time it didn't take effect as it had for the earlier match. He suited up for the game, but he didn't feel well. His back screamed that he couldn't play.

He went out onto the ice at forty percent and played at forty percent. He was rigid and tentative. There was no fluidity, no leaning forward, no eternal reach. When he got the puck, he didn't even try to move far with it and create opportunities. He looked instead for the outlet pass. He harmlessly dished it off.

Early in the game Kevin Stevens collided with an opponent, fell face first to the ice, and was carried off on a stretcher. Barrasso collapsed, allowing two soft goals to let the Islanders take a 3–1 lead in the third period. The Penguins miraculously rallied in the final minutes to tie it. But in overtime, Ulf Samuelsson was caught up ice, the Islanders bore in on a two-on-one break, and the puck slid over to David Volek. Barrasso came out to meet him, but he mistakenly went down too early. Volek's shot soared over him into the goal.

In the horrific silence that followed, Mario skated slowly over to Al Arbour, the New York coach, and tapped him on the shoulder and shook his hand. He went to his dressing room, but by the time the media entered, he was no longer there. He was hiding in the adjacent trainer's chambers where he wouldn't have to see anyone.

While Mario's Penguins fell, Wayne Gretzky surged. Lemieux thought he had dispensed with Gretzky. Like others, he thought Gretzky could never challenge for number one again. But now Wayne Gretzky played impressively as the Kings defeated Calgary and then Vancouver. Now Wayne Gretzky took the scoring lead in the playoffs. Now Wayne Gretzky single-handedly eliminated the Toronto Maple Leafs in game seven of their semifinal series. Gretzky was back and the Anti-Gretzky, he who had touched the stars only weeks earlier, was gone. The hockey world was progressing as it should.

After the defeat, no one heard from Lemieux, still his own worst PR man, for several weeks. With his new contract, he was supposed to become a more marketable Mario. With the traumas he had experienced, he was supposed to have matured. But what the critics didn't understand was that his intensely private nature was not something that could be changed.

He went to Toronto to collect his awards, no fewer than three of them—the scoring title, the Hart Trophy, and the Masterton Trophy for perseverance. It was a nice moment. It had been a long time since anyone had won three. (The next day he also added the Lester B. Pearson Award.) But Mario being Mario, he had to spoil it. He encountered Bertrand Raymond, one of the most widely read hockey writers in Quebec, in the hotel lobby. Raymond asked him if he had a few minutes for a short interview. Mario had time, but he didn't want to talk. He told Raymond he had learned to say no and was saying it now.

The next day a full-page article appeared in *Le Journal de Montréal*. It was entitled "Mario the Magnificent—My Eye!" It went on to denounce Lemieux for all the things he had always been denounced for: not giving anything back to the game, not working hard, not thinking of others. Even those in the Pittsburgh media, who hadn't heard from him since the Islanders series, wondered why he had chosen to ignore all the home-town fans who had cheered him and loved him for so long. A column appeared, asking, Mario, where are you? Are we not entitled to a word, just a word about what had happened? Wayne Gretzky, the column said, wouldn't treat his people this way.

Following the defeat by the Islanders, Lemieux had surgery scheduled for the purpose of removing some of the scar tissue thought to be the reason for the intermittent back pain. He could have been operated on immediately following the early play-off exit, giving him four months to recuperate and prepare for the new season.

However, there were other considerations. Given what he had been through, Mario didn't want to risk surgery again unless there was absolutely no alternative. The memory of the surgery in 1990 was still fresh in his mind. The doctors still weren't exactly sure of the specific nature of the problem, but assured Mario that all would be well, that these operations had a fantastically high success rate. No one spoke of the possibility of an infection settling in during or after the operation that could cripple him for several months and put in doubt his future in the game.

This time, the surgery was to be a very minor procedure. Even so, Lemieux wanted to wait a couple of months in the hope that his back would feel normal again. He'd bounce back from the loss of the Cup, play some golf, not think about the cancer, get married, fawn over his new baby girl, see how his back felt, then decide whether his condition warranted another operation.

By the end of July, still in pain, Mario decided to undergo surgery once again. It appeared successful. Mario was told he would be able to attend training camp and then play in the regular season opener in Philadelphia on October 5th.

Rehabilitation, however, was slow. Two weeks before the first day of training camp, Mario told reporters he was, "a little behind schedule." Complications had arisen and Lemieux was again on his way to California, as he had been three years before, to have another specialist look at his back. The specialist concluded that Mario would not be able to start the season. The disc herniation had been corrected, but there were other problems: "localized arthritic changes" and an old stress fracture. For the long term, the doctors said, the prognosis was bright. But Lemieux had now been in the league almost a decade and it was getting too late to start talking about the long term. The dismal news was that he was again a part-time player, a maybe-player. Yet another dispiriting chapter in his hockey life had begun.

He worked at getting into shape in the hope of beginning to play by the end of October. Mario was in a hurry. Even though he would miss close to a month of the regular hockey season, he still felt he could take a run at the scoring championship. He thought he could spot Gretzky or any other leading player 20 points or so and still catch them. He'd done it the previous season; missed 24 games, then put on the miracle finish to surpass LaFontaine. This season, Gretzky wasn't injured and had immediately sprinted to the scoring lead, a fact which made Mario even more eager to return.

He did return within a month, played satisfactorily for a couple of games, but it was soon apparent that he was hurt and out of shape. When the club went on a west coast swing, he got the flu which made him look so weak that Craig Patrick and the Penguins brass decided to pull him from the game. What was the use in playing Mario at quarter-speed and leaving the team in a constant state of quandary as to his availability? The club was easily good enough to make the playoffs without the megastar, so they decided to rest him through most of the regular season, then get him into shape for the playoffs. The previous spring, the consensus had been that a contributing factor to the playoff loss to the Islanders had been that the team had overworked itself in winning the regular season championship. Why risk repeating that mistake?

Lemieux realized he wasn't healthy enough to achieve anything spectacular individually and didn't object to the plan. Patrick refused to give reporters an estimate of when Lemieux would be back. The Penguins had made that mistake before, he acknowledged, putting undue pressure on the player and creating unwarranted expectations among the fans.

Mario devoted that winter to his new life's work—rehabilitation. He watched a lot of games from the stands and press boxes but, as he later said, didn't enjoy them. The game, as Mario saw it, was being given over to marginal players. It was the hackers that the rules favoured. They were allowed to club and maul the talented skaters without sufficient penalization. The big stars suffered injuries as a result. In this, the 1993–1994 season, Eric Lindros was sidelined, Steve Izerman was out, Mario Lemieux was down, Cam Neely went down again, Ray Bourque was felled, Pat LaFontaine was out.

Mario came back to play in March but not full time. He'd play a game, then sit one out, especially if they were on consecutive days. He was effective, scoring close to an average of two points per game, but he couldn't light up the hockey skies like he had following his cancer treatments the year before. The cancer had been stilled and now that there had been a year without recurrence it was unlikely it would return. But the deteriorating back pain worked insidiously on him. He simply never knew from one day to the next how he would feel. The story had become tiresome, lugubrious. People were as bored of talking about Mario's back as he was. An agreement was reached between the Pittsburgh players and media that no one would mention the word "back."

Playing most of the season without Lemieux, the Penguins posted a good record, maintaining a lead in their new division, which included Montreal, Boston and Quebec. Jaromir Jagr played strongly in Mario's absence and there was a feeling that, given the inherent strength and the experience of the Penguins without Lemieux, the prospects with him were boundless. Coach Eddie Johnston said that without Lemieux his club was on equal footing with several other strong NHL teams. With Lemieux, he knew, the Penguins could go all the way.

At the end of March, two weeks before the playoffs opened, Lemieux, who had missed sixty-one games, spoke confidently.

"I'm feeling pretty good. My back is in decent shape and my conditioning is much better than it was. This reminds me of the year when we won our first Cup [1991]. I had back surgery, then played only twenty-six games during the year. Hopefully, history will repeat itself."

There were moments when it looked like he was at the height of his hockey powers. On April 3rd, Easter Sunday, the Penguins played the Boston Bruins at the neutral site of Cleveland. The clock had changed the evening before. Mario forgot to change his and missed the team plane. He drove to Cleveland from Pittsburgh, but arrived fresh. He stood behind the Bruins net, took a pass and, as if pre-programmed, instantaneously knifed it through a maze of players onto Kevin Stevens' stick, who took it fifteen feet from Mario and scored. What was astonishing was the speed with which Lemieux had read the play and reacted to the puck. It happened so fast, like a carom in pinball. Onlookers could only wonder how the mind, the eyes, the hands, the imagination could all work together so instantaneously and so perfectly.

Moments later, during a Penguins power play, Mario stood with the puck about ten feet to the side of the Bruins net. The experienced Boston defenceman Glen Wesley stood between Lemieux and the goaltender. In such situations, from a stationary start, it is extremely unusual for the offensive player to manage to get around the defenceman for a clear shot on goal. Lemieux gave a couple of feints and induced Wesley to lunge for the puck on Lemieux's right side. He then moved the puck to his left, stepped around Wesley and jammed in a goal on the short side. He scored two goals and two assists in Pittsburgh's 6–2 win.

During the month of games he played before the season ended, Mario was again riled by the tactics of muggers from opposing clubs. Playing against Tampa Bay, he was being repeatedly fouled, as he saw it, without penalties being called. Finally, he retaliated by high-sticking Lightning defenceman Roman Hamrlik. Assessed a minor penalty by Kerry Fraser, the normally laconic Lemieux erupted into a degree of rage few had ever seen him reach. He flung his stick onto the ice from the penalty box, then charged from the booth at Fraser. Teammates Stevens and Ron Francis intervened to calm him.

The incident made headlines for days in NHL cities. NHL senior vice-president Brian Burke studied films of what had happened and assessed Lemieux a meagre $500 fine. Veteran observers complained that had most any other player behaved in this manner, they would have been suspended for several games. The $500 fine meant that Lemieux, whose salary equated to $73,000 a game, made only $72,500 in the Tampa Bay encounter.

The brouhaha gave him a chance to broadcast his case against the league. He had done so a few seasons earlier when he called the NHL a "garage league" for allowing the cheap fouls. Now he repeated the charge. "They have to do something," he said. "I've been watching games from the press box this season and it has not been very good hockey. I don't know if the fans have enjoyed it. There has been a lot of clutching and grabbing and I don't think that's what the players want." He noted that players had been able to score seventy or eighty goals a season until a few years back. Now the stars were being man-handled so much, he said, no one was scoring over sixty.

Lemieux coupled his complaints with a threat. He wasn't, he said, going to do anything to promote the NHL as long as it continued to condone the type of hockey currently played. Since Lemieux's off-the-ice contribution to promoting the league had been negligible in his first nine years, few among the NHL fathers were moved to panic.

This tempest aside, Mario was feeling good when the Penguins faced off against the Washington Capitals in Round One of the playoffs. He had been using a new exercise machine the last three weeks of the season which he said was doing a great job of reinforcing his muscles and ligaments. He vowed to play in all the playoff games, the situation made easier by the fact, as he noted, that none of the games would be on successive nights.

The Capitals were coming off another lacklustre season and though they had finally fired coach Terry Murray, replacing him with Jim Schoenfeld, they were widely viewed as easy prey for Pittsburgh. The Penguins, it was thought, were hungry this year, following their elimination the previous season. But the team, for some reason, played the Capitals with an utter lack of abandon and inspiration. The Penguins looked aging and slow. They suffered, detectably, from an absence of speed on their defence. The Samuelssons were big cruising oceanliners with no zest. Larry Murphy was not the offensive threat he used to be. No one could ignite a spark and if some imagination from the coaching staff was required (mixing up the lines, bringing in a couple of new faces to shake things up), it wasn't to come from the conventional veteran, Eddie Johnston.

The Penguins were defeated by the Capitals in six games. A more legitimate result might have seen them out in four. The two games they won were more by dint of lucky breaks than a high level of play. Lemieux played in all six games, scoring four goals, and there was little evidence that his back was restraining his ability to be effective. Nonetheless, his play was mediocre. Much of the time, he wasn't meshing properly with his line-mates, Stevens and Tocchet. They seemed out of sync. No flu-idity embraced their play as they tried to move up ice with the puck. So often when Lemieux got possession of the puck, it seemed there was no one available to pass to and no option but to dump it into the Washington zone. On other occasions, he showed a disconcerting tendency to rid himself of the puck the moment it came onto his stick. Why would a player with the magnificent one-on-one skills of Lemieux not choose to use them, especially when no one else was clicking, especially when the team was on the way down, especially when only he could ignite a comeback? Periodically in Mario's career, coaches had complained that he didn't play the game selfishly enough. The same could be said of him in this series. He didn't use the talents with which he was blessed.

In previous series and Stanley Cup victories, the Penguins had relied heavily on their power play. Against the Capitals, the power play vanished. In twenty-seven power play opportunities, the Penguins scored only twice. "Again, the power play didn't do the job," Lemieux said. "We pretty much lost the series on the power play."

The failure spelled the end of hopes for a Lemieux-led dynasty in Pittsburgh. As Mario said after the loss, it was a team that would never be the same. Veteran big-salary earners would have to be unloaded. For a market so small, the payroll was far too high. And besides that, the Penguins needed revitalization.

There was still the matter of Lemieux's future. He'd been hinting and gave more hints now that he might not return. He wasn't interested, he said, in going on the way he had been the last two years. "I don't want to be limited to twenty-game seasons anymore. I still love to play hockey—providing you can play it without being tackled all the time—but there remains a chance I'll retire. Playing one match in four, that doesn't interest me."

As everyone knew, it would be a wait-and-see situation. It had been this way with Lemieux for years. But while no one could predict the health of an athlete so vulnerable to setback, there were some encouraging signs. He had finished the disappointing Stanley Cup campaign in relatively good physical shape. No back operations were planned for the summer. No radiation therapy was on the schedule. And challenges still confronted him.

Deep inside, as everyone knew, this was an athlete unfulfilled. This was an athlete too frequently deprived of his genius. This was an athlete to whom the gods of fate still owed something; the chance at a season free of pain, the chance to demonstrate there was no one better.

CAREER PLAYING RECORD

(*league-leading figure)

1981–82	Laval	QMJHL				Playoffs			
GP	G	A	PTS	PIM	GP	G	A	PTS	PIM
64	30	66	96	22	18	5	9	14	31

1982–83	Laval	QMJHL				Playoffs			
GP	G	A	PTS	PIM	GP	G	A	PTS	PIM
66	84	100	184	76	12	14	18	32	18

1983–84	Laval	QMJHL				Playoffs			
GP	G	A	PTS	PIM	GP	G	A	PTS	PIM
70	133*	149*	282*	92	14	29*	23*	52*	29

1984–85	Pittsburgh	NHL				Playoffs			
GP	G	A	PTS	PIM	GP	G	A	PTS	PIM
73	43	57	100	54	—	—	—	—	—

1985–86	Pittsburgh	NHL				Playoffs			
GP	G	A	PTS	PIM	GP	G	A	PTS	PIM
79	48	93	141	43	—	—	—	—	—

1986–87	Pittsburgh	NHL				Playoffs			
GP	G	A	PTS	PIM	GP	G	A	PTS	PIM
63	54	53	107	57	—	—	—	—	—

1987–88	Pittsburgh	NHL				Playoffs			
GP	G	A	PTS	PIM	GP	G	A	PTS	PIM
77	70*	98	168*	92	—	—	—	—	—

1988–89	Pittsburgh			NHL		Playoffs			
GP	G	A	PTS	PIM	GP	G	A	PTS	PIM
76	85*	114*	199*	100	11	12	7	19	16

1989–90	Pittsburgh			NHL		Playoffs			
GP	G	A	PTS	PIM	GP	G	A	PTS	PIM
59	45	78	123	78	—	—	—	—	—

1990–91	Pittsburgh			NHL		Playoffs			
GP	G	A	PTS	PIM	GP	G	A	PTS	PIM
26	19	26	45	30	23	16	28*	44*	16

1991–92	Pittsburgh			NHL		Playoffs			
GP	G	A	PTS	PIM	GP	G	A	PTS	PIM
64	44	87	131*	94	15	16*	18	34*	2

1992–93	Pittsburgh			NHL		Playoffs			
GP	G	A	PTS	PIM	GP	G	A	PTS	PIM
60	69	91*	160*	38	11	8	10	18	10

1993–94	Pittsburgh			NHL		Playoffs			
GP	G	A	PTS	PIM	GP	G	A	PTS	PIM
22	17	20	37	32	6	4	3	7	2

	NHL Totals					Playoffs			
GP	G	A	PTS	PIM	GP	G	A	PTS	PIM
599	494	717	1211	618	66	56	66	122	46

Awards and Honors

QMJHL Second All-Star Team (1982–83)

QMJHL First All-Star Team (1983–84)

QMJHL Most Valuable Player (1983–84)

Canadian Major Junior Player of the Year (1983–84)

Calder Memorial Trophy (1984–85)

NHL All-Rookie Team (1984–85)

NHL Second All-Star Team (1985–86, 1986–87, 1991–92)

NHL First All-Star Team (1987–88, 1988–89, 1992–93)

Lester B. Pearson Award (1985–86, 1987–88, 1992–93)

Hart Trophy (1987–88, 1992–93)

Art Ross Trophy (1987–88, 1988–89, 1991–92, 1992–93)

Conn Smythe Trophy (1990–91, 1991–92)

Bill Masterton Trophy (1992–93)

Canadian Athlete of the Year (1993)

NOTES ON SOURCES

THE SOURCES FOR MUCH OF THIS STORY ARE EVIDENT FROM THE wording in the text. These additional notes cover cases where the sourcing is not clear or needs to be elaborated. In some cases, information was provided only with the understanding that the source not be identified.

Prologue

Hazlitt's opening quotation is from *The Plain Speaker* (1826). Mario's embarrassing experience in the dressing room was compiled from interviews with Doug Shedden, Mike Bullard, and Warren Young, and also from Mario's own description of it to his then agent, Bob Perno. Other material in this chapter is from author interviews with Shedden, Paul Martha, and Ron Stevenson.

One: The Natural

The description of Mario's early days on the ice is from an interview with Fernand Fichaud. The story of Mario playing hockey on the living-room rug was confirmed by Pierrette Lemieux in a conversation with the author. This anecdote was also told earlier in a short photobiography on Lemieux, *Mario Lemieux:*

Hockey's Gentle Giant by Jean Sonmor (Toronto: Macmillan of Canada, 1989). Carl Parker's humiliating moment in goal was recounted to the author by Parker.

Two: "By the Sound of His Skates"
Memories from the boyhood hockey days, as told to the author, differ in detail depending on the source. In some instances there was disagreement on the scores of games in atom and peewee, or on exactly how many goals Mario scored. In such cases, the author took what appeared to be the most legitimate consensual information. Material from Father Fortin is from an author interview. All other quotes are from author interviews with the subjects.

Three: The Black Machine
Mario's quotation about always being the best is from an article by Bruce Keidan in *Pittsburgh Magazine* (August 1992). The wonderful moment when Mario told Carl Parker not to worry if he flubbed the next shot was told to the author by Parker.

Firsthand evidence proves that Mario did write out lines of punishment as a peewee player. Coach Ron Stevenson still has some copies of Mario's handiwork. Sylvain Nantel remembered J. J. Daigneault brawling with Sergio Momesso in a restaurant, but Daigneault, who now plays for the Montreal Canadiens, said he could not recall whether it happened. Daigneault was one of several players who know Mario well and were hesitant to say anything for publication about Lemieux. Daigneault phoned the author to ask that he not be quoted on anything.

Information from Wayne Gretzky's early career is taken from his autobiography, *Gretzky*, written with Rick Reilly (Toronto: HarperCollins Publishers, 1990), and other sources. Harold Ballard's famous remark about Inge Hammarstrom was told to the author in an interview with Ballard in 1974.

Four: Number 66

In several long conversations with the author, Bob Perno detailed his relationship with Mario and described the various experiences they went through together. Perno was eventually let go by Mario. The fact that some of his views may have been colored by this incident was taken into account. His version of events was measured against the opinion of others, who were very much in Mario's court and put a positive spin on his actions.

Five: A Breed Apart

Marc Lachapelle of *Le Journal de Montréal* was interviewed at length on his experiences covering Lemieux throughout his junior hockey career. Lachapelle also kindly supplied the author with his entire file on Mario.

Six: Heir Apparent

The scene at the Chez Paree bar was recounted by Bob Perno. Perno reluctantly revealed that this type of establishment was the venue for Gretzky's congratulatory toasts in honor of Mario's outstanding season. He wished to emphasize that, in going there, Gretzky was only doing what many NHL players and coaches did. Reporter Tom Lapointe thought nothing of Gretzky's frequent visits there, saying the Chez Paree was a classy place, not a typical strip joint.

Seven: My Way or the Doorway

There are many varied accounts of the moment when Pittsburgh scout Albert Mandanici approached the Lemieux box at the NHL entry draft and demanded that Mario come down to put on the Pittsburgh jersey. Who got the better of the exchange depends on whose version of the story one chooses to believe.

The story about Peter Mahovlich's complaint to management is from Dave Schultz's book *The Hammer* (New York: Summit Books, 1981).

Eight: First Season

Penguin front-office employees who knew Mario well, most notably Paul Steigerwald, contributed significantly to the portrait of Mario's early days in a Penguin uniform. *Pittsburgh Press* reporter Dave Molinari's newspaper accounts also supplied color for this chapter.

Nine: Sixth Sense

Mario's thoughtful observation comparing hockey to golf is taken from Jean Sonmor's *Mario Lemieux: Hockey's Gentle Giant*.

Ten: The Anti-Gretzky

Jimmy Maggs has an interesting habit of saying "you know" two or three times in every sentence. After the first couple of references, the "you knows" have been deleted from his remarks.

The term "Anti-Gretzky" came out of an interview with Paul Steigerwald, the Penguin's marketing director and later a TV analyst for the team. Steigerwald began thinking of Mario this way in the late 1980s.

Eleven: Mario's Cup

The observations on Soviet hockey here and elsewhere in the text were drawn from the author's three-year stint as a correspondent for the *Globe and Mail* in Moscow and from *The Red Machine*, his book on the history of Soviet hockey.

Pierre Creamer gave his account of his season as the Penguin's coach in an interview with the author.

Twelve: Severing the Tie
Mario's feelings on Gretzky's trade to the Los Angeles Kings are from an interview he did with William Houston in the *Globe and Mail*.

The snippets of conversation reported in this chapter are from Bob Perno's memory bank, nothing more.

Thirteen: "Ace"
The view in Pittsburgh that the French–English problem in Canada was roughly equivalent to black–white racial tension in the United States is widely held. Several people in the media and in the Penguins' organization mentioned this and attributed a good part of Mario's image problems to the English-Canadian bias against him.

Though Mario and Wayne Gretzky gradually grew apart, they maintain cordial relations on the surface and have the utmost respect for one another's abilities.

Fourteen: A Christmas Present for Tony O
The anecdote about Mario's performance at the NHL players' association meeting is from an interview with William Houston of the *Globe and Mail*, who attended the meetings.

Mario's role in Tony Esposito's dismissal was confirmed by Paul Martha, Jimmy Maggs, and Paul Steigerwald. It is difficult to comprehend how Tony Esposito could go to such lengths to alienate Lemieux without realizing that he was cutting his own throat.

Fifteen: Career Threat
The doctors' performance did spawn rumors in Pittsburgh of possible legal action. Mario's agents sometimes worried about the quality of treatment he was receiving. The Pittsburgh media did not aggressively pursue the story.

Sixteen: *Lord Stanley, Lord Mario*

For the account of the 1991–1992 season, the author is indebted to Dave Molinari, who smoothly chronicled the year in *The Best in the Game* (Champaign, IL: Sagamore Publishing, 1992).

Ken Dryden was interviewed by the author for his thoughts on Mario's abilities. Dryden, who was categorical in his opinion that Mario's talent was superior to Gretzky's, thought it unlikely that Lemieux would ever be able to unlock the mystery of his game and put it into meaningful words.

Seventeen: *Tragedy and Triumph*

Paul Steigerwald was amazed when, later in the season, some Pittsburgh players complained about Bowman not even bothering to show up for practices. Bowman would have shown up and run them, said Steigerwald, whose inside sources included Mario, but was following the wishes of the team by staying away.

Dan Quinn's friendship with Mario was not a temporary thing. Months after the incident in Minnesota, Mario told interviewers he still regarded Quinn as his best friend.

The incident in which Mario plowed into another car was told to the author by Jimmy Maggs. Mario's description of his feelings while undergoing radiation are from an interview he gave to Jennifer Frey of the *New York Times*. His statement about his need for privacy and his difficulty in talking to people is from an interview for CBC Television's "The Fifth Estate."

Epilogue

The column questioning Mario's failure to communicate with his public was written by Ron Cook of the *Pittsburgh Post-Gazette*.

ACKNOWLEDGMENTS

BECAUSE MARIO LEMIEUX IS SUCH A POWERFUL FIGURE AND because he wields considerable influence in his hockey environment, it was difficult for some who know him to speak their minds. There was a fear, particularly among those in Pittsburgh, that any assessment bearing slightly negative overtones would impact against their best interests.

I am therefore most appreciative of the many who agreed to speak candidly about the subject of this book. Little has been written about Lemieux in an in-depth way. Jean Sonmor's short book, *Mario Lemieux: Hockey's Gentle Giant*, was a helpful guide, particularly for his pre-Pittsburgh years. Dave Molinari's *Best in the Game* captured the feel of the Penguin team and Mario's place on it. Molinari, a reporter who has covered Lemieux since the athlete's arrival in Pittsburgh, provided me with good background information on him.

I am very grateful to Tom McMillan, who has also covered Mario's every year with the Penguins. McMillan performed consultant duties for the book, filing background reports and kindly offering any insights he had gathered on Lemieux over the years.

My thanks to Marc Lachapelle of *Le Journal de Montréal* for supplying me with his huge file on Mario in his junior hockey days. The same to all Mario's minor-league coaches and those who played hockey with Mario in Ville-Emard beginning at age six.

In recent years there have been a spate of unauthorized biographies on athletes, books that have their limitations. Publisher Malcolm Lester was confident that an unauthorized bio on Mario Lemieux could work, perhaps even better than the other format. I am grateful to him for this confidence and his helpful editing suggestions, and also to editor Janice Weaver.

L. M.

INDEX